WANDERING PROFESSOR

By the same author

Poetry

Domestic Interior (Hutchinson, 1959)

The Directions of Memory (Chatto & Windus, 1964)

Selves (Routledge, 1969)

A.R.T.H.U.R. The Life & Opinions of a Digital Computer (Harvester, 1974)

A.R.T.H.U.R. & M.A.R.T.H.A. The Loves of the Computers (Secker & Warburg, 1980)

The Man I Killed (Secker & Warburg, 1980)

Chapter & Verse: Bible Poems (Secker & Warburg, 1984)

Selected Poems (Secker & Warburg, 1984)

Rembrandt's Mirror (Secker & Warburg, 1987)

Fiction

The Englishmen (Hamish Hamilton, 1959)

A Free Man (Chatto & Windus, 1968)

My Grandfather's Grandfather (Secker & Warburg, 1985)

Criticism

The Truest Poetry: An Essay on the Question, What is Literature? (Hamish Hamilton, 1960)

The Truthtellers: Jane Austen, George Eliot, D H Lawrence (Chatto & Windus, 1967)

The Uses of Nostalgia: Studies in Pastoral (Chatto & Windus, 1973)

An Introduction to English Poetry (Edward Arnold, 1975)

Love & Marriage: Literature in its Social Context (Edward Arnold, 1979)

The Literary Imagination: Essays on Literature & Society (Harvester, 1982)

The Frontiers of Literature (Blackwell, 1988)

Angels & Absences: Child Deaths in the 19th Century (Vanderbilt University Press, 1997)

LAURENCE LERNER

Wandering Professor

CALIBAN
1999

Published in 1999 by Caliban
an imprint of Book-in-Hand Ltd
20 Shepherds Hill
London N6 5AH

Copyright ©Laurence Lerner 1999

ISBN 0 9536307 0 6

A catalogue record for this book is available from the
British Library

Typeset in New Century 11/13pt
by Scriptmate Editions

Manufacture coordinated in UK by
Book-in-Hand Ltd, 20 Shepherds Hill, London N6 5AH

Teaching can be a scholarly, passionate, frustrating, rewarding and infinitely varied activity. It can burn you out or enrich your life beyond the dreams of intellect. Teaching literature should be the most rewarding of all, since literature is not a specialist branch of knowledge, but the expression of the whole person. And literature now — in the 1990s — has also become the seat of ideological controversy as never before, as the traddies argue with the trendies. This book is the story — one man's story — of the experience of teaching in institutions all over the world.

I owe everything to my students: without them, it often seems to me, I'd have led a drab, uneventful life. Surely a lawyer's clients, a doctor's patients or a banker's customers do not enrich his life as my students have enriched mine. Some of them, if they happen to read this book, may recognise themselves; some may feel they hardly recognise me. The conclusions to be drawn from my experience go to the heart of our culture; but readers may of course often draw conclusions different from mine.

The chapters are arranged in groups — Travelling, Teaching, Acting, Writing, Politics, but such arranging is only an arrangement: teaching, scholarship and personal life interact constantly. I have moved from one country to another, always learning something new; and readers who prefer to move about, following their fancy, rather than read straight through, are positively encouraged to do this.

The book owes much to my friends, many of whom have read parts of it and told me not to make a fool of myself, not to show off, not to be so humble, not to be so solemn, not to be so flippant — but all, I am glad to say, have read on, and always found something to take issue with. I hope the same applies to my readers.

Contents

INTRODUCTION

The view across the Cape Peninsula from the University of Cape Town is magnificent. After the walk up through the woods you crossed the rugby fields, and looked up at the statue of Cecil Rhodes gazing northwards, with the verses from Kipling inscribed on his plinth: I dream my dream, By rock and veld and pine, One empire to the northward, Aye, one line, From Lion's Head to line. This celebration of British imperialism imprinted itself on me each day with something of the innocence of the fresh morning air. Rhodes looked down benevolently on the stream of students arriving for classes, and beyond them across the Cape Flats warming slowly in the haze towards the smoke curling from a cooling tower in the distance. The haze seemed as infinite as the unmastered knowledge waiting for me in the library. Sitting on the wall we looked down and dreamed our dream, of girls and lectures, exams and political arguments, what made Shakespeare valuable today and whether Roy Campbell was a true modern poet, rehearsals for the arguments I have gone on with all my life. Because of my success in exams, my friends would sometimes ask, Do you intend to be a university lecturer, and I would usually say No: sometimes through modesty (Me? Lecture in a university?) sometimes through vanity (I'm going to be a writer), sometimes through idealism (I want to do something useful, teach the deprived not the privileged).

Like so many students, I began by doing a lot of things more or less badly: playing rugby, acting in plays, climbing mountains, editing the literary magazine. From W S Mackie, Professor of English language, I learned about the first Latin borrowing and Elizabethan inkhorn terms; with Oswald Doughty, Professor of English Literature, I read Rossetti's sonnets, and was informed that they were written not to his wife but to Jane Morris; with the classics department I picked my way slowly through books of the *Aeneid,* trying to feel distress at Dido's grief when Aeneas left her and she was driven by Furies into rhetorical lament (heu furiis incensa feror), trying not to share my friends' amusement when the lecturer translated 'heu' as 'dearie me'. Far away to the north were real furies,

9

where the war was raging, first in North Africa, then in Italy: it filled the newspapers but played little part in our lives. It had prevented me travelling to England with my mother between school and University, it caused the government to put up some lurid anti-Japanese posters, but our lives were untouched by it, as they were untouched by fascism, communism, psycho-analysis, structuralism or feminism, what have come to be the great intellectual upheavals of the twentieth century. We read *The Waste Land,* we read Auden and Spender and Graham Greene (our teachers never mentioned them), but I was growing up in a previous age.

Now it is April 19th, 1995, 7.30 in the morning: fifty years since I graduated from the University of Cape Town. I am about to retire as Edwin Mims Professor of English at Vanderbilt University, Nashville, Tennessee, and today is my valedictory lecture. I caught an early bus, and the campus was quiet as I walked past the Law School on one side, the School of Management on the other, comparing the shades of verdure on the trees: long fingers of pale green on the Osage Orange, darker green on the oaks (though none of the in-and-out curving edge that I associate with oaks), even darker green alternating with yellow on the magnolia leaves, which look as if they're dying, though I know they aren't, because the buds are there, waiting: waiting till I step on the plane before they reveal their white calyxes, pink tipped, as they do every year once they're sure I'm about to leave for the summer. It's not botanical knowledge that makes me so well-informed about the trees, it's the munificence of a Vanderbilt alumnus who left a legacy, not to endow a lectureship or build a chapel, but to put plaques on the campus trees announcing their names to the ignorant — of whom, here in Tennessee, I am definitely one.

It feels like spring, and will do so for another hour or so. For the most part, Tennessee spring feels to me like summer (and summer, if I stayed to experience it, would press and batter me with blunt heat); but for an hour or so in the morning, if you get up early enough, there is the slight tingle, the cool welcome not quite burned off by the sun, that announces the freshening of the year. In two hours the students will scurry to classes and the sun will bludgeon, spring will be over until tomorrow.

For ten years we have lived in Nashville during term time, and escaped the summers, catching the plane home to England at the beginning of May and not returning until the next semester starts at the end of August. We have lived in Nashville without making it our home: children and grandchildren are in England, our house in Lewes contains almost all my books, and because of my frequent study leaves I have spent almost five of the ten years in England. Yet I have enjoyed Vanderbilt: for all sorts of reasons I took the right decision when instead of seeing my time out at the University of Sussex and retiring at 65, I accepted the chair they kindly offered me and became a transatlantic hopper. I was of course not alone among English academics in doing this, and the 'second brain drain' of the 1980s is widely regarded as due to the Thatcher government's policy of university cuts, driving English academics to greener pastures and bigger salaries across the Atlantic. I obviously belong with that movement, but I doubt if I was really part of it. I did not come because I thought British universities were collapsing, or to register a protest against the government (who, anyway, heeds such protests? As my wise friend Barry remarked to me, when a politician resigns in protest, it doesn't take long before people blink when his name is mentioned, and ask Who's he?). Much as I disliked the University cuts, I found I disliked the response of some colleagues and students quite as much, so I did not feel I was making a political statement. Of course I doubled my salary, but that seemed curiously unimportant at the time: more important was not having to retire at 65. The eighteenth century actor Charles Macklin is said to have lived to 99. More doubtfully, he is said to have played Shylock at 99. More doubtfully still, he is said to have dropped dead on the stage playing Shylock at 99. In the United States, where compulsory retirement on the grounds of age has been abolished, one can go on teaching until 99, and it has occurred to me that Macklin would make a good role model: teaching the Shakespeare course to Vanderbilt students in 2025, I could drop dead in front of them while reading 'Hath not a Jew eyes', and it might be a good way to go. Not having to retire to order seemed one reason at least to make the change. More important still was the feeling of having been at the same institution for 2 years and needing a change: 'time for a change' — the expression dreaded of politicians in office, and irrationally strong in academics. Other things were important too: Natalie my wife had retired from teaching science and become a painter, and one can paint anywhere, the children had left home, her mother, who'd lived with us, had died, even the cat had died. We were free to act on a whim and go to Vanderbilt.

And now, on April 19th 1995, it is about to end. Term is not quite over: I have three more classes, some exams and some graduate papers to mark (sorry, to grade), and today I have to give my Valedictory lecture. Before that, at 9 o'clock, I have to talk about Hopkins to the Survey course. Nothing is so beautiful as Spring, When weeds, in wheels, shoot long and lovely and lush. I won't reminisce to them about my morning walk across campus, I won't say how strange I find the paradox of the magnolia leaves looking dry and dead when they are so very alive, I'll talk to them about Hopkins' verbal acrobatics, the elaborate collapse and restructuring of language as he alliterates, dances, rhymes and overrhymes in order to praise God. Then I can read and think for a while, take an old dissertation student to lunch, and ponder the lecture — though since it's written, there isn't really much to ponder.

Valedictory lecture. It was Paul's idea, once I'd decided to retire. Paul is (or then was) chair of the Department, and he said, You must give us a valedictory address before you go. After all, I came in with a public lecture, so why not go out with one. Actually, I gave two inaugurals, and have often felt that was a modest claim to appearing in the Guinness Book of Records — two inaugurals in the same university. I came to Vanderbilt as the Kenan Professor of English (all the best jobs in American universities have handles to their name); then they wanted to give a chair to my colleague Cecilia to stop her from leaving, and it was felt she would be more suitable as Kenan professor, and I was more suited to filling the conveniently empty Mims chair, so I was switched sideways, and Paul said, Well, now we can have another inaugural from you. And now the Valedictory: that makes three times in one university — surely a record? Then will come the farewell party, and various other smaller parties, and then the end. No-one really believes it's the end. I expect you'll go on teaching, they all say to me, or writing, or reviewing, or lecturing, or — well, what will you do, they ask? Write your memoirs?

According to Arthur Koestler there are two impulses which make people write autobiographies, the 'Chronicler's urge' and the 'Ecce Homo motif' : the fact that one has been witness to great historical events, and the belief that one's inner life is important and worth exploring. No doubt there is always a touch of the latter in any book of memoirs, but this book derives from the chronicler's urge: not the chronicler of great historical events, but the chronicler of one of the central activities of any society, more important in the twentieth century than it has ever been — the activity of teaching. For I have perhaps another claim to the Guinness Book of Records — the number of universities, and the number of different countries, I have taught in. A student at Cape Town, then at Cambridge; a teacher at the (then) University College of the Gold Coast, then Queen's University Belfast (first in the extra-mural then in the English Department), then the University of Sussex, then Vanderbilt. A visiting professor in Munich for two years, in Dijon (twice) and in Paris, once. Several visiting posts in the United States and Canada. A month at the University of Kashmir. A semester at Würzburg. Most recently, a semester as Visiting Professor in Vienna (I'm spoilt, I told the Viennese, since my past visits to the German-speaking world have been to Munich. Well, they replied, we consider Munich a passable imitation of Vienna). Lecture tours for the British Council in France, in Germany, in Spain, in South America, in Turkey, and twice to India. With no more than normal powers of observation, I must have found out something about how university teaching can vary from culture to culture; what are the problems inherent in any teaching situation, what are those that depend on the society where it is taking place? I must, surely, have stories to tell. And walking across campus at 7.30 on a spring morning, I leap in memory over more than fifty years, walking up through the woods (but the woods have gone now, there are broad roads there) to meet Cecil Rhodes and Professor Doughty, to dream of the future and argue with my friends. The leaves coming out on the trees — signal, in both hemispheres, to start revising for exams.

From one spring to another. This book is about that journey, and all I have learned in between. The journey from dogmatic ignorance to the self-doubts of knowledge. From what are you going to do when you graduate to what are you going to do when you retire.

The Valedictory lecture is over now. It went very well. I spoke on 'Representing the Oppressed', and tried to show that I was neither a conservative nor a radical; I claimed that my constant aim as a teacher, here as always, was to ask simple questions and give complicated answers. When it was over, the audience applauded long and loud. Everyone at the reception asked, as I knew they would, And what are you going to do now? I went out to dinner with one of my best friends, and a poet who had just won the Pulitzer prize, and we told comic and entertaining anecdotes. I came home in the deepest depression I had known for years, hating myself, feeling unloved and unlovable, not wanting to retire at all, wanting to retire that instant. If I had sat down then to write some of this book, it would have been very explicitly about the inner life, but (fortunately) I didn't. It is time now to yield to the chronicler's urge.

TRAVELLING

A Change in the Weather

The Gold Coast

October 1949. I stepped off the plane at Accra airport, and was wrapped in heat. I looked round for someone whom I could ask to switch it off; and for the next four years, the thought that it couldn't be switched off lay just under the surface, and could become frightening if one stopped and thought about it. The heat was a smothering presence, a constant reminder that we were only there temporarily. I loved the feel of West Africa: the fierce, predictable showers of rain, always announced by a premonitory gust of wind, and the huge sky, with its bold sun-sets. We could sit on our verandah and watch William Blake painting evening cloudscapes for us in huge streaks of colour. But one could not actually *live* in a place that was never cool. Just as one could not permanently live in a place where you could not be anonymous. If the car broke down and I took a bus into Accra, I was the only white person on it; people smiled at me and said 'Has your car broken down?' If I drove to an inland town to give an extra-mural class, passing through a village was an event: hundreds of children appeared out of the ground, surrounding the car, laughing, cheering, waving, miraculously not falling under the wheels. It was impossible to be inconspicuous, to be a passer-by, or a neighbour who hap-pened to teach in a college, not a representative of the colonising power. Sophisticated Africans would refer with a smile to the time, soon to come, 'when our guests have gone' : in the age of colonial freedom I was no longer an invader, just a guest, and guests do not stay long.

Was not the very idea of teaching English Literature in West Africa artificial? To read *Murder in the Cathedral* with those who had never entered a cathedral; to read nature poetry with those who had never seen a daffodil or heard a nightingale; to read Dickens with those who had never wandered the streets of London or seen 'gas looming through the fog in divers places in the streets': was that not obviously artificial? But I had grown up in Cape Town, far from nightingales and London fogs: that had not impeded my love of English literature, and my conviction that it was *my* literature. Why should it be more artificial for a West African to love English literature than for a South African? Indeed, there are thousands of English people who have never heard a nightingale and some of them must enjoy Keats; none of Dickens' readers today have travelled in a stage coach, and only the very oldest have seen gas lighting. Why should it be more artificial to be separated from the world you are reading about in space, than to be separated (as we all are reading Shakespeare and even Dickens) in time?

What we are taught at school doesn't seem artificial to us. We may dislike it, we may be reluctant pupils, but the fact that it's the syllabus suggests that if anything is to be learnt at school, this will be it. And plenty of West Africans had learnt Shakespeare at school. Speaking at a meeting in Accra once, I quoted the conclusion of *Julius Caesar* ('This was the noblest Roman of tham all'), and most of the audience joined in. There is a famous story of a speaker in the House of Commons hesitating over a Latin quotation, and the whole house prompted him with one voice. Latin poetry was at least as foreign to 18th century England as Shakespeare to twentieth century West Africa, but this did not make it inappropriate for the syllabus. My friend Jormby, an adult education organiser, would talk lovingly about how poems (English poems: what else?) made him see the world anew. Once in a class, when he was present, I read Frost's 'After Apple Picking', and he described vividly how this poem about physical exhaustion had a shadow poem lurking behind it, that was about death. I had nothing to teach Jormby about poetry.

***

C and J: The Englishman Abroad

What makes an African university African? It seemed a natural enough question, but to C it was merely wrongheaded. C was the first principal of the University College of the Gold Coast; before that he had been the classics don at a

Cambridge college. His view of universities was that they had been invented in the fourth century BC in Athens, and had not changed since. Whether they were situated in Cambridge or California or the Gold Coast was just a superficial detail: no doubt the botanists would do their research on local plants, the sociologists (if there had to be sociologists) would design their questionnaires around local issues, but the essential academic function of dispassionate rational inquiry into timeless problems would not change.

This is now a deeply unfashionable view; and for that reason, worth thinking about seriously. But when I thought about it, I could not fail to notice how closely the timeless idea of a university, as C set it up in the Gold Coast, resembled the actuality of the Cambridge where he had been teaching. In my very first term, C announced a series of lectures on Greek thought; they were the lectures he had given in Cambridge, and were announced in the same wording ('the lectures are open to all members of the university without fee' followed by details of time and place). All the students came: they drew no very clear distinction between requirements and extras, and if the principal put up a notice, that looked like a requirement. They listened patiently to his account of the pre-Socratics, the difficulty of being sure what Anaximander really thought, and what exactly was meant by 'logos'. Remote, yes, but was it any more remote than Chaucer — or for that matter plant physiology?

The opposite view was represented by J, who was director of extra-mural studies. In an age when adult education has become soberly professional, he stays in my memory as a rugged and colourful entrepreneur, vulgar, enterprising, energetic, tactless. J was vividly conscious of the fact that he was in Africa, and everything he did was directed at the local community. He set up a People's Education Association to represent the consumers of his extra-mural courses: it was democracy by fiat. He interfered in everything. At one of his innumerable weekend schools, he had invited an engineer from the Public Works Department to discuss village water supply. The talk was simple enough for the most impractical listener to follow, and included a careful description of digging a well by hand — all you needed was a metal cylinder and a spade; you stood inside the cylinder and dug and dug until you found water. No expertise was needed, only muscle. J was thrilled by the talk; 'now I'd like to go and dig a well,' he said. Any of us might have said that; but two weeks later I happened to walk past his house, and saw him loading his car with suitcases, baby cart, wife, assistant and (presumably) tools. 'I'm off to dig a well,' he said. He not only dug a couple of wells; he described the experience in his annual report, and added a section on how the government was mismanaging village water supply. It began, I remember, 'most of the well-digging in the Gold Coast today is being wasted for want of a ha'porth of educational tar.' The PWD were not pleased, and I think J had to make some kind of apology.

So there was C, pretending he was still in Cambridge, and J, intensely curious about every detail of local politics and local life — up to a point: it would not have occurred to him to start learning Twi, or Fante. C wore a tie, designed himself a kind of cassock to wear at official functions, and required us all to wear gowns when teaching (and the wearing of gowns, he pointed out, presupposed the wearing of long trousers). He played the piano and never raised his voice; he gave dinner parties — at which the ladies withdrew after dessert, and at which his wife whispered in the ear of my wife (aged 26) 'Remember you are the senior married lady, and you have to give the signal to leave'. J gave no dinner parties and was indifferent to the pre-Socratics. He was friendly to everyone and rude to everyone — his assistants, his colleagues, his wife. He set up a local equivalent of the Workers Education Association, which he called the PEA (P for People), because he believed in democracy, but he was the most prominent figure in it. He liked to do everything himself: when one of the temporary huts in which his department was housed seemed to be leaking, he climbed onto the asbestos roof, fell through and chipped a piece off his backbone.

What did West Africa need: the scholar and Hellenic rationalist, who disapproved of my attempts to set up a school to teach stewards how to read, because we were an academic institution and should not distract ourselves? Or the go-getter rushing around the country in his huge white Chevrolet, who was in favour of everyone who taught anything to anyone else? At least you could say for C that by not making any attempt to

Africanise the university, he was admitting that he was not the person to do it: a new generation would come along, and Africanising would be done by Africans. C would hope that they would Africanise the personnel but not the syllabus, but by that time he would be gone, and it would all have passed out of his control. J would be there still, loved and hated, shouting and chivvying, falling off roofs.

***

Christianity has several claims to distinction among the world's religions; and perhaps the most striking is its anti-humanism, its devaluing of pride. That we should turn the other cheek, that we should forgive our enemies, that there is no health in us: for the ordinary self-respecting person, this, if it were not so familiar, would be an affront.

In West Africa I found that apologising is not a natural human activity. An African I knew came to London on a work-study project, and found he did not like the way his workmates treated him. One said to him in the washroom, pointing to his face, 'Does it was off, then?' It was no doubt meant as a joke, but it was neither witty nor kindly, and Mark, understandably, did not care for the universal facile excuse, 'I was only joking'. He was angry and showed it, and was willing to fight the man. 'I'm sorry, Mark,' said the workmate, but this was not enough; 'You English,' said Mark, 'you always say you're sorry, and you think that makes it all right.' Mark clearly did not see apologising as a difficult and valuable exercise in humility, he saw it as an easy verbal gesture for getting out of a tight corner. He was, perhaps, being very observant.

My first year class, like any first year class, wrote essays that were full of errors in grammar and idiom. I decided that the best way to make them conscious of this was to use an actual ex-ample, so I typed out and duplicated one of the essays, leaving out the student's name, and handed it out. I explained that it was a typical example of their common mistakes, and that we were going to rewrite it correctly and idiomatically. I sensed an uneasiness even before someone put up his hand and said, if this was my essay, I would not like being picked out publicly in this way. I said that the essay had been chosen more or less at random, and was no worse than many of the others, but I could still sense the uneasiness, so I put it to the vote. How many think we should go on with this, I asked, and how many agree with Mr Mensah that it is unfair? Everyone voted no, so I collected the copies back and did something else.

Of course I should have handed out, not one student's complete essay, but an assemblage of sentences from different essays, and I have never repeated that mistake; as a result, I have never discovered whether English or German or American students would have reacted in the same way.

A third example concerns my poetry-loving friend Jormby. When I took our student production of *The Tempest* to the Accra Community Centre (more about this in a later chapter), I asked him to help, and he took charge of ticket sales. On the last night there was a gratifyingly long queue at the entrance and Jormby was late; when he arrived he told me, very calmly, that he had unfortunately forgotten to bring the cash box, containing the money and the unsold tickets, and would have to go home for it. I exploded, cursed him, and told him to hurry; somehow I managed to handle the queue, took their money, and scribbled some sort of ticket for them. I even discovered that I had a talent for mental arithmetic under pressure. Jormby returned with the cash box just before starting time, and I was able to rush backstage and encourage the actors.

A few days later, when Jormby and I met to sort out the money, he said in a dignified voice, 'I did not take much notice of what you said to me the other night. I knew you were excited, and could not have meant it all.' I said something dismissive, and we remained friends, but as I looked back I found something sublime about his assurance. He had offered no word of apology for his mistake, and had graciously indicated that he would spare me the need to apologise to him — thus making it clear that he had been insulted. What mattered to him most was his own dignity, and if he was gracious enough to overlook my attempt to dent it, he had all the same to make clear that it had been dented.

William Empson's book *The Structure of Complex Words* has influenced me as much as any work of literary criticism I have read. By exploring the implied statements in particular uses of important common words, Empson not only analyses poems and plays, he offers a version of cultural history. In his discussion of the colloquial use of 'dog' and 'rogue' and of Shakespeare's use of 'dog' in *Timon of Athens,* he wrote:

> The web of European civilisation seems to have been slung between the ideas of Christianity and those of a half-secret rival, centring perhaps (if you made it a system) round honour; one that stresses pride rather than humility, self-realisation rather than self-denial, caste rather than either the communion of saints or the individual soul.

'The web of European civilisation': what of other civilisations? If they are not slung between these two ideas, it is because they lack the ideas of Christianity, not because their sense of honour is any weaker. A society without Christianity, or a society where it was only a set of beliefs, not (or not yet) a cultural presence, would be much more uninhibited about the need for personal dignity and defending one's honour. West Africa was perhaps such a society: Britain is becoming one.

***

A bus ride represented my reluctant special status as a white man in West Africa; and as it happened, a bus ride remains in memory as the essence of my return to Britain. At the age of 27 my wife and I decided we'd seen enough of Africa. She had given up her job when our second child was born, and the following year I gave up mine; she went to Cape Town to show the children to grandparents, and I went to London to hunt for a job. So I stepped off the plane alone on a bright May afternoon, and took the coach to Victoria air terminal, as it then was.

Outside the windows lay the rest of my life. England seemed small, tidy and domestic; the flowers and the fruits and the sunshine were kept in gardens and greenhouses. Rows of terrace houses, ornate and three-storeyed, or tidy, modern and minute, stood up and looked down at their gardens; grocers and chemists and newsagents waited for customers who would spend small sums in cash and go on their anonymous way. A traffic light stopped us in front of the

Oak and Eagle, where a couple sat drinking outside in the cool sunshine, the man stretching his tweed suited legs in front of him, the woman in a cotton dress with a cardigan (I had forgotten that one wore cardigans with summer dresses), revealing, I was sure, no undergarments or bare flesh beneath straps and gaps and buttonholes, as the white women did in Accra. (Things have changed, since 1953.) Future busrides were dissolved in that hour of welcome, busrides in very different weather, sniffling with a cold or to a drearily familiar destination, and I accepted them all. In the endless domesticity of London I did not seem to have done anything rash, arriving back with two children and no job. If no university wanted me, I thought, I would teach in a school. Fortunately a university did.

Belfast

Reminiscences of Belfast should, one expects, deal with religious tension and tribal hostility, with soldiers on the streets and the terror of walking past a parked car; but in the 1950s it was a peaceful city, marked by its lilting accent and horse-drawn drays, patches of pre-war poverty and a few jokes about the Troubles of the 1920s, which nobody thought would ever recur. Reminiscences of teaching at Queen's University in those days of lost innocence must, inevitably, have a nostalgic air — nostalgia for peace, along with the nostalgia of looking back on early married life, my wife pushing a pramful of clothes to the launderette, the children speaking with broad Ulster accents (which they soon lost when we returned to England). Touches of nostalgia, too, for the dead: Eric Ashby, the perfect Vice-chancellor, tall, gracious and tough-minded, or Philip Larkin, tall, lugubrious and witty in the library; and the nostalgia of teaching for the Workers' Education Association when it had workers.

It took me two interviews to get a job in Belfast. In 1952 I applied for a post in the English Department, which I did not get (I sometimes comforted myself with the thought that Kingsley Amis was one of the other unsuccessful candidates); the following year I applied for a job in Extra-mural studies, which I did. Eric Ashby began the second interview by saying 'Ah, Mr

Lerner, we saw you last year. So good of you to come over again.' The candidates, as tends to happen in British universities, sat around in the waiting room, during the interviews and after they were over, trying to like each other; one of the others grew interested when I said I'd been in the Gold Coast, though it wasn't till later that I discovered that he'd applied for (and indeed got) the job I'd just left. When the secretary appeared to announce that I'd been appointed, he did not make the little formal speech I expected, but shook my hand and whispered into my ear 'Seven-fifty. Plus children's allowances.' I had become a lecturer in extra-mural studies.

Extra-mural teaching should be the perfect job. To be employed by the university without any of the chores: no examinations, no essays to mark, no committees, just lectures to give to those interested. And what better subject than literature? An extra-mural class on geology or history could be considered parasitic on the research and teaching within the university, but George Eliot and Keats wrote for the people in my adult education classes, not for academics and their students. Literature turned out, however, not to be as popular as I'd expected, and some of my classes were very small: in (was it?) Ballymena the local secretary described delightedly how the room had not been big enough to hold the crowd who'd come for geology the previous evening; looking round at my 6 or 7 auditors, scattered through the room, I did not take great comfort in the contrast. I found too that I missed the chores that bind us to our institution, the tedious tasks that establish a bond of common grumbles with one's colleagues. The extra-mural department never met as a body: our sensible director thought we all had better things to do than to discuss administrative arrangements and departmental policy; but when I listened to ordinary lecturers describing a tedious faculty meeting, or complaining how many exam scripts they had to mark, I felt a touch of envy.

When the Workers Education Association began, its purpose was to enable intelligent working men (seldom women) to make up for their lost educational opportunities. Gradually it lost its working-class flavour, and it ought now to be called not the WEA but the BEA or even the RB (retired bourgeoisie) EA. This change had taken place by the 1950s, but not yet, or not completely, in Belfast. There I had storekeepers and artisans who loved reading and had left school early, who being Ulstermen did no domestic chores and so had plenty of time to read, and who were proud of their democratically run association and its collaboration with the university. They came to my classes on Shakespeare, on the Victorian novel, even on the metaphysical poets, expressed lively views on Shakespeare's politics, and said how pleased they were that I'd decided to discuss Vaughan as well as Herbert. They were sophisticated and at the same time innocent; they loved literature, and did not want to use it for any purpose except itself. When I moved into the English department four years later I became a professional, though fortunately I could still teach my beloved Mr Willis and Mr Macateer of an evening.

It was Terence Spencer who pulled me into the English Department. He had been appointed the second professor of English a year or two after I came, because everyone was so dissatisfied with Professor B. B had been appointed in 1930 as a young and (presumably) promising scholar. He did not fulfil the promise, and by 1953 he had settled into a routine that included a little lecturing and a great deal of grumbling. His conversation was invariably polite and invariably trivial. He would talk about the price of coal, the weather, and the fact that his wife liked to listen to the news on the radio whereas he preferred the newspaper. The appointment of Terence was an attempt to prise the department out of the flabby hand of B, and one consequence of this was that I was invited to join it. For this a formal interview was necessary, and so for the third time I was summoned to the Vice-chancellor's committee room. Terence had discussed the move with me in some detail, and assured me that it would go smoothly, but B was, after all, still head of department. 'Does Professor B know that I am joining his department?' I asked, a little nervously. Terence was evasive and reassuring: 'don't worry about that.' 'Will he be at the interview?' 'Oh yes; but there's no need to worry.' On the day of the interview I met B emerging from the little shop opposite the university. 'I've been buying pipe cleaners,' he remarked. 'They keep the right kind here, I don't seem to be able to get them anywhere else.' I let him finish his explanation of what made a good pipe-cleaner, then paused for him to say something about the impending interview. 'Splendid weather,' he said, waving his hand at the sky, blue for once (though never the enormous blue sky of Africa). 'Belfast weather has a bad press.' Another pause, and he turned away. Desperately, I said, 'I think — I believe — we'll be meeting soon.' 'Soon' was only fifteen minutes away. B seemed to search his memory, to discover why he had come into the university, and nodded. 'I believe so,' he said vaguely, and walked on — to the same committee room as me.

B was nothing if not affable. Shortly after arriving I had bumped into him in a corridor; he greeted me warmly, and started telling me how sorry he was that he hadn't appointed me the year before, so effusively that he must have realised he was painting himself into a corner, and pulled up short to say 'Of course in Carnall we have a very good man — very good indeed' — as he had. Soon after that we received a formal invitation to dinner from his wife. This gave us a glimpse of his lively, childless marriage: it was then I learned that he needed his study to escape from the fact that she liked to listen to the radio, whereas he, as he put it, 'had learned to read' (it was hard to know if he was putting his wife down or not). The excellent dinner was followed by a choice of dessert. 'Would you prefer apple fool or lemon solid?' she asked each of us; and when it came to her husband, 'Ric, which will you have? They've both been started.' 'In that case my dear,' said Ric, 'I'll have a bit of each.' 'Very well,' she answered grimly, 'you may have both.' 'Oh ho,' chortled Ric to the table, 'put my foot in it again, haven't I?'

Much of what is said about Ulster Protestants is true (or was true in the 1950s): that they all go to church, that on Sundays they wear their best clothes and don't work in their gardens, that they think in religious terms. The Protestant students knew their Bible, the Catholics could handle theological ideas, and reading Milton was easy for them. To that extent, as with the WEA, they hadn't quite slipped into the post-modern age. Once, when a student seminar was limping, as any seminar does from time to time, and no-one seemed to have any interest in *Dr Faustus,* I tried in desperation the crudest question I could think of: 'Do you think it's blasphemous? Do you think

Marlowe is in Hell now, for writing it?' Suddenly they all woke up: whether Marlowe was in Hell turned out to be a question they cared about, and there was a lively argument.

I must have remembered that argument, more or less unconsciously, twenty years later, when I wrote a poem about Faustus:

Faustus, from Hell

The mortgage must be paid by now,
The bond expired,
Those endless documents
No longer needed
We used to write in mirror-Latin,
In Greek, or blood,
Saying, with diabolic cunning,
'To Hell with God',
Hoping the mumbo-jumbo might
Catch Nature unprepared,
And we'd find on the parchment
'e=mc squared.'
It's over now: the stars
Have lost their influence,
They're on the run; astronomers
Can see them blush.

Come, sing the new Credo:

The sun's a ball of gas; the heart a pump;
The earth is very old;
The arm's a lever and the eye a lens;
Belief's a bubble;
The sun stands still; the solar system moves;
The moon is cold;
The universe is finite without end;
And Hell's a fable.

Can I come out now?

Not sharing my students' concern about where we all go after death, I had dropped the interest in Marlowe: the Faust story is about Faust, not about its author. But I realised that Faust, as the centuries passed, would have kept up his interest in science, and I trusted that they took all the latest journals in Hell. To my delight, a colleague at Sussex who taught the history of science read the poem in the TLS, and wrote me a note saying that he would be putting it into his lectures. I did not tell him that he should thank the bored students of English 2a.

***

Only after I had joined the department did I discover that Terence had been less than open: he had accepted a chair in Birmingham, and had invited me into a department that he was leaving. And within a year B too had resigned, so a new professor was appointed; and then I went to America for a year, and soon after my return I left for Sussex. Nothing gives me a clearer picture of the lost world of the 1950s than the remark of a friend when I told him I was leaving: 'Seems strange, doesn't it, for there to be a *new* university?'

Orientation

My first visit to America was in 1960. I had been awarded the John Hay Whitney fellowship for visiting academics. The main condition of the fellowship was that one should teach in two different institutions, one semester in each, both of them off the beaten track, the sort of place that did not usually have distinguished visitors. My function would be to go there and pretend to be distinguished. I realised that when asked why I had been assigned to that particular institution, I would need to be tactful.

But first came orientation: that is, three days at Sarah Lawrence college, along with a host of other foreign visitors, being lectured to by American deans, college presidents, and even a few actual teachers, on the ways of American academia. We were told a lot of stock jokes which, since I hadn't heard them before, seemed rather witty: one college president explained that he had three main functions, to see that there was sex for the students, football for the alumni, and parking for the faculty. And since families were invited too, and most of the other visitors had come unencumbered, our four children (ranging from David, who was 10, to Richard, who was not yet talking) attracted a good deal of attention, and one speaker congratulated me publicly for being such a productive scholar: everyone smiled, and I realised that the remark was meant to be friendly, yet it still sounded like a put-down. (Yet a short while earlier, writing to a former head of department, I mentioned some of my recent books and articles, and received the reply 'You seem to be tremendously prolific.' Write a little, write a lot, and if you are paranoiac enough you will feel put down.)

On the very first evening of the orientation session I encountered a small — and revealing — misunderstanding. Hosts as well as visitors had been invited, and we were to meet Wayne Booth, then head of English at Earlham College, where I was to spend my first term. At the reception desk I overheard an

American registering and saying (I thought) 'My name is Booth', so I accosted him and said 'Hello, I'm Lerner.' He nodded, asked hesitantly if I'd had a good trip, and after a few awkward moments muttered 'Well, I'll be seeing you around,' and took his leave. My heart sank: this offhand person was to be my colleague for the next four months, and the American warmth and friendliness of which I'd heard so much didn't seem any part of what we were orienting to.

All was soon well. The man's name was not Booth but Bush (or Bull or Tooth or some other half-homonym); Wayne Booth turned up shortly afterwards, was as warm and welcoming as one could wish (and has become a lifelong friend), and before long we were discussing *The Rhetoric of Fiction,* which had just been accepted for publication. So the next day I sought out Mr Tooth, who was a professor of mathematics in a big university, and apologised. He was gracious, and we exchanged pleasantries. As I was moving off I said, 'You must have thought it very odd, that a stranger come up to you and introduced himself.' 'Oh,' he answered, 'I thought you were Max Lerner.' So this is America, I thought. Famous academics accost total strangers and announce who they are: 'I'm Schlesinger, I'm Oppenheimer, I'm Bloom.'

The year was, as one would expect, full of stimulus. Both institutions to which I was sent turned out to be of high quality, so there was no need after all to be tactful when asked why they had been chosen to receive my visit. The three older children attended the local schools, and we had our first encounter with school reports in which the pupil was asked to assess his own progress. We once stopped for lunch at a fast food restaurant where I felt the children were being even noisier than usual, and as we left the waitress asked my wife, 'Is your husband a college professor?' 'Yes,' she said, 'how did you know?' 'Because the children are so well-behaved.'

***

Oriented at last?

Since then thirty-five years have passed. I paid two other, briefer visits to the USA, before finally coming to Vanderbilt as a regular faculty member. By now, surely, I must be oriented. I must be capable of answering the questions I have so often been asked: what are American students like? How do American universities differ from British (or French or German) universities? Or as capable as I'll ever be.

Once, as I walked across the campus during my first year at Vanderbilt, my eye was caught by a notice pinned to a tree. 'Everyone is invited,' it said, 'to my 21st birthday party, next Friday evening' — followed by date, time and place. The student was in my survey class, but I didn't go to the party; I did however realise that I had found a way to answer the question, what are American students like; for I could not imagine seeing such a notice in any other country. And what does the notice tell us? That the girl was the spoilt darling of a capitalist daddy, throwing her money round to impress? Or that she was open and generous, unable to believe there was anyone on campus she would want to exclude? And if the latter, did that mean that all of humanity was welcome at her party, or that there was no danger of undesirables turning up because she realised she belonged to a privileged institution that had done the excluding for her? Or are all these alternative formulations just different ways of saying the same thing?

***

What one learns

In a good teaching situation, learning takes place in both directions, but just what one learns from one's students is not easy to pin down. I don't learn much from them about the English literature I have been reading for a lifetime, but I do learn a lot about them — and about myself. Both pieces of learning can be unwelcome, as when a girl in the survey class reading Hopkins' poems of religious despair, wanted to know what had happened to make him so upset; my attempts to explain that he felt shut out from God, and then to talk about the theology that lay behind such a conviction, led her to say, 'But it's all so *vague*', and then to add, 'Still, it was written a hundred years ago, what can you expect?' She belonged to the most assiduously church-going nation in the world, but she had not learned about the dark night of the soul. When Hopkins referred to the 'sweating selves' of the lost, and I explained that they were the damned, she referred to them as the people who don't go to church: religion, to her, meant church-going. 'Worship at the church of your choice,' ran a notice opposite our house in Nashville. Should one, I wondered, rejoice at the spirit of tolerance there shown, or shake one's head over the marketing of religion (We know you have a choice of religions: thank you for choosing Presbyterian).

Or there was the occasion in my seminar on women in the 19th Century, in which we discussed the convention that proposals of marriage have to come from the man. I produced my theory that the reason for this is that in a society in which the position of old maids was so bad, it was far more urgent for women to get married than for men; and therefore the pretence was maintained that the woman was doing the man a favour. I asked whether this practice is still alive in the American South today, and from my small group of one man and half a dozen women (one married, two engaged, some unattached) I got fascinating answers. If the group was representative, it was clear that the practice is moribund, but the habit of the young man consulting the girl's parents is very much alive. 'John asked my father before he asked me,' said the married woman; but added that he already knew her answer. Most striking was the response of the young man. 'I don't want any girl proposing to me,' he declared. 'I can tell you now, if anyone does, the answer is no.' He grew eloquent, even indignant, to the amusement of all the women. So what had I learned? That at least one Southern man lived further back in the past than the women? That Southern eloquence for a lost cause is still alive? Or that one shouldn't generalise?

The more individual the student the less one can generalise from her case. Was anyone ever as individual as Jo? Jo's talent was for writing excuses — a universal practice, surely, but perhaps more prevalent, or at least more urgent, in a system where your teacher is also your examiner, and a missed essay can pull down your all-important Grade Point Average. I kept Jo's excuses, and I now quote them, hoping that she will never read this book. I have corrected the spelling as a gesture of friendship, and abridged them slightly, but they are otherwise unchanged.

Monday

Professor Lerner,

I've come by already once early this morning and missed you, so I decided to leave you a note. You gave me an extension on the Donne paper. Well, obviously since it is not attached to this note, it is not finished. Although the reason probably does not matter to you all that much, I would like to briefly explain. Last night I went to the Peabody library to study. It was a convenience since I live on Peabody so I went there to try to concentrate on my paper. I took a study break around 9.30 and went to get something to eat. I ended up going to my room to get some money where I was detained by a phone call. It was 10.45 before I returned to the library, and it was closed! I assumed it stayed open till midnight like the rest of the libraries on campus. So all of my notes and the pages I had written were locked up... If you want to verify my story, I talked to a young woman with a bright pink sweater on and glasses when I went there today. She helped me find my book bag and papers... I am sorry for having so much trouble again. I really do want to major in English and would like to do fairly well in your class so am very disturbed.

Thanks,

Jo

Thursday

Dear Professor Lerner,

Here is my paper finally. I apologise greatly about all of the confusion and the inconvenience which I have caused you to suffer. I appreciate your patience and understanding too. I had wanted to get this to you as soon as possible, but being that typing is such an overwhelming task for me, I did not have time to do it until last night, mainly because I worked Monday and Tuesday nights until midnight. With early morning classes I just cannot stay up all night typing after work.

I said above that last night was my first chance to type, yet you will soon notice that this paper is not typed. I once again am sorry. I have a Physics lab from 7-10 pm on Wednesdays. Last night I had planned to arrange with my professor to do it on another day so I could work on typing the paper. Well, he wouldn't let me because it was a long and complicated lab. So I called a friend of mine who said that he's meet me after lab and help me type. Well I did not get home from lab until almost 11.00. He did not show up until 1 am. That part did not bother me. The bad part is that he had gone out beforehand and was quite intoxicated. Indeed, he passed out in my room last night! Not what I needed! I tried to start typing about 3 am, but knew it would take me forever, so I finally wrote it very neatly for you, which still took up most of the night…

As you'll see, I was headed towards some of the same ideas as you explained to us, but never totally grasped them. I was not in class today because I was in Student Health (Student Death as we call it). I stopped by there on my way to class to get something for my allergies and one of my hall mates was in there. She had fallen down the cement stair by the main library and really hurt herself. She was really upset because she had a test and they wanted her to get X-rays and everything else. So I stayed with her to calm her down. It turns out she broke her ankle although it took us from 9.30 am until 12.15 to find this out. Sorry again for all the trouble. My next paper will be early because I never want to go through this much trouble again!

Thank you,

Jo.

When I retired from Vanderbilt I read this letter at my farewell party. I'm constantly being asked, I remarked, how American students differ from English (or German or African) students; the best answer I can think of is to read you this letter, and say that I can't imagine getting such a letter in any other country. The reading was a huge success: everyone roared with laughter and applauded furiously. I began to feel I had stolen Jo's copyright: they seemed to be applauding me, not her. And a lot of people remarked afterwards that Jo had a good deal of literary talent; I hope you didn't penalise her, they said, after such a lively letter. So perhaps I don't after all hope that Jo never reads this book.

Visiting South Africa

To be a visitor in the country where you were born and grew up is not, of course, peculiar either to the twentieth century or to academic life; and for those who have fled persecution it has meant something far more painful than the little ironies and readjustments I am now to record. In 1978 the Christian Fellowship Trust asked me to go to South Africa. That worthy body arranged for professionals in Britain and South Africa to spend a few months working in the other country. They paid the fare, arranged what contacts they could, and helped you find hospitality in the homes of sympathisers and former Fellows. Their contacts were mostly with churches and social workers, but they would be delighted, they said, to do what they could to put me in touch with writers and academics. They wanted me to see as much of South African society as possible, and of course not to confine myself to the whites.

I told them I could only go for 6 weeks, not the three months they preferred; that I would be able to make my own contacts, and that I wanted to go only to Cape Town. The more you travel round a country, I claimed, the less you really see. A lot of the people I knew were in the Cape, and it had three universities, within easy reach of each other, one of each kind: Cape Town (my Alma Mater) belonged to the white liberals, Stellenbosch was the traditional centre of Afrikaner intellectual life (six of the first seven prime ministers were Stellenbosch graduates), and the University of the Western Cape at Bellville was for the Cape Coloured. The CFT agreed, though it was arranged that I would spend the last week in Johannesburg, and I arrived on the 19th of July.

It was 31 years since I'd left, and I had been back twice, in 1950 and in 1969. I was, I felt, completely anglicised by now. Speaking to strangers, I would be able, if I wished, to play the innocent outsider, inquiring about local customs, probing people's opinions, inviting whatever mixture of hostility, deference or condescension was proffered by my interlocutor to the interfering foreigner. When I spoke to those who knew who I was, I received conspiratorial winks, or patient explanations ('a lot has changed since you left, you know'), or well-concealed envy ('some of us have stayed, of course').

I had left to continue my studies at Cambridge, with no intention of returning (I did not tell my mother that, but she realised). Both my parents had grown up in England, my mother, indeed, belonging to that now (surely) extinct group who not only never learned Afrikaans, but actually referred to England as 'home'. She had been seventeen when she left her village in Surrey to join her brother in Cape Town, and since my birth she had been back to England twice. (Visiting us at the age of 70, she actually died where she was born). There are several poems about her in my book *Rembrandt's Mirror,* published in 1987, for it took a long time before I could write about my family.

Full Circle

Born in this village, left at seventeen,
Returned at seventy, died. Her parents' house
Shrunken and sold. Watercress still for sale
At Peaslake farm: penny a bunch it was.
Limp from the stream, it tore your mouth. The owls
Still hooting nightly, 'Home. Go home.' Her cousins
Living in Guildford. Weeds in her sister's garden.
Born here. Come back here. A biography.

That leaves out everything: sun on the rock,
White on the water. The last thrust of sea,
The sight of Cape Town lurching in the wind.
Her brother at the dock: 'That's Table Mountain'
— The towering presence she would learn to live with.
No owls, no watercress. At first, no letters.
Grapes, naartjies, proteas. Suburban gardens
With huge black harmless gardeners. Dark hibiscus
In its green wall, and dahlias exploding.
Weeping for letters, weeping when they came.
On Sundays the young men, handsome or clever,
But never both. Her brother's wife, her brother,
Carefully saying nothing. The stony mountain

Carefully saying nothing. No-one to ask.
The young men growing more importunate,
Then less. And so she chose the clever one.

She watched her son steal all the cleverness
And hide himself in words. She watched him leave
Into the thrusting sea, and dared not ask.
The sun flared on the water, hurt her head,
Shouted his absence. Again, she wept for letters.

She woke with morning. Day like a spider's web
Was sticky on her face. As the hours passed
Her skin grew drier, she could feel the village
Throbbing inside her: watercress for tea,
Draggled and sharp. Mother in tears. 'Where's Will?'
'Your brother's gone to make his fortune, dear.'
'Can I go too?' She felt the room go still.

If it would rain, if it would only rain.
Fifty three years, and back in England. Rain
Would wash the stickiness, would still the owls,
'Come home,come home,come home.'
While her son watched, her hand
Wavered and dipped, trying in vain to tear
From her dry skin the spider-web of air.

***

I left on the Carnarvon Castle, still equipped as a troopship, amid rain, mist and wind, gripped by sea-sickness and exhilaration, and arrived at Southampton 17 days later amid sunshine and birdsong: the weather had committed an inversion to welcome me. I set off to find the aunt I hardly knew, whose address had elicited roars of delight from the friends I gave it to: High Hobby, Hackhurst Lane, Abinger Hammer, near Dorking — it sounded more English than Howards End. I delighted in the address, in my ration book, in cycling round Surrey. I felt my new life was beginning, and my new friends would all be English.

In fact a good number of them were South Africans who, like me, had looked forward to shedding their past selves and meeting the English. We used to spend long hours discussing whether we should go back. Some said yes, some said no: the politically involved, the politically indifferent. But which was which? You stayed away because you did not care about the oppression of Africans, or because you cared so much that it was not safe to return. You returned because you felt a duty to teach in the country that had educated you, or because you could not bear to live without the sight of Table Mountain, and the white horses stirred up by the south-easter on Table Bay. One of our number tried to sum up the endless argument: 'If you're going back because of sunrise in the Karroo,' he said, 'or to see the heat haze over Table Mountain, is there anything useful you can do?' But when my friends grew nostalgic for the landscape, I thought about the Alps, and Wordsworth climbing Snowdon, and Tennyson and Catullus at Sirmio.

That is some at least of the background when I stepped off the plane on the 19th of July 1978. So much has changed since then, that any sketch of the South Africa of 1978 will seem like an exercise in historical imagination, a leap back into the bad old days of apartheid. Yet almost everyone in the ensuing anecdotes is alive and well and the same person — if one ever is the same person twenty years later. No-one is yet sure just how much the world around them has changed.

During my six weeks I gave sixty talks — poetry readings, formal lectures, discussions, whatever was asked for: it was the most strenuous lecture tour I have ever done. I lectured to anyone who asked: high schools, church groups, literary societies, as well as the three universities I was supposed to be visiting. One of the talks lasted three hours: it was to a group of teachers from coloured schools, for whom hearing a visiting professor from England was the chance of a lifetime. In theory it was a one-hour lecture followed by discussion, but the discussion consisted of someone saying, every now and then, 'Now will you please talk about...'

I went three times to the University of the Western Cape. This was one of the colleges set up by the Nationalist government when they segregated the universities. The theory of apartheid was that each racial group should be educated separately, so there was a college for Africans in the Northern Transvaal, for Indians in Natal, and for the Cape Coloured at

Belleville. Politically conscious non-whites naturally disapproved of them. Richard, a short story writer who taught at Hewatt Training College, where coloured teachers studied, explained to me that he would have nothing do with the segregated education the government had introduced, had refused the invitation to set up an African literature department there, and even refused to set foot in the place. I objected that he was himself teaching at a segregated institution. That was different, he claimed: Hewatt was a long-established college, it wasn't set up as part of a systematic move to apartheid. But it was financed in the same way, by the same government: Richard was taking his stand on history, not on politics.

The logic of boycotts is always tricky. In 1978 Cape Town had two fine modern theatres, the Nico Malan, in the town, and the Baxter, attached to the university. Kathryn, the secretary of the Arts Centre at the Cathedral, a young coloured woman who had helped arrange my programme, would not go to the Nico Malan. Of course if it had been for whites only she could not even have decided not to go, but it had a permit, allowing it to take racially mixed audiences. If the theatre applies for a permit, she explained to me, this implies an acceptance of the system, so we will not go to a place with a permit. The Baxter theatre, which was more recent, began by admitting non-whites without a permit, and was then informed, by some authority or other, that they'd been granted a permit. Should it too be boycotted? Kathryn and her husband went to the Baxter, but I discovered that the students at the non-white university were boycotting it. They gave as their reason the fact that it had been built with the labour of squatters. But it was government policy to force African squatters out of the Cape: was it not a good anti-government gesture to use squatter labour? At what point does one give up seeking a logic behind boycotts, and simply say that the lunacies of apartheid necessarily bred counter-lunacies?

And I had after all broken a boycott myself, since the British Association of University Teachers had asked its members not to go to South Africa. When my first lecture was introduced at the University of Stellenbosch, the professor referred to this. 'Mr Lerner has shown great courage,' he said, 'in defying the boycott and coming to South Africa to lecture.' Of course that was nonsense: no courage at all was required to do something my left-wing colleagues did not wish me to do, and that I had often argued against. It was no surprise to discover that white South Africans were against the boycott: what mattered, I was aware, was how the non-whites felt.

Gertie was a middle-aged African woman, now trying to take a correspondence degree. She had been politicised by her children, several of whom had gone into exile, and one of whom had died abroad. She was the only person I met, in my six weeks, who told me that I shouldn't have come (but then staunch believers in total boycott probably wouldn't even have spoken to me). 'We do not altogether trust you,' she said. 'You come here and say that the Africans are happy, that they wear shirts and trousers, not blankets, that you haven't seen anyone shot in the streets. You say, look how much press freedom there is in South Africa.' We had just been listening to a South African newspaperman, a respected progressive, saying 'in sorrow' that there was more press freedom in South Africa than in any other African country; and Gertie had not liked him saying it, she felt the comparison was unfair, but she had not succeeded in persuading him that it wasn't true.

Gertie was in favour of all that the young blacks had done in the Soweto uprisings, including the burning down of schools. To the suggestion that it would have been more logical to burn down the police stations she reacted with angry contempt: 'How do you get to the police stations, past all the guns?' I asked if she wanted the schools rebuilt.

'It doesn't matter,' she said. 'You don't think they're *our* schools, do you?'

'Don't you want your children to learn to read?'

'They'll learn, somehow or other,' she said. 'We'll have street schools if we need to.'

That evening, pondering what Gertie had said, I met Alice. She was baby-sitting for the friends I was staying with. Alice was coloured, Muslim, also middle-aged. She had had nine children, eight of them living. She acted as companion and did 'general work' for two retired doctors, both called Cohen, both bed-ridden.

'Dr Cohen said to me one day, "Come over to the bed, Alice, so

I can bless you. You have made my day. I can bless you because I'm a Cohen, it's like being a rabbi." ' Why had he said that? 'Because I made him laugh. He said, "No-one has made me laugh like this for ages." So he blessed me. I can count myself really lucky, because I work for two Cohens.'

I asked if she had had a hard life. 'You know, we didn't realise how hard it was, only now when it's got a bit easier, the children all grown up, four of them married, only now we can realise we never had time to stop and think about it.' None of her children would have nine babies. 'You know, people nowadays are so clever, they can decide when to have children, we never knew anything about that.' So all hers will only have one or two, but they are so close they're all growing up together like one family. Alice had just had a hysterectomy (was it Dr Cohen who taught her the word?), and as thanksgiving for her recovery she intended to go and help in an orphanage.

Two women, one African, one coloured. Both had lost a child. Both had worked hard all their lives, mainly for others. Both were friendly, and both (it was clear) were better people than me. One of them politically conscious, the other totally uninterested in politics. I found it impossible to say that one was right, the other wrong.

***

The Coloured University

In 1978 the University of the Western Cape was staffed by Afrikaner schoolteachers, staunch Nationalists who believed in apartheid and were glad of the opportunity to move from school to university teaching while also acting on their beliefs. They were not, I felt sure, altogether pleased to see me. I'd have been fascinated to be a fly on the wall when the English Department received my letter, announcing that I was coming to South Africa for the Christian Fellowship Trust, and would love to visit their university; that I would do any teaching they might find useful, and it would not cost them anything. Whatever they said to one another, they received me nervously. They were all huge: I felt sure they had been rugby players in their youth. I am only 5ft 7, and they towered over me, but they were terrified of me. I was academia, come to see through their pretensions; I was scholarship, come to discover what they didn't know; I was a British visitor, come to denounce them to the world. Professor Potgieter was the biggest of all, but he shook when I asked him anything. The more polite I was, the more nervous he grew. And what part of English literature are you most interested in? I asked, choosing my words carefully. He hesitated; beads of sweat were forming on his brow. 'What about a cup of tea?' he said, in an urgent voice.

The students were, of course, very different. They showed no inhibitions about talking to me, and none of them said that I ought not to have come (or were they just polite?). Some of them said they were at the institution under protest. One girl objected indignantly that she was happy there, and thought it a good university. The government spent money on it, the rector was coloured, it was allowed to take members of all racial groups (but of course there were very few except Coloureds). I looked round the refectory and remarked how filthy it was, and added (with a touch of smugness) that in my university everyone was asked to take his dirty dishes back to the counter, and did.

'It is part of our protest,' one student explained.

'Nonsense,' said the girl who liked it there, 'it is an excuse for their own slovenliness.'

Mr R, the rector, was the most interesting man I met. He began by telling me that we had been fellow students at UCT, and I felt ashamed that I did not remember him. He was the first coloured rector, and had been appointed after the 1976 riots, when one of the demands of protesting students had been for a coloured rector. He had been an opponent of the institution at first, but he decided to take the post, so he moved (as he explained with amused pride) from being the head of a primary school to being the rector of a university. And now that he was there, he intended to make the place work. The students went on protesting (this was the seventies, student protests were dying down in America, but they were still flourishing at Sussex); and I was familiar with the problems of walking through picket lines, resisting disruption, controlling violence, and (for a rector) whether to call in the police. Richard, I remembered, had been very scornful of this rector, calling him a time-server; speaking to me, he appeared earnest and well-meaning. During the last protest he had addressed the students, telling them he was ready to resign if they insisted, but that it was student insistence on having a coloured rector that had led to his appointment: did they want to go back to having an Afrikaner?

R's problems, it was clear, were and were not the same as those of an English vice-chancellor. The police he would call in were not the fair-minded, scrupulous English police, these were the thugs of apartheid, glad of a chance to beat up 'coolies'. But the radical students in England would hoot at the claim that their police were scrupulous, just as the South African government would get indignant at the suggestion that theirs were thugs.

The very beginning of my visit to UWC will serve as an epilogue. One of the Afrikaners (more friendly and relaxed than the giant Potgieter) introduced me at my opening lecture. He told the audience something about me, and I saw him looking round for something more personal to add. 'I should tell you, he said, 'that Mr Lerner wrote and said he wanted to come here. We didn't invite him, he wrote and asked to come.' With a friendly smile, he sat down and left the platform to me. Perhaps, I reflected, there are some people in favour of a boycott, after all.

***

The Calvin Daybook

At Stellenbosch the most interesting member of the English Department was Stan, a serious minded, politically aware person, far more fluent in Afrikaans than most English-speakers, and, because he had grown up on a farm in Natal, fluent in Zulu as well. I found our literary tastes were not the same (he thought little of Richard Wilbur, and far more than I did of the Soweto poets: but it's impossible to disentangle how far that's a political and how far a literary judgement). Stan and his wife had been all ready to leave for Canada a few years earlier; he even had a job arranged. While negotiations were going on about the job, Soweto exploded in the riots of 1976, and they found that all their friends now assumed they would leave as quickly as they could. The result of all this was that they stayed, and he took the job at Stellenbosch. Just before I left, he told me that he had been offered the chair of English at UWC (presumably Potgieter was retiring — or had R turned out a tougher rector than expected, and eased him out?) Much later, I discovered that Stan took the job, then became Dean, and watched the institution turn into something very different from what was originally planned, with a Marxist rector, who announced that he wished it to become the intellectual centre of the Left in South Africa. Stan is a devout Christian, but had no difficulty in accepting and supporting this programme. I last met Stan in 1992, and recognised what, if all goes well, the new South Africa will be like

Professor Van Rooyen, in contrast, represented the old South Africa. I had asked my liberal friend Johann at Stellenbosch if he could introduce me to a real *verkrampte*, and he took me round to spend an afternoon with this newly retired professor of Theology; then, after mentioning that Van Rooyen was looking forward to the opportunity of putting his case to me, he prudently withdrew. Van Rooyen was delighted to have a visitor from England, and I never confessed to him that I was a renegade South African. He explained the government's policy lucidly and politely, and now that policy is in ruins, I find myself fascinated by the recollection of hearing it defended when it was flourishing. It was all based on stewardship, Van Rooyen explained: the whites saw themselves as helping the blacks take their place as a civilised people, and the Afrikaners had done more for blacks than anyone else had ever done; but they had a long way to go. It was not possible for the government to move too quickly, because it had its own rural voters to think of. If too much money, raised by taxing the whites, was diverted to educating the blacks, there would be protests. I queried the term 'diverted': what are taxes for, if not to set up schools for the poor as well as the rich? He nodded, but after a little thought he continued to use the term, for his position was based on the belief that South Africa is not one nation but many. He did not object to the idea of Africans acquiring political power (slowly), and running their own affairs (though he seemed never to face the problem of the dependence of white South Africa's economy on black labour); but he could not tolerate the thought of Africans exercising political power over whites. Do I hope that Professor Van Rooyen is still alive today, and is watching Mandela's South Africa coming into being, or would it be kinder to think he has been spared the adjustment? He was a gentle and thoughtful man, and if he is not too old to bear the thought, I would like to think he is seeing how wrong he was.

But we did not spend much of our time discussing politics. His political opinions were, after all, more or less predictable; and the chance to meet a real seventeenth century Calvinist in the flesh was too good to miss. A year or two earlier, I had taught a seminar on English Literature and the Civil War with my colleague Willie, who is a distinguished authority on seventeenth century Puritanism; not surprisingly, Calvinism had figured prominently in our syllabus. After the second meeting, one of the students stayed behind and said, 'I think I ought to tell you that I am a Calvinist.' We were delighted, and told him that we looked forward greatly to his participation in the discussions, but alas, he turned out to be a very twentieth century sort of Calvinist, so that we found ourselves saying, time after time, no, that's not really what Calvin believed. Now here was the chance to meet the real thing at last.

So I questioned Professor Van Rooyen at length about his theological beliefs, which he set forth with care and logic. He described the break between the Dutch Reformed Church in South Africa, and the parent church in Holland, which had only recently been made final. The South African church had broken away because of what they saw as Dutch support for terrorists, and because of their unbiblical theology: those Dutch theologians who saw Jesus Christ as human model, and denied the doctrine of His propitiatory death, should in Van Rooyen's view have been disciplined. I asked about predestination, and he replied, 'What about a cup of coffee?' But he was no Potgieter: he simply wanted to insert a natural break while he prepared his answer to this all-important question.

Predestination, he explained, was not to be conceived mechanically. It was not a matter of a reward or punishment imposed arbitrarily at the end; the whole life of the elect was a closeness to God, the reprobate led the life of the damned all through. All the same, I protested, didn't he find the idea of everlasting punishment almost unbelievably cruel? Yes, if he allowed himself to be led by his human thoughts and feelings he would not be able to accept it, but Scripture made it quite clear (of course Scripture is far less clear on the matter than Calvin, but I did not press that point). I could not help admiring the careful reasoning that informed all his theology, but when he encountered a real problem he did what theologians always do, he explained that God's ways are supra-logical. How, I asked, do we distinguish the supra-logical from the merely illogical, and he replied by discussing the nature of God: there is nothing in His nature that is against logic. This was a neat dodge: if the difference between the supra-logical and the illogical was a matter of different thought-processes by us, it would not be difficult to show that they are really the same; but by invoking the nature of God he moves us from reason to faith when reason is in trouble. The only objection, of course, is to wonder why you should not do this from the start, thus eliminating theology completely, and basing the whole religion on faith.

I asked Professor Van Rooyen why God has made it so easy for an Afrikaner to be saved (by placing the true church on his doorstep) and so hard for, say, a Russian. His reply shows that he is a genuinely humble man: he insists that no individual should ever be sure of his salvation. But in general terms he has no difficulty in accepting that God has chosen the Afrikaners: it would not, after all, be the first time He had chosen a people.

As I left, Professor Van Rooyen showed me, with some pride, the task that kept him busy during retirement: he was compiling a daybook of passages from Calvin, a page of text (mostly from the *Institutes,* occasionally from the letters) for each day. That is the gift he hoped to leave to his people. It's not easy, he explained, to translate Calvin's Latin into Afrikaans, but he'd done 220 so far.

'I suppose you're going to do 365,' I said, feeling my remark to be banal in the extreme. But it wasn't, for he answered, with just a shade of reproof, 'Three hundred and sixty-*six.*' Everything in this world is decreed by the Calvinist God, including the leap-years.

The Gift of Tongues

It should hardly need saying that one wants to know the language. Unfortunately, the most useful skill is also the hardest. Any language learner knows (or are all language learners not the same? Am I speaking only for the deaf?) that of the four processes — reading, writing, hearing, speaking — the most difficult to master is hearing: easy enough when the foreign speaker is addressing you, but frustratingly difficult when they speak among themselves, all at once, interrupting, leaving sentences unfinished, using modish slang, drastically reducing the redundancy that we need for communication. And in a teaching situation in a foreign country where the medium is English, the students will make their official statements in English and their asides in their own language. The nugget of insight that the student offers the class is wrapped in a coating of prejudice, half-understanding and irony: how useful it would be to catch a glimpse of that coating by hearing the asides. Alas, pupils are skilled at mutters and whispers that evade the teacher even in a monoglot situation: 'If I *have* to answer pompous questions like that.' 'He thinks he knows all about women.' 'If we believe an old bore like Henry James (or Wordsworth, or Milton, or Auden, to taste).' 'Go on with your verbal masturbation.' 'What is she wearing underneath?' 'Oh God, not again.' 'Will that be in the exam?' (though this one may well be out loud). 'Wait till the revolution comes.' When the situation is bilingual, how easy for them, how hard for the visiting teacher. I am convinced (on no real evidence) that all these remarks have been made in my classroom in a foreign tongue incomprehensible to me, perhaps accompanied by a polite, even deferential smile.

Lecturing on modern literature in an Indian university, to quite a large group of students and, in the front row, the faculty of the English Department, I recognised, as soon as question time began, the old and inevitable dilemma of the visiting lecturer: who is to ask the questions? If the faculty, then there is a good chance of a lively discussion, but one from which the students are excluded; if the faculty hold back, so that the students can speak, there will be long pauses while no-one has the courage to risk exposure — and a particularly long pause before the first question. A mild joke from the lecturer about the difficulty of being the first to speak may seem to relieve the tension, but only at the cost of reimposing it, perhaps stronger than ever, when the nervous titter has died down. That is why it is often better to talk to a group of faculty only, or a group of students only, but neither is easy. University teachers are proud and busy people: to persuade them that they can and wish to gather together on Friday at 3 o'clock to hear a visiting speaker of whom they have never heard is not an easy task, especially in a remote university without the habit of colloquium and visitors. To talk to students only is easy to arrange — you simply arrive at an ordinary timetable hour, when they would normally be studying Shakespeare or Romantic poetry with Dr X, and you have something closer to a normal teaching situation: closer to, but still far from, for you do not know the students, do not even (if the hosts have been unco-operative or embarrassed or deferential) know what texts they have read. And of course Dr X is there…

At my Indian lecture on modern literature there was a student willing to speak — and to go on speaking. 'Sir, is it not true that modern English literature is written to justify colonial oppression?' Asked to elaborate, he said the same thing again, in predictable abstract clauses: English literature is a way of making us feel that white men are all very civilised, and coloured men are savages. 'It makes us believe in the white man's burden, but it is the black man, or the Indian, who carries the burden. It shows us what the English think of the Indians, but why doesn't it tell us what the Indians think of the English?' It has a political programme, though it pretends not to. And so on. I remember he was very naive, and even the crude remarks I have just attributed to him would have been beyond his powers: I'm sure he didn't refer to the black man's burden. There was a certain amount of laughter and nodding from the other students when he finished.

How does one reply? The lecturer has enormous advantages: he is standing on the platform, in a position of authority, he has heard it all before, he has certainly read more than the student. In a situation of real political crisis these advantages all become drawbacks, as the audience will readily identify with the un-authorised, the anti-official, the unlearned. But this, I sensed, was not the case here: that student laughter relaxed the situation, and anyway this was 1981, the student revolution was over, and there was no political crisis in India. The young man was not threatening to lead the audience in chanting slogans or marching out of the room. I had several options. I could have pointed out that most modern English literature has nothing to do with colonialism, and challenged him to interpret Norman McCaig or Ivy Compton-Burnett as an imperialist apologist: but he would certainly not have read them, almost certainly not have heard of them. Or of course I could have done the opposite: I could have feigned to accept his position, and talked about Ki-pling, or cited hostile Indian essays on *A Passage to India*. I could have congratulated him on his understanding of neo-Marxist criticism, and suggested that Ted Hughes' fascination with violence, Graham Greene's subtleties on the problems of the ex-patriate Englishman, though they might not mention colonialism, were subtly suggestive of something like a white man's superior consciousness — and under the guise of accepting his view, gone on to show the difficulties in such a reading. We have all been here before.

I did none of this. I asked him who he was thinking of. More student laughter. 'I am not thinking of anyone in particular,' he said in the rhythmic Indian English that sounds so like a Welsh accent. 'I am just thinking in general terms.' It was growing clear that he didn't know much. I suggested that the argument would be more meaningful if we had some examples, and that I'd like to talk about a book he'd read, so would he suggest one. 'I am not an expert in English literature,' he said, unnecessarily; 'I am thinking in general terms, I am saying the political basis of it must be imperialism' (he had stopped using the interroga-tive). I began to feel sorry for him: the more confrontational he got, the easier it would be for me. I indicated gently — or rather, made him reveal that he knew nothing about modern literature, that he only knew political clichés. I was careful not to insult him. I may have tried to show how hard it is to find imperialism in Margaret Drabble or Penelope Mortimer, or how anti-colonialist Doris Lessing can be. And the student laughter grew stronger and stronger, they turned in their seats to grin at one another, they called out remarks to the speaker — all of course in Hindi (or Punjabi, or Gujarati: I forget where we were).

What I wanted to know, of course, was what the other students were saying. Were they rallying to his side? 'Good old Vishnu, he's showing this visitor that we aren't doormats.' 'Don't let him put you down, Vishnu, you show him there's an Indian point of view.' Or were they enjoying his discomfiture? 'Vishnu's put his foot in it again.' 'Shut up Vishnu, you don't know anything.' It could have been either, and over lunch I asked the faculty. But alas, they were so embarrassed about the whole episode, they just wanted to change the subject. 'Most of our students are not like that, they assured me. 'I am sorry he was so rude. He is not even a student of English.' That was all they wanted to say, and then went on to what an interesting lecture I had given.

I longed for the gift of tongues.

***

They order these things [differently] in France

My first really thorough attempt to acquire foreign tongues was by going to Dijon. In 1956 I was an extra-mural lecturer at Queens University, Belfast; ashamed of my lack of languages, I decided to do something about it, and so I sat down and wrote two letters. One was to the Academic Board of Queens, saying that I'd been invited to do some lecturing in Dijon, and would they please give me leave for that purpose; the other was to Professor Henri Talon in Dijon, saying that I had a term's leave from my university and wanted to improve my French, and would he like me to come to Dijon and do some teaching? I chose Talon because he was the only professor in France who might possibly have heard of me. I had read his book on Bunyan, and thought it likely that he would have read my article on 'Bunyan and the Puritan Culture' in the *Cambridge Journal,* one of the two scholarly articles I had so far publish-ed. He had.

The plan worked perfectly, the only complication being my family, consisting at that point of three small boys. Should we all go? Natalie could feel no great enthusiasm either at being left or at coming: where would we live, where would David go to school, what would we use for money? Talon wrote to say that I must not dream of bringing my family unless the question of ac-commodation was settled in advance, and there seemed little chance of that; so we decided I should go alone. Looking back, I am astonished at my wife's generosity in agreeing to this: it set what was to become a pattern in our family, but in all my sub-sequent trips abroad there was at any rate something for her: she was able to come out for a holiday, I was able to come home, or a child might go with me. This time there would be nothing but four months of being a single parent, no communication ex-cept by letter (I don't think I had in 1956 ever made a long-distance telephone call in my life). I realised later that the purpose of the trip would have been half-defeated if they had come, since I'd have spent half my time speaking English, not only to the children, but for everything we did together (my wife is a living proof that you can be very intelligent without having any gift for languages). As it was, apart from giving my classes in English, I was able to immerse myself totally in French.

I spent a few days in Paris, where a colleague in French from Belfast was staying; I found a room in his hotel, and nodded gratefully when he corrected my grammar. I had a room off which another room opened, in which an old lady slept. She had to tiptoe through my room to go to work in the morning: I was invariably in bed still, and she excused herself softly and humbly. Once or twice she spoke to me in the evenings, apologised once more for coming through, offered me tea, and told me how *sérieux* I was for sitting reading a book. She ex-plained that she worked in a home for the blind, a job which led one to count one's blessings and be grateful for sight. It will be clear that my French was progressing, and that the old lady had a sweet nature.

I must have taken an early train to Dijon, since I remember

making my way to Prof Talon's lodgings in the early morning, when his room was not yet done. The landlady appeared on the balcony, informed me that M Talon was out, and asked who I was. When I gave my name the little man sitting next to her leapt up, said 'Aha', and asked me in. Because his room was not yet done, he explained, we would go up one floor to his neighbour's room. He told me where the university was, that my French was very creditable for someone who wasn't a specialist, and invited me to lunch the next day. Then the neighbour came in, a former student of his now teaching at the lycée, who seemed embarrassed but welcoming: he was tall and thin, slightly younger than me, and carried a loaf of bread as thin and almost as tall as he was. And so I met the two most important people of my days in Dijon.

Talon took a fancy to me. He tended to take a fancy to young men, indeed he was capable of becoming very emotionally (but not sexually) involved with his male students, past and present. He seemed altogether less interested in being paternal towards the women. He was a middle-aged bachelor, hypochondriac, excitable, dogmatic and warm-hearted. He gave me some of his articles to read, and read much of what I wrote; when I made a mistake in French and he corrected it, he would misremember the incident, and be convinced that I had corrected myself. He sent a copy of my article on Marvell's *Horatian Ode* to Pierre Legouis, doyen of French anglicistes, who had occasion a year or two later to write a review article about recent studies of Marvell, in which I figured with the gratifying judgement that 'the poem emerges comparatively undamaged from his discussion'.

Jean-Claude, the neighbour, became my fast friend. He too was a bachelor (and has remained so), and was basking in the glory of having come first in all France in the previous year's agrégation. Or rather he wasn't basking, since he is the most modest of men, but Talon basked on his behalf, proud of the glory it brought to Dijon. Jean-Claude and I had meals together, went sight-seeing together, and translated bits of Stendhal into what we tried to tell ourselves was the style of Jane Austen. He did not enjoy teaching at the lycée, and had great difficulty controlling the fifteen-year-olds: he obviously belonged in the university, and made the transition a few years later. He even came to visit us in Belfast, which I regarded as a true sign of friendship, and we spent time together in London. Once he took our son Edwin (then six) out for a day at the Tower, where he received a lesson in English manners. He decided, in all innocence, to go to a pub for lunch: he would try English beer, and Edwin could drink lemonade. The two of them sat down at an empty table, and for a long time no-one took any notice of them. Eventually the waitress came up to the table and said with a steady stare, 'Do you realize you could go to prison for this?' It was like that in the 1950s.

Talon had found a few addresses where I might get a room, but did not wish, naturally enough, to do the choosing for me, so I set off to visit them. The third one was a tiny flat belonging to Mme Delmas, a widow of 64 who had lost three of her four children. The remaining daughter, of about my age, slept in one room and she in the other. When I explained that I wanted a room for three months the daughter said, 'No, that's too long,' but they agreed to let me stay for a month, the daughter sharing a bed with the mother, while I looked for somewhere else When the month was over, I remarked that I'd better start looking, and they were quite surprised. Puisque vous êtes sympathique, said Mme Delmas, you should stay. They introduced me to their friends, Lise took me for rides on her scooter, and Mme Delmas felt grandmotherly towards my children, whom of course she knew only from a photograph. She died many years later, in her nineties, a grandmother and an enthusiast for the British royal family. I remember being puzzled by her reference to la-di-di (till she produced a picture of the [then] Lady Di), and being shown her treasured letter from Giscard d'Estaing. Lise has two sons and the most absurdly happy marriage I know, and occasionally I visit them still.

Eleven years later I went back. This second stay was similar and different. The Delmas had long left Dijon, but Talon was still there, as were Jean-Claude, and the other professor, Michel Grivelet, a Shakespeare scholar of real distinction. There were half a dozen new members of the department, and the rather pleasant old-fashioned building in the middle of the town had given place to a huge new structure on the edge: Faculté des Lettres, Dijon had become l'Université de Bourgogne. No chicanery had been necessary this time to persuade the University of Sussex that visiting a French university was a good reason for getting a term's study leave, and once again I did some teaching. Talon asked me to lecture on two of the books on the agrégation syllabus for that year, Newman's *Apologia,* and *The Catcher in the Rye*. When I mentioned this to a colleague in Sussex he replied, 'That should produce the most unusual critical article of the decade.' Unfortunately it didn't.

There is nothing like the agrégation in other countries. Formerly the gate of entry into teaching at a lycée, it later became the entrance ticket to university teaching. It is an exam, but is described as a contest, which in a way it traditionally was, since passing entitled one to a teaching post, and the number of those who passed (who were received, as the eloquent French idiom has it) was determined by the number of jobs there would be in the ensuing year. It was — is — also a contest in that all the successful candidates are ranked in order. The syllabus is a list of about ten books, ranging over the whole of English literature (or whatever other field is in question), and for a year English literature, at least in the academy, consists of those ten books. There were three agrégation candidates in Dijon in 1967, and I lectured to them once a week for a term. They sat round a table, and I told them about the Church of England and the Tractarian controversy, about how Newman saw his face in the mirror 'and I was a Monophysite', about his need for dogma and his determination, in matters of religion, to be guided by reason and not imagination, even how the invasion of privacy by newspapers had already begun in 1842: '"Why did I go up to Littlemore at all? For no good purpose certainly; I dared not tell why." Why, to be sure, it was hard that I should be obliged to say to the editors of newspapers that I went up there to say my prayers.' We were a tiny, tightly-knit, academic community. They seldom interrupted, but they were fascinated to learn about the history of English religion, of which they knew nothing. It was some of the most rewarding teaching I have ever done. Two of the three passed, and I still have a letter from one of them, telling me with delight that both Salinger and Newman had turned up in the exam (there is no choice of questions in French exams, so the examiners' decision what questions to ask gives them some of the excitement of a horse-race. There were some gratifying remarks in the letter about the breath of fresh air blowing from Brighton, the non-conformism so different from what she had hitherto experienced in her studies. And I had felt how French and formal my teaching had been.

A Passage to India

Prologue: My 'Most Unfortunate Student in India'

Before I went to India I had, like many of my colleagues in Britain, examined some Indian Ph D theses. There is nothing unusual about being the external examiner for a Ph D: every doctoral candidate in Britain has his thesis read by one. To their credit, many Indian universities require an overseas examiner from an English speaking country for a Ph D thesis, and so I entered the life of Mr Baruah (that is not, of course, his name) in a story which stretches over two and a half years.

The bulky volume (bad theses weigh as much as good ones: they are as much of a burden to the postman, and a greater one to the examiner) arrived in January 1979, accompanied by a letter from the Academic-Registrar-Cum-Controller-of- Examinations, which had the honour to acknowledge with thanks my acceptance of the Examinership for the thesis, asked for my report in about three weeks, and added, in ink, that I was very cordially requested to send the report within the time allotted.

Mr Baruah wrote pedestrian but fluent English, and had read Hardy's novels; most of his thesis was devoted to summarising them. He then turned to his subject, 'modern elements' in Hardy's fiction, and pointed out that most of the novels ended unhappily, that Henchard supplied a misleading sample when a corn-factor and Fanny Robin had an illegitimate child, that they depicted religious scepticism and (in *Jude)* modern urban life. All these were modern elements. He quoted promiscuously — and abundantly — from critics of Hardy, showed no awareness of modernism as a literary movement, and no sign of having any ideas of his own.

There are pedestrian students everywhere: they recur as regularly as the harvest. What complicated this case was the encounter of two different university systems. I was asked by the Academic Registrar to state whether the thesis would be awarded a Ph D in my University. I wrote that Mr Baruah's command of English was very good, that he was familiar with Hardy's novels, and would probably be perfectly competent to teach them to his students; but that the level of literary criticism was very low, that no general argument was being advanced, and that the thesis would have no chance of being awarded a Ph D at Sussex.

The University reacted by inviting the candidate to rewrite and resubmit his thesis. In most British universities that recommendation needs to come from the examiners, who can judge whether there are particular faults or omissions that the candidate should and can remedy, or whether the whole approach is misconceived or the candidate's ability inadequate, in which case there seems no point in rewriting. So when the university took the easy option and asked Mr Baruah to resubmit, the new thesis that arrived 8 months later was not really any different from the old one. It still said that Victorian fiction accepts married life as a state of perfect bliss: for him, George Eliot, Dickens and Trollope had written in vain (or perhaps he had not read them). It still summarised plots and quoted other critics. I was also sent the (very brief) reports of the two internal examiners, which made some criticisms but recommended that the degree be awarded, despite 'certain lapses in the use of the comma'.

I repeated my previous remarks, and told them that I could not possibly say that the thesis would earn a Ph D in a British university. Perhaps I should have left it at that, but it seemed too cruel; yet the only way to be less cruel to the candidate could be seen as insulting the system. I wrote that since I had no first hand knowledge of Indian universities, I could not compare Mr Baruah's thesis with others; so if the internal examiners were in favour of awarding the degree, I would withdraw my objection. That really set the cat among the pigeons. The Academic Registrar (who had now become the Academic Registrar-Cum-Controller-of-Examinations In-Charge, and was a different person: had I cost the other one his job, I wondered uneasily) wanted a 'categorical decision' from me. I was, no doubt, displaying all the liberal evasions, I was showing cowardice, sitting on the fence, having my cake and eating it. I repeated what I had said before.

Next came the intervention of Prof Sarma (again, not his name), the candidate's supervisor. His letters were cool and sophisticated, referred in passing to his time at Cambridge, and made complimentary remarks about my books. He referred patronisingly to 'poor Baruah', admitted that he was not brilliant, but felt he was 'up to the job'. He informed me that 'communal turmoil' had disrupted the postal service, and at least one of my innumerable letters had not reached the Academic Registrar. He carefully refrained from asking me to change my verdict, but he inserted these two sentences: 'The academic world unfortunately is also not free from racial prejudice. I think they have taken good advantage of the reservations you have made and found a situation for giving this prejudice full play.' I never found out what the prejudice was: was Mr Baruah a Muslim, or an untouchable, or just from another part of India? Was it even prejudice against Professor Sarma? I felt, by now, that the situation was beyond me, and next time I was asked to act as external examiner by an Indian university I would be too busy.

'Schrecklich ist die Verführung nach Güte,' says the singer in Brecht's *Kaukasischer Kreidekreis.* 'Terrible is the temptation to goodness' — if, that is, you know what goodness would be, in any particular situation. It would be so easy to show compassion, and alter my recommendation. Yet what had I to offer the Indians except my tiny share of academic integrity? They were paying me 150 rupees (about £10), which was probably what it was worth. Integrity is cruel, and I would have to stick by my £10 worth of cruelty.

I did stick to it, and I never found out what finally happened. But about a year later came a letter from the candidate himself, which I must give verbatim, and without comment.

To
My most esteemed Professor
Lawrence Lerner,
The University of Sussex,
Arts Building, Brighten, Sussex,

Honourable Sir,
        Sub:- A Thesis on: "Modern Elements in Thomas
        Hardy — A Study of His Major Novels" —
        submitted to ———— University
        by Vikram Dutta Baruah

With a respectful submission and with a sense of extreme delicacy I am approaching your honour for which I may kindly be excused. I am forced under a compelling necessity to write to you in spite of myself. Perhaps your honour may be able to recall my name as I am that unfortunate Indian student of Thomas Hardy who, like a Hardian figure, particularly like a Jude, have been bufetted by an unkind destiny.

I have before me two opposite versions about my Thesis. — ——- University holds that my thesis was not recommended by you for the award of the degree. But Prof Sarma, my Guide, holds that your honour has no objection to the award of the degree if it was recommended by the other examiners.

Under the circumstances, I shall deem it a great favour and shall remain grateful if your honour would kindly enlighten this unfortunate fellow as to which version, whether of the University or of my Guide, is correct.

With the best of regards,
Your most obedient student in India
Vikram Dutta Baruah

***

'If I lived in India'

'If I lived in India,' I remarked (not adding 'Which God forbid') 'I would keep my body in Simla and my spirit in Bombay.' I had discovered Simla, as the British had done a century or so earlier: its comparative coolness, several thousand feet up, its spacious views, its impudent situation perched on a tall mountain, citied to the top, and if not quite 'where meteors shoot, clouds form, Lightnings are loosened,' at any rate where provinces were governed, plays acted, and Indian servants kept as far out of sight as possible. A tunnel through the mountain, a hundred feet or so below the colonised top, enabled them to do their errands without trespassing on the Mall or even sullying the view with the sight of a brown face.

It was in Simla that I learnt about audience response at poetry readings. Instead of the reverent hush that prevails in England, where a small audience of initiates allows every word to drop into a silence (awed or bored), the Indian audience, it was explained to me, enjoys its poets, and talks back at them, murmuring appreciative Hindi noises, laughing or clapping. In my case they obligingly murmured in English, and I was surprised at how brightly a line glowed and shone after one of the audience said 'Let's have that one again' — even a quite ordinary line (if a poet will ever admit that he writes quite ordinary lines).

Next day the positions were reversed. Reading my own poems I had been totally exposed, and the relaxed audience of academics had held all the cards. At the lectern as the British Council's visiting professor, with students in the audience, I commanded a certain awe, and when I found myself running a seminar for the faculty only, in which they were turned into students, then there was no doubt from which point power radiated. I did not realise how much, until Yasmeen pointed it out to me (Yasmeen was the British Council education officer in Delhi, whose presence was such an invaluable help on my academic wanderings). I had decided to run the seminar on some questions of poetic technique, handing out poems in which some words or even phrases are replaced by dots, and inviting the students to suggest what the words might be (the method will be discussed in a later chapter). Whatever its faults, this is an exercise that always engages the students' attention, and they usually enjoy it; but Professor A in Simla didn't enjoy it. After two or three minutes of silent wrestling with the blanks, he spoke. 'Professor,' he said, 'I suggest we move to the discussion. We want to compare our opinions about the purpose of this exercise.' I said, in surprise, that we couldn't compare opinions until they'd done it. 'We wish to discuss with you,' he said, 'we wish to exchange ideas, that is why you are here.' I said nothing would delight me more, but that I couldn't talk about this task until I had some material. 'Just write anything down that seems to you suitable,' I continued, and repeated my assurance that this wasn't a test, and it didn't matter whether the answers were right, indeed that there was no 'right'. He conceded, and finished the task, and we had our discussion.

Afterwards Yasmeen congratulated me on sticking to my guns, and explained that Professor A had been afraid his dignity was at stake. He didn't want to be reduced to a student, she remarked, and he was afraid of getting some answers wrong, even getting them wrong when some of his juniors got them right. I objected that there were no wrong answers. 'I know, and you did right to say that, but he could still lose face if some of the others gave better answers than his.' I realised that more had been at stake than I had (naively) realised, but the discussion went well enough. If I remember correctly, the professor didn't proffer many suggestions, but commented freely on those of others.

And I realised that I had, after all, shown much the same behaviour a week earlier. I had given the same exercise (though with other poems) to the assembled English departments of several Punjabi colleges, and as they settled down to it I realised that I had left the text of the poems in my hotel. I need to have it, I thought, or I can't tell them what the poet actually wrote (I might actually have done so, from memory, but wasn't sure enough). So with Yasmeen's help I persuaded one of the faculty to take me back to the hotel on the back of his motor scooter; clutching a sonnet by Daniel, a sonnet by Shakespeare, a Browning poem in one hand and holding on to my driver's waist with the other, I shut my eyes as we threaded through a tangle of children, cars, other scooters and cows (surely, I thought, it isn't so far from hotel to college, but it was), risking our lives (and that of the pedestrians) for the sake of textual accuracy. Cow or child: we were certain surely to hit one or other (fortunately, miraculously, we didn't); and I thought, Well, this is a Muslim town, so it would be worse to hit a child; if it was Orissa, predominantly Hindu, we would get into worse trouble if we hit a cow.

And why had I done this? I could have improvised. I was after all in the same position as they were, having to guess or suggest what words to put in the blanks — in a stronger position, since I knew the poems, and might well remember what the word had been. I could even have confessed that I hadn't brought the text, and everyone would have enjoyed the fact that I had to guess too. But like Professor A, I had preferred to retain my authority.

**

'Who will come from England?'

Kashmir was peaceful when I arrived, ruled by a Muslim doctor with an English wife, seemingly content to be a part of Hindu India. It did not last, but how often it's been my fortunate fate to stumble on peaceful interludes (had we not lived calmly in Belfast in the 1950s?), and so to remain convinced that there is no real need for communal strife or bloody revolution. But bigots and revolutionaries reason not the need.

I was to spend a month in Srinagar. My friend D, seconded from Delhi to be head of department there for two years, had invited me, and his friendliness, along with the Shalimar Gardens, the Dal lake, and the high altitude to counter the summer heat, led me to accept eagerly. We arrived on a Friday, and I was promptly informed that for some complicated reason the university would be on holiday all the following week: we would now have a holiday before I did any lecturing. But, I suggested, why don't I meet the students today, before they go away, so that I can tell them what to read. D seemed a little less enthusiastic about this than I'd have expected, but agreed that it would be a good idea for them to learn who I was. I had been asked to teach two classes, one of them studying *Bleak House,* the other *Nostromo* — two nice meaty novels, on which there was plenty to say, and two of my favourite books. So I brought my notes and thoughts, and told each class what I'd be talking about in 10 days time: Had anyone read either novel yet? No-one had, so I remarked how fortunate it was that there was now a week's break, which they could spend reading the text. I explained that it was very important that they finish the book before I started lecturing, so that they could treat what I said critically, and they all nodded and smiled. Off I went, to spend a few days with my wife exploring Srinagar and walking in the hills.

When I entered the classroom ten days later, three girls in Class A had read *Nostromo;* no-one in Class B had read *Bleak House.* It was not much use asking why. The students could not get the book, because the local bookstore had not ordered it; the bookstore, I was told, refused to order books unless the university assured them that the book was prescribed and it was compulsory for the students to buy it; the university, I was told, did not consider it was its function to interfere with commercial transactions: it was the students' responsibility to get hold of the texts. There was a similar merry-go-round, I discovered, about the buses. The university was several miles out of the town, and the municipality provided buses to bring the students to campus. Classes began at ten o'clock, and the first bus left town at ten o'clock. The municipality claimed that before 10 o'clock the buses were needed to transport workers to work. The students claimed that they could not arrive until a bus brought them. The university claimed that it was necessary to start teaching at ten, and it was the students' responsibility to find a way of arriving on time. Round and round went the grumbles, and if you had a ten o'clock class it filled up gradually in the course of the first half-hour.

So no-one had read *Bleak House* and hardly anyone had a copy. It was no use going home in disgust, so I modified my teaching. There were two ways in which it still seemed worthwhile discussing the book: I could tell them about the law's delays, the industrial revolution, and the position of women in 19th century England, which they would have needed to be told even if they had read the novel; and I could discuss the way Dickens used the language, beginning with the marvellous opening about the fog, the smoke making a soft black drizzle, with flakes of soot in it as big as full-grown snowflakes, and as much mud in the streets as if the waters had but newly retired from the face of the earth, and it would not be wonderful to meet a Megalosaurus, forty feet long or so, waddling like an elephantine lizard up Holborn Hill. Dickens' megalosaurus may have had impeccable scientific credentials, but he waddled between the biblical flood and a very modern Holborn Hill, for Dickens' style bridged the conflicting worlds of 1852. I could ask the students if they had ever seen a fog like that — they had certainly seen plenty of mud. I could ask if they noticed the shift of register at 'waddling' or if they realised that 'elephantine lizard' was close to being a translation of 'dinosaur' or that the existence of dinosaurs was a recent discovery in 1852. I could usefully talk about all this to people who hadn't read the book, and I did. So I handed out passages from the un-read novel (getting them typed and duplicated was not easy) and I talked about English social history, reading them bits of Ruskin and Cooke Taylor, Macaulay and Mill, that I had brought with me. The students were docile, wrote everything down, and seemed appreciative. The day before I left one young man spoke to me. 'You have told us all about the social background of *Bleak House*' (not all, I murmured deprecatingly, but he did not pause). 'And you have told us all about Dickens' style, and explained how it works' (tried to explain, I murmured, but he went on inexorably). 'But you have not told us the plot, you have not explained the characters, and we need that too.'

The answer was obvious, and I made it. 'I told you to read the book', I said, 'but you didn't. It's no use discussing plot and characters with someone who hasn't yet read the book.' There didn't seem anything he could say in answer to that, but he was unabashed. He smiled plaintively, ironically, even pityingly, and said, 'Who will come from England to tell us about the plot of *Bleak House?*'

The situation in Class A had one difference: the three students who had read *Nostromo*. They all came from the women's college in the town, where I also lectured, and where the atmosphere reminded me of what Cheltenham Ladies' College must have been like in its early days. The girls all wore white dresses, the teachers were dedicated and caring, and the atmosphere of politeness was as thick as the fog in *Bleak House*. It was one of the most paternalistic (or rather maternalistic) institutions I have ever visited, and it produced students who actually read the books. I decided that my last class on *Nostromo* would be for these three students only. So I announced that though I had modified my classes to fit the unhappy fact that they hadn't read the book, I would talk about plot and character and anything else they wanted on the last day, but only those who had read the book would be allowed in. No-one sat up all night in order to get in, so all I had was three shy Muslim girls, who had no questions or comments to offer, but listened and nodded and wrote things down and (I hoped) would later talk about them among themselves. When I left a week later, Dr D, taking a fond farewell, uttered the expected thanks for my coming, and for what I had done for their department during my month's stay. Moments like that feed one's vanity, and sometimes produce satisfying compliments to one's teaching skills or brilliant insights. But Dr D ended by saying that the most valuable thing I had done was to refuse entrance to the last class to those who had not read *Nostromo*. It made a tremendous impact on the students, he explained.

I would like to think (but I have no real reason to do so) that as a result of my visit the bookshops order the texts, the buses run at the right time, and Srinagar is now full of graduates who have read *Nostromo*.

To Poland — and back

Every three years the Jagellonian University in Krakow holds an English studies conference. When I went in 1987 the atmosphere was fairly free, and very much more so in 1990: the difference between relaxed Communism and post-Communism showed itself in what the elderly professor said. In 1987 Professor X, a devout Roman Catholic, made a speech of welcome to the delegates, a delicately ironic speech, paying homage to the realities of power, and indicating delicately what he'd like to be able to say. Three years later, no longer head of department, he was on the sidelines, but came to the conference and joined in the discussion at least once: this time his attacks on Communism were direct, straightforward and crude. Rhetorically, he seemed to have lost all his skill.

Why, I ask. Because he was three years older — 68 not 65, or 73 not 70, as the case may be? Because he was no longer head of department, and did not need to watch his words? Or because there was no longer a government of threats and censorship at which he needed to glance over his shoulder? What destroys rhetorical subtlety — age, or shedding responsibility, or freedom?

In 1987 I gave the closing lecture at the conference, in 1990 the opening one. The opening lecture took place in the wonderful 16th century hall in the old university building, arranged like a cathedral choir, with carved wooden seats on both sides and a good deal of gilt scattered about, gloriously inconvenient for lecturing. You stood up in an awkardly shaped pew, with no lectern, the audience of colleagues facing you in long tiers, and the important local people at the side, visible only out of the corner of your eye. But who cares about convenience when offered a beautifully preserved Renaissance hall to lecture in? The concluding lecture was in a dull practical building nearby, so my regret at not getting the chance to lecture first time round was only compensated for three years later.

The reason I almost gave the opening lecture in 1987 was that Bernard Bergonzi, who was meant to give it, had announced that he would be arriving by train from Lodz at (I think) 2.30, half an hour before the lecture. That train is always late, the locals moaned, they know that in Lodz, they should have told him: what do we do if he doesn't turn up? I remarked that as the other plenary lecturer I could always change with him: if I spoke first, he could speak at the end. The hosts were delighted: would I really be willing to do that, or rather to hold myself ready in case he didn't come in time? So I sat in the front row with the text of my lecture, feeling like the substitute in a football match. What should I do, I wondered: ought I to warm up, sprint up and down the centre of the hall in case I was called on to play? I found myself hoping the train would be late, and I can still feel the stab of disappointment when I saw Bernard, relaxed and smiling, chatting to his hosts in the entrance. Reduced to a mere member of the audience, I sat back and prepared to dislike the lecture.

Of course there was nothing to dislike: he talked about the first World War and its literature, and offered plenty for the conference to chew on. That is presumably the purpose of an opening lecture, as I found three years later, when what I had said kept cropping up in the form of polite dissent from subsequent speakers. The purpose of a closing lecture is less clear, but the potential is richer, everyone filled with the mixture of relief and disappointment that marks the close of a conference. As the audience gathered for the final session, I sensed an inaudible hum of expectation, rendered audible for a moment when a plump bald affable professor from Malta, standing next to me as we waited to go into the hall, smiled and remarked 'So now we have Lerner.' Uncertain how to respond I smiled back, nodded, and waited to hear if he was being eager or sarcastic. Sensing, no doubt, that I wasn't responding with some lively anecdote, he nodded and moved off. Ten minutes later I was standing on the platform, unfolding my notes and waiting for the audience to settle, when the plump and now blushing Maltese came bustling up to me. 'I did not realise you were Professor Lerner,' he said in an embarrassed hiss: he may even have said 'the eminent Professor Lerner.' His confusion was so great that I felt sure he had intended to be sarcastic, and didn't realise how harmlessly little he had said. The unspoken part of his remark will now remain among the great unuttered sentences I wish (or think I wish) I could have heard.

What happened at the conference in 1990 was however dwarfed by what happened on the way home. I had decided to fly to Krakow via Vienna. My friend Z, professor at the University of Vienna, was also going to the conference; so I would stay a few days in Vienna, give a lecture to his students, and then we would travel to Krakow together. Booking a train ticket and a sleeper from Vienna to Krakow was too much for my travel agent in Brighton, so Z did that for me. But when I arrived he was ill: I gave my lecture (and then gave another to his class because he was ill), and travelled with his assistant instead. As the train crossed the border into Czechoslovakia I was told that as a foreigner I needed a transit visa (the travel agency in Vienna had obviously not thought to mention it, since the ticket was being booked by an Austrian). The woman official sold me one for quite a sizable number of Austrian schillings, and remarked (with what turned out to be misplaced kindness) that she would not sell me the return visa, since it would be much cheaper for me to buy it in Poland.

At the conference I forgot about visas — I did remember the matter once, and discovered that I would need to go to Katowice, which would take half a day, so I shrugged and decided to buy it once more on the train. Getting onto the right train at nine o'clock on the last evening turned out to be no easy job; the colleague from the Jagellonian who took me to the station, bewildered by the lack of information, was reduced to asking the waiting passengers on each platform where they were going to. I realised that if I'd come alone to the station I'd never have caught it, and when it drew out I felt only relief. Visas were far from my thought — until we reached the border.

The Czech frontier official was plump, neatly uniformed, and unsmilingly efficient. Looking at my passport, he asked, in immaculate German, for my transit visa, and shook his head on learning that I hadn't got one. No, he could not sell me one; I must go back to Katowice. 'Get off the train,' he said brusquely.

'Go back and get a visa.' 'How can I get a visa at midnight?' I protested. He shrugged. 'That's your affair. You must get off the train.' It was clearly no use arguing, so I simply said I wouldn't. He patted his buttoned up pocket, and pointed out that he had my passport. At that point the Polish woman in the compartment joined in, on his side. She had explained to me, in very halting German, that she lived in Vienna, and was evasive about what she did there; she had seemed nervous but friendly, but suddenly she toughened, nodded vigorously at everything the guard said, and stammered fiercely that when you travel then, of course, you must have a visa. I wondered if she had run into similar trouble herself in the past.

The guard got off the train, and I pondered. What would happen if I went on without a passport? The Czechs at the next border would surely let me out of their country — eagerly perhaps — but would the Austrians let me in? I would have to talk my way past the frontier police, and then onto the plane in Vienna. Once at Gatwick, I would surely be able to talk my way into Britain. I'm not sure why I didn't risk it. Perhaps a passport is the modern traveller's viaticum: he feels too vulnerable without it. I picked up my bags, nodded curtly to the woman, and got off the train.

The guard had vanished. There were several of his underlings around, who seemed to speak nothing but Czech. I found the frontier office, which was locked. I watched my train beginning to move, setting off for a Vienna I began to feel I would never reach. There were various other trains around, but no indication which direction they were going in. I had no idea where I was. I had walked into one of Graham Greene's early novels, or a pre-war poem of Auden's, travelling across Europe and getting lost, and I thought light-heartedly, Perhaps I may never leave this place. Z will wonder why I haven't turned up for our lunch appointment, but he will never find out. I will simply vanish, and not even know the name of the town I have disappeared into. I felt completely carefree: there was nothing I could do, so no reason to worry.

As I stood among the railway lines looking up at the longest train in sight, a woman approached me and pointed to it. 'Katowice?' she asked, hesitatingly. We seemed to have no language in common, and I shrugged. A moment later a guard arrived, pointed to the train, gave me my passport, and stood behind me to make sure I got on. There seemed no particular reason not to.

The woman got in with me, and turned out to be American. She had left Warsaw that evening, and she too had no transit visa. Her name was Sandy, and she was of Polish ancestry; she had visited a distant relative in Warsaw, and was now off to join her husband on holiday in Vienna. With her few stammered words of Polish, Sandy discovered that the train was going to Warsaw, and announced that she would go all the way: there would be an American consul in Warsaw, an airline, her cousin, and — what seemed to give her most comfort — the Marriott hotel, right next to the station. As we drew up in Katowice station I looked out of the window: deserted platforms, darkness, incomprehensible notices. What would I do there at three in the morning? I had no Polish money, I didn't know the telephone number of any of the colleagues in Krakow. I decided to go to Warsaw too.

We had forgotten that there would be a ticket collector. When he came, and saw that we both had tickets to Vienna, he grew very eloquent — in Polish. We were, after all, travelling directly away from Vienna. Sandy's few words of Polish were soon left behind, and we smiled idiotically at him. This moved him to further eloquence: he disappeared, and fetched a colleague, who also spoke only Polish. I had spent all my zlotty, and neither English nor Austrian money interested them. Sandy, searching her bag, found some zlotty, but not nearly enough. She searched further, and found more. As long as there isn't another stop before Warsaw, I thought as we raced through the night, they can't do anything. It began to look as if he would accept the situation, and be satisfied with the number of zlotty he could get. After he'd finished counting for the third or fourth time, Sandy produced a dollar, and said 'Tip': she seemed to have found an English word he understood.

Once we were in Warsaw all was easy. I took Sandy to a splendid — and expensive — breakfast at the Marriott, and then we booked seats on the 2 o'clock flight to Vienna. I managed to telephone Z, and he agreed to get a message to

Sandy's husband. Suddenly, thanks to credit cards, technology and capitalism, all our problems disappeared, and we had four hours to spare in Warsaw. Sandy announced that she would go back to her cousin's. Wanda was an unmarried woman in her sixties. She had put Sandy onto the train the previous evening, and when she answered the door and saw us her face fell. She had lived under Communism for forty years, and immediately she thought of disaster. Sandy held her hand and explained that she was quite all right; as she told her story, Wanda began to weep. Their embrace said not only that Sandy was safe, but that tyranny really was over, that you could turn up unexpectedly without any reason to be frightened. All that was left was the petty tyrants at the frontier posts, and nothing would unseat them.

There is a brief comic postscript. Wanda's mother came into the room, a frail old lady with wandering wits who (of course) spoke only Polish. She looked at the vaguely familiar Sandy, and turned inquiringly to her daughter. 'It's Sandy — from America. You remember Sandy, she was here yesterday'; she began to explain the complicated family connexion. Slowly the old lady nodded, smiled, and embraced the half-known second cousin twice removed; then she noticed me, and turned to Wanda, clearly asking, 'And who's he?' Wanda looked at us both, and gave a helpless shrug; explaining was obviously hopeless. 'That's Sandy's husband,' she said, and the old lady nodded, satisfied.

That was how I married an American in Warsaw, and never saw her again.

The Wrong End of the Applause

When I was an undergraduate at Cambridge, it was the custom for the audience to applaud each lecturer at the end of the term. Though never tumultuous, the clapping was loud and sustained, and everyone joined in. I liked the practice, since it made things clear. Lectures were voluntary and contained no element of discipline; their purpose was to help the students pass their exams — they were for us, and so we showed our appreciation. One member of the history faculty, Kenneth Pickthorn (who was also a conservative MP, and so lectured only on Saturdays when Parliament was sitting), asked his audience not to applaud, giving two reasons: that since the practice was more or less automatic, and all lecturers were applauded, there was no way of showing disapproval, which rendered the applauding more or less meaningless; and second (one suspected this was what really mattered to him) he was not an entertainer but a scholar.

There is no doubt a certain logic to the convention which now obtains almost universally: that no-one is applauded for his ordinary teaching, but everyone is applauded for a special occasion — a visiting lecture, a conference paper, even a public lecture in one's own university. Few of us like to admit it but I think most lecturers are highly sensitive to the length and nature of the applause they get; and when a lecturer holds up his hand to indicate that's enough, he is surely as pleased to be required to do so as he is desirous that the clapping should stop. Applause, of course, is undiscriminating: there is no way of conveying just what elements you really liked, so that all it can indicate is general approbation; but as part of the ongoing dynamic of a conference, it can be very eloquent, and when there are ideological tensions, it can be a weapon.

***

I arrived in what was then East Berlin at 2 am on a Saturday night in February of 1969 — in the middle of a blizzard, and without a visa. It was a good way to arrive, for it brought vividly home to me that the most striking thing about communist countries was not violence, or repression, but red tape. Before the night was out, I had grown very familiar with the entry point in Friedrichstrasse station. The last returning Pole had been let through; Italians and Arabs, working in West Berlin, had drifted back from a night out in the East; and still I waited, while soldiers kept disappearing to consult with one another or make telephone calls about me. The friend with whom I would be staying had come to meet me, but had left in despair two hours after the train was due. He left a letter explaining what a fine fellow I was, and hoping all would be done to smooth the formalities; but a letter, even though on official stationery, is not a visa. The soldiers were friendly, but rules are rules. Could I go to a hotel I asked, and start again in the morning? Well, no: you can't spend a night at a hotel unless you have an entry permit, and you can't (of course) get that at 3 in the morning. In the end, a soldier said I'd better take a taxi to my friend's house and he would come with me. So out we tramped into the snow, and joined the eight people waiting at the taxi stand — a small enough queue, but the man in front had been there an hour and a half. The big beery woman who told us this looked the soldier up and down and shouted 'Schätzchen, wo ist der Mantel?' — Darling, where's your coat? He wasn't the Stasi, and we didn't know much about the Stasi in those days: I decided that I wasn't among a repressed population.

In the end, the soldier sent me off by myself. I waited in another taxi queue; I tried to telephone, but a public telephone that worked was a rare find in East Germany in 1969; I caught a train; I trudged through snow — new snow, two feet deep, carrying my bags; it was nearly six o'clock when I got to my friend's house, which was right on the outskirts of the suburb, on the edge of a forest. It was still dark, and snow was scurrying all round me; the bell didn't work, and there were no footprints in the snow on his front steps. I banged on the door and no-one heard; I wasn't even sure, by then, if I wanted anyone to hear.

Suppose a stranger put his head out of the window, and I had to tell him, in my hesitant German, that I was an Englishman, that I wasn't a spy, that I was cold and hungry, and that I had no visa (no doubt he would ask that first!). I ate one of the bananas I'd brought because fruit was dear in East Germany. I walked to the wood, where I saw neither Valkyries nor troops. Perhaps this wasn't even Berlin, perhaps the train had taken me to Siberia without my noticing. The snow kept falling.

After that night, nothing seemed difficult. There was a good deal more red tape, and actually getting the visa took most of Monday; I only got it, I felt sure, because I said to the woman at the travel bureau that I couldn't wait any longer, I had to take a little girl to the children's theatre. This was true (the girl was my host's daughter), and though I didn't manage to get to the theatre in time, I did get — well, not my visa, but a form to take to the police station in order to get another form and so, at long last, a visa.

I didn't spend the whole week getting visas. I went to East Germany to talk to people, to go to the theatre, and (on a second visit, two months later) to attend their annual Shakespeare celebration in Weimar. There used to be (and now, once again, there is) a single German Shakespeare-Gesellschaft, but in the early sixties the West Germans decided that they'd had enough Marxism, and they walked out and founded their own, which met at Bochum. I went twice to the Shakespeare meetings at Weimar, where you could see both plays and communism — plenty of both — listen to lectures, take part in discussions, meet literary people from other Communist countries, and even hear a recital of Elizabethan songs by two fiercely formal middle-aged musicians in dark suits. 'Tobacco, tobacco is like love,' sang one of them, holding the music stiffly in front of him, and acknowledging the applause with jerky Germanic bows.

The plays on offer included *A Midsummer Night's Dream,* in an almost wholly delightful production, fast-moving, graceful and without tricksiness. Bottom was self-satisfied, Peter Quince was fussy, as they should be; Flute looked duly ridiculous as Thisbe, and the workmen were helpless without Bottom. 'If he come not, then the play is marred, it goes not forward,' they lamented, showing a thoroughly unsocialist personality-cult. But the production was followed, the next day, by a pious lecture from the director, telling us that the course of true love was interfered with by class conflict (though all the lovers actually belong to the same class, a point he didn't mention), and which sang the praises of Bottom and the mechanicals — the ancestors of his own theatrical company, he remarked, with what to a Westerner seemed self-mockery, or at least excessive modesty, but seemed to be a kind of boast. There had been only one moment during the production when the theses of the lecture reared their heads. This came at the end, when the mechanicals danced their bergomask, and Theseus and the courtiers walked out, in irritation or disapproval, leaving them in possession of the palace, as if they had somehow triumphed over the nobility. And even that soon gave way to Purcell's music and Puck's poetry.

Several speakers the next day, in praising the production, remarked that they had enjoyed it more than the lecture. Two of the Soviet delegation said this; and as it happened the last to say it, just before the lecturer replied, was me. I remarked that it had reminded me of the best English productions and that without the lecture I would not have known how it differed from them. I should have known better. The director, when he rose to speak, was obviously moved; his irritation may well have been building up all day; and most directors are probably offended when told that their productions are reminiscent of others, even if it is intended as praise. Since the man was, of course, an actor, his performance was brilliant. He paid tribute to all he had learned from theatre in the West, but disassociated himself firmly from it. It was clear, he said, that what Herr Lerner had been looking for was sensationalism, but the trouble with capitalist theatre was precisely that it was too fond of sensational effects, and of cynicism. He had seen a *Merchant of Venice* in which no-one was happy at the end, a *Troilus and Cressida* in which Thersites was murdered. That sort of thing would not happen in a socialist country. In the end, the differences between one production and another, socialist and bourgeois, might be small; but, he concluded, they were crucial. I am sure he was absolutely sincere, and moved; and he placed every syllable with care and polish. When he sat down, the applause was thunderous. It was no use leaping up to protest that I hadn't implied any wish for sensationalism, indeed that I disliked it quite as much as he did, and thought it the bane of the English stage (twenty-five years later I saw *The Tempest* at Stratford, and am still wincing at the fact that Ariel, on being given his freedom, spat at Prospero). Nor was it any use protesting that a cynical interpretation of *The Merchant of Venice* is one thing, a cynical intepretation of *Troilus and Cressida* is quite another. Even if my German had been up to such an intervention, which it then certainly wasn't, I saw how easily he'd have managed a triumphant riposte. The day was his, and I sat and felt what it's like to be at the wrong end of the applause.

There was one other moment that brought as much applause, though of a very different kind. There was a lecture on the previous day by a Professor at the Theatre-university in Leipzig. It was called Tradition, Present and Prognosis. It contained quotations from all the East German scholars of English who were present, quotations from Marx (the usual ones, remarked an East European delegate to me), and a good deal about the decadence of the capitalist West. The lecturer read a paragraph from a newspaper account of a production of *Hamlet* in Bremen, full of gimmicks and costumed in jeans, and observed that such was the lamentable state of the late-bourgeois theatre. There was a good deal more about bourgeois society, the war in Vietnam, the problem of leisure (only a problem under capitalism) and a number of East German productions of Shakespeare were named and praised. Shakespeare was of course described as a humanist; and socialism, the culmination of the humanist tradition, was therefore a prerequisite for his full understanding today. Several speakers the next morning mentioned this lecture with approving nods, and the first critical note came from one of the two West Germans present. He was a student from Göttingen, and when he spoke he did not pull punches. 'We heard a thoroughly unscholarly performance yesterday,' he said, 'from a professor who read us a quotation from a newspaper without giving us the date or the name of the paper.' German Gründlichkeit crops up everywhere! 'As it happens,' he continued, 'I saw that production in Bremen, and it was by no means all bad. It's too easy to score such cheap points.

How many of you have ever had the chance to see for yourselves the Western productions that you are always hearing condemnations of?' He, of course, got less applause than anyone; and what there was must have come largely from foreigners. Even the West German professor sitting next to me remarked, 'No, he's too angry, too personal', and certainly there were more important criticisms to be made of Professor K than his lack of footnotes — as the young man knew, for I heard him saying to some of the East German students at lunch-time, 'If we got a lecture like that from one of our professors, he'd be hooted down in ten minutes.' It was 1969, and for the first time I began to feel some sympathy with the disrupters of lectures.

A short while later the West German professor also spoke. He began by saying, 'I'm going to be scholarly (wissenschaftlich); some of you may consider me formalist.' He spoke of the dangers of twentieth century interpreters looking for their own opinions in Shakespeare; he documented a number of Elizabethan views of history that are unacceptable to us today; and he showed very competently how some Marxist readings of Shakespeare easily become misreadings. Finally, he added a complaint about the constant assertion that only socialism could provide the basis for a true response to Shakespeare today. 'I don't find that tells me much,' he said. 'Not out of hostility but in genuine bewilderment I have to say that there are so many socialisms. We must not gloss over the differences.' He sat down to mild applause; he had been sober, controlled and — it seemed to me — moderately sympathetic to the prevalent Marxism.

Both the West Germans were attacked by speaker after speaker. The unfortunate student got nothing but kicks — solemn, patronising or caustic. Everyone told him that he had offered provocation, that Western guests were welcome but not if they came to provoke. No-one was patronising to the professor (hierarchy is, after all, ineradicable — even under socialism!) but no-one supported him either. Most of all, he was criticised by a tall elderly professor of Marxism, a speech that had even less to do with Shakespeare than any of the others. After shaking an avuncular head over the Göttingen student for his fanaticism, he began answering the point about there being so many socialisms. He leaned over his desk and pointed at the

West German professor, whom he kept addressing by name; and after a while his victim rose and said he would like to ask a question. It was 1969, and the question was about Czechoslovakia; and it was as if he's thrown pepper in the speaker's eyes. 'Did we imagine there were no links between the so-called reformers in Czechoslovakia and the West,' he shouted. 'And what about Yugoslavia? I could prove to you,' he thundered, 'that the World Bank controls Yugoslavia's economy, and what is the World Bank but Western capitalism?' Things began to get alarming. He showed no sign of stopping, leaning over the rostrum, waving his arms, throwing his zeal around the now restless hall. There were whistles and stamping; then the president of the Shakespeare-Gesellschaft, a Professor of English who had decided that if you couldn't beat them you join them, got up from the front row and interrupted. 'We are supposed to be discussing Shakespeare,' he said. 'You objected to fanaticism, and now look at you.' This was the other moment that brought thunderous applause and it was certainly the one round of applause in which everyone joined, East and West. I have to hand it to the old professor of Marxism. He waited till the noise had died down, leaned forward on the desk, and said, 'Pater, peccavi.' Then he went on in an academic voice to make a point about sixteenth century capitalism that seemed to me trite, but went down well, and by the time he left the platform he had been forgiven, at least by his countrymen, and there was applause left for him.

Finally, *Gammer Gurton's Needle*. A main reason for my going to Weimar had been the chance to see this anonymous Elizabethan farce in which an old woman loses her needle, Hodge her labourer tears his breeches, Diccon the Bedlam beggar sets a quarrel going for fun, Dr Rat the curate is made a fool of, and the needle is finally found in Hodge's buttocks — the whole thing written in doggerel, slow-moving, simple-minded and bawdy. The play is mentioned in all the histories of literature, and for the most part it has stayed there. I never expected to see it anywhere, least of all in East Germany. But, as the producer, a young Englishman living in Berlin, told the conference, it is largely a play about the social and economic relations of capitalism. Gammer Gurton is poor; therefore the loss of her needle is serious. We are seeing, he observed, the new poverty brought about by capitalism. Because of capitalism, he asserted with bold Marxist confidence, the land was unfertile and the village had fallen on hard times. As for Diccon, his little prank of telling Gammer Gurton that Dame Chat has stolen her needle serves 'to divert attention away from the basic problems and contradictions of capitalism, so that the ruling class can preserve its hold over the people.'

There is nothing to be said in favour of this interpretation; and not much more, alas, for the production which preceded it. Gammer Gurton is in fact not poor: she has a brown cow and a sandy sow, she employs a labourer, and at the end she stands all the village to drinks. The play is crude and condescending and won't stand too much interpreting, but if there is any explanation for the fuss she makes over her needle, it may be just that she's a fussy old woman; such a reading however, would of course be a late-bourgeois error. As for the production, one should clearly not be too hard on the attempts of East German students to act in sixteenth century English. It had been carefully rehearsed, with no imagination whatever; and it went down wonderfully. No joke was too simple, or too often repeated. No bit of business was too clumsy to please. When actors came through the audience to get to the stage, the result was electric; the two worlds rubbed against each other, and trembled. Almost everyone there had read the work of Robert Weimann, the East German Shakespearean scholar, who has written so well about the English popular theatre. I realised how right Weimann is in his belief in the power of breaking out of the world of the stage into that of the spectators, even if it was done as crudely as here. What I was seeing might be a scholarly reconstruction, but it was, in its way, popular drama; and the scholarly audience was clearly enjoying the experience of going naive. They liked the young Englishman, naivety and all; he was so firmly on their side. They liked the thought of producing a neglected Elizabethan play. They were prepared to like the play itself. They applauded, they made speeches they made a presentation, they went off in a wave of euphoria. And I, the bourgeois outsider, once again at the wrong end of the applause — how could I be anything but envious?

***

Going out with a Bang

For the summer term of 1994 I was a visiting professor at Vienna; and while I was there, Professor K retired. He had been professor at the university for 37 years (is that a record?) He must have taught half the English teachers in Austria. He'd been dean, then rector, and some of his old students and present colleagues described him as an inspiring but temperamental teacher. He gave a farewell lecture, which I propose to describe, but first a word on him and me. I had met him twice before, on two occasions when I had turned up as a visiting lecturer, sent once by the British Council and once invited by one of his colleagues. On both occasions he was polite and remote, the courteous host, adept at concealing the fact that he'd heard it all before. His English was beautiful, and the pleasure of letting you see how exquisite it was seemed indistinguishable from the pleasure of making your acquaintance. The host professor, when you come as a visiting lecturer, often feels he's heard it all before, then congratulates you on how well the students responded, or tells you how he is burdened by administration, and wishes he had more time to keep up with his reading. There are variants, of course: the all-too-rare host who really enjoyed your lecture and tells you so, or the slightly less rare host who feels you've done untold harm to his students and tells you so with varying degrees of politeness. But Prof K kept his distance and on the second occasion didn't come to the lecture. He knew, no doubt what I was going to say (or, if I did not say what he expected, he knew that it wouldn't be of interest). When I turned up as a visiting colleague in 1994 I bumped into him in a secretary's office. He brushed aside the introduction: 'Wir kennen uns schon,' he remarked. 'You are visiting us: Sie sind hier zum Besuch?' By speaking German he was treating me as a real colleague — and also making it clear that too much courtesy would not be required. 'For how long?' he asked. When I said it was for the whole semester he raised an eyebrow: 'so long!' But he would put up with it, as long as he didn't need to trouble too much about me.

I decided to go his farewell lecture although it involved some rearrangement. After all, I was myself due to give a farewell lecture at Vanderbilt a year later, and curiosity could not resist the glimpse of a possible preview. The Ministry of Education had decided to take the occasion seriously, and wrote to all the secondary schools in Vienna and nearby districts, perhaps in all Austria: people came, I was told, from as far as Salzburg. K's former students came in droves, along with his colleagues (many of whom were former students too), and a good sprinkling of present students. The lecture took place in Hörsaal 7, in which K had given his first lecture course (on Elizabethan drama, he told us), and for sentimental reasons he wanted to give his last lecture there. The room was far too small — people sat on the steps, stood in every corner, packed the doors. When K stood up there was applause. He then began to reminisce, in German, and told a story about Byron and Grillparzer ('the Austrian with the unpronounceable name') facing each other in opposite boxes at the theatre in Venice, greeting each other formally, and weeping over the play. Then he said, mischievously, 'Ich lasse Byron und Grillparzer für mich weinen': more applause. Then he switched to English for the lecture proper, which was called 'Literature. What it is, how it works, and what I have learned about it.' A title which allowed anything, and he did indeed allow himself anything. There was a handout consisting of photocopies of many of his favourite passages which he urged the audience to take home and read, so that they would be sure to get some profit from the lecture: bits of Vonnegut, of Golding, Ulysses' speech on degree, Herbert's 'Love bade me welcome', Goethe's most famous tiny lyric (über allen Gipfeln/ist ruh'), which he read to us. The Herbert poem he didn't read, but said it was his favourite poem, the finest poem known to him. It was no good settling back in your seat (or on your piece of floor) in eager anticipation of learning something new about each text, since he discussed none of them, but paid his compliments and moved on to the next one.

Did the lecture have an argument? If any, it was that literature should not be mistaken for anything else. It's not ideas: he didn't quote Mallarmé's famous put-down of Dégas, 'Ce n'est point avec des idées qu'on fait des sonnets, Dégas, c'est avec des mots', but he made, or tried to make, Mallarmé's point. In the last and most interesting part of his lecture he compared literature with recent science, and claimed that Einstein's theories (of which he hastened to disclaim any real understanding) had deeply influenced modern literature, citing Durrell's Alexandria Quartet and the fact that Durrell had visited his seminar, and told them how deeply he'd been influenced by the theory of relativity. Whether Durrell understood it any better than K was not asked. Gone now was the insistence that literature was not made of ideas.

He sat down, and everyone applauded. It began, as German applause does, with rapping on the desk, then they all stood up and clapped, and clapped, and went on clapping. I have never heard so much applause in my life. A week later Zerbinetta brought the house down in *Ariadne auf Naxos* at the Staatsoper, and it looked as if we'd never get on with the second act because of the endless rapture of the audience: but Professor K beat Zerbinetta by a comfortable margin.

What were they applauding? Not, surely, that heartfelt but platitudinous lecture. They were applauding a career (K has published nothing, he had made teaching and administration his life). They were applauding an institution, the University of Vienna, where they had studied and learned all they knew and were passing on, and which had been courteous — and sentimental — enough to invite them back for this occasion. And — no doubt too — they were applauding their own youth.

***

Introductions

The lectures which are followed by applause are also preceded by an introduction. How many introductions, lecture-going reader, can you recall? Why should you remember any, since you went to hear the lecturer, not the introducer? But the lecturer, however experienced, however free from vanity, is more likely than the audience to pay attention to what is said about him, to admire the skill with which quite ordinary achievements are made to sound distinguished, or to wince at the inaccuracies. What causes a lecturer most pain is, I believe, the naive question from a (usually young) chairman as they walk together into the lecture hall: 'Please tell me something about yourself, so that I can introduce you.' I have (so far) resisted the urge to say, 'I prepared my lecture; you should have prepared your bit'; but I have at any rate refused to answer, simply saying 'You're the chairman; you must decide what to say.' So far, no-one has retaliated by getting up and saying, 'This is Laurence Lerner. I don't know anything about him, and he wouldn't tell me.'

The standard formula for introducing a speaker in American universities is rigid: 'Professor X received his BA from Harvard (or Columbia), his Masters from Columbia (or Chicago), and his Ph D from Chicago (or Harvard); he has taught at the University of Virginia, at the University of Illinois, and is now the John Smith Distinguished Professor of Allerlei-Wissenschaft at the University of Weissnichtwo.' Then comes a list of his publications, and the fact that he's held a Guggenheim award and a fellowship from the National Endowment for the Humanities. How often I have sat in the audience and longed for a speaker who'd published nothing, who didn't have a Ph D, who'd failed to get a job at Chicago. Or for my favourite introduction, received in the Linguistics Dept at the University of Delhi (the only time I have spoken in a linguistics department, or ever expect to). The young professor who had invited me said: 'This is Mr Lerner. I met him at a party last week, and he seems an interesting fellow, so I've invited him to come and speak.'

I do not remember my introduction at the Shoreham Poetry Society, meeting in the local public library, but I remember vividly the conversation that preceded it. I was greeted on arrival by the secretary, who was busy taking the money and handed me over to her husband to be entertained until she was ready. The husband made three remarks, all engraved in stone on my memory. After a minute of awkward silence he looked round the room, and said, 'Not many people here tonight.' Another silence, and then he added, 'It depends on the poet, you know, how many come.' Another silence, and he said, 'I have to say, I'd never heard of you.'

Before you start, you are introduced; after finishing, you are thanked, and that too can be memorable. Memorable because unwelcome or because so very welcome. When I was an extramural lecturer in Northern Ireland, in the mid-fifties, the last meeting of my class in Portadown (or was it Dungannon?) was followed by the usual vote of thanks. 'Mr Lerner is one of the best lecturers we've had,' said the secretary. 'We all know the lecturers who lose their place, and keep us waiting while they hunt through the pages of their book and can't find the quotation they want. Now look at those little bits of paper marking the place in Mr Lerner's books: that's what I call a lecturer who knows what he's doing.' And it may have been in the same town that an admiring member of my class told me that what was really impressive about my lectures was not just how much I knew, but my command of the English language — 'the way you can say the same thing over and over in different words.'

And the best? Very recently, in April of 1994, I lectured to the Hungarian Shakespeare Association in Budapest. Twenty-odd lively and able people, lots of questions and discussion. Towards the end one or two people got up to go. A middle-aged woman who'd said nothing stood at the door, while one of the younger women was speaking. She put up one hand, the other already on the door handle, and when a pause came I nodded at her. She said: 'Please. Come again. Then come back again. And again,' and opened the door and left.

I wish she could read this, and know what she did for me.

TEACHING

Lectures and other Forms of Behaviour

When I taught in Paris, at the Sorbonne nouvelle, in the Spring of 1982 I was not given very much to do. This was not unwelcome since it obviously made it easier to explore Paris, improve my French, and go home for occasional weekends, but it could easily lead to uneasiness about whether one is really earning that comfortable salary — along with wondering how much one's French colleagues are doing for theirs. Professor B, at any rate, if we are to judge by the time he spent on me, was doing a good deal of organising. He was arranging a lecture series for the CAPES (le certificat d'aptitude pour l'enseignement supérieur — a sort of junior version of the agrégation): everyone who has had to arrange a lecture series knows that it sometimes seems much easier to give all the lectures yourself — for one colleague Thursday morning is the one time he really can't manage, another is being pestered by an editor to finish some great project which — it is made clear — dwarfs into triviality your request to give a mere lecture, a third has an ailing mother who calls on him at the most inconvenient — or convenient — times. How much simpler to sit down in the library and read the material rather than listen to excuses from the colleagues who would have loved to help if only. But my colleague B was not the sort who shrugs and writes the lecture himself; he treated making arrangements as an art form, even to what time of day one should meet and sort things out, along with careful discussion of how best to take the metro to meet him. After several conversations, a visit to his house and a great deal of 'si cela vous convient', it was agreed that I would give one lecture on Larkin. Each student, B explained, would only be required to write on (I think) two of the texts on the list, and they do not all choose the same ones, so not everyone needed to hear all the lectures; but it was necessary to offer them all, and a lecture on Larkin would surely be of great interest, coming from our distinguished visitor, who was himself a poet and knew — n'est-ce pas? — M Larkin personnellement. Quelle honneur pour nos étudiants, et quelle occasion d'en profiter. The flattery was a kind of lubrication for a creaking and rather confusing conversation about whether notre cher collègue X was going to lecture on Dickens or had chosen to do Auden instead, in which case the Auden lecturer might want to do Larkin, but of course he had not the advantage of personal knowledge, to say nothing of being a native speaker...

In the end it was agreed that on Friday the 21st of April I would turn up in the main building of the Sorbonne at ten o'clock. It was a 2 hour session, explained B, and he himself would be lecturing for the first hour. He would finish at ten, there would be a short break, then he would introduce me, and I would have until 11 for my lecture — not enough time of course, mais nous sommes contraints par l'oraire, comme chez vous, cher collègue, j'en suis certain. It would be best he explained, if I came to the little room used by the professors, and he gave me even more elaborate directions than for the Metro, up this staircase, down a tiny corridor to the right — easy to miss — up three steps (it may be rather dark) and then the second door on the right, I will fetch you from there — just after ten.

I found the room with some difficulty. Could this dusty cupboard be what B had meant? There was a man sitting in it — colleague or caretaker? It seemed impolite to ask, so I never found out. He was profoundly uninterested in my stumbling explanation that my colleague B was to collect me here, and when I asked if this was right for Salle D-2 he pointed to one of the three doors. It was 10 to 10 (I had of course arrived absurdly early) so I sat and waited, trying not to think about Larkin or get impatient. Ten long slow minutes later no-one had appeared, so I cautiously opened the door. It turned out to give directly into the lecture room, and I glimpsed high tiers of benches and the back of B, who was holding forth eloquently on Keats. What he was saying didn't sound like a peroration. So I shut the door again and waited: 5 past 10, 10 past 10. I might be constrained by the timetable, but B clearly wasn't. I wasn't meant to walk in and interrupt, surely? Wondering which poem to leave out when I gave my now truncated lecture, I shut the door and stared at the clock, which had now ceased to move altogether. At 10.17 the door opened and B walked into the cupboard, greeted his cher collègue warmly, and explained that it would take a few moments while the students who had decided not to study Larkin left, but perhaps I would not mind being patient for a moment. At 10.20 he accompanied me back to a now rapidly emptying room. It was an honour and a rare opportunity, he announced to the backs of the departing students, that Mr Lerner, lui-même poète, would be lecturing for the benefit of those who had decided to offer Larkin as one of their authors. It was clear that not many had so decided. The rows of empty seats were evidence that Keats mattered more than Larkin, or (more probably) that B mattered more than me.

I now had 35 minutes in which to interest the remainder in Larkin, but neither Larkin nor I rose to the opportunity. Most of the audience seemed to be packing up their papers, or chatting to their neighbours, or — worse — to someone three seats away. And what they were chatting about I realised, was whether to stay or go. Invariably, they decided to go. The friend three seats away got up, tapped his friend on the shoulder, and they walked up the aisle to the greedy exit. 'Why should I let the toad *work* Squat on my life?' I declaimed, and one student mouthed to another 'café?' and they threw the brute off.

One couple sitting four rows from the bottom had not looked round for friends, or packed up their notes. True, they had not brought a text of Larkin (no-one had) but they were listening. Well, I thought, where two or three are gathered together. I would speak to them, and if I managed to interest two people in Larkin, out of the whole of Paris, then though I would not feel I had earned my handsome salary, at least my morning would not have been wasted.

The couple stayed until 10.45: then after some act of telepathic communication they both folded their books, put them in their bags, and got up. I managed to take no notice, and went on lecturing to the now almost empty hall, relying on the act of faith that lies behind every lecture, that someone, somewhere, wants to hear it. It was obvious that I hadn't lived up to

B's introduction. Poet? Poet who knew Larkin? What I needed to do was to tell Larkin about the occasion, in the hope that he'd write a sour and witty poem about it. Or should I have written that poem myself — written it extempore, and cut into my lecture to read it to them:

> Who's that performing
> Those verbal feats
> Footnoting Larkin
> (Or is it still Keats?)
>
> Ironic distance,
> The self-mocking ham:
> How much of all that
> Will be in the exam?

I did none of this: I went on lecturing, since it was, after all, a lecture. Words spoken into the void for any who cared to listen.

Here is a definition of a lecture: it takes place because the lecturer has something to say, gets up on a dais, and says it. If anyone wishes to come and listen, they are welcome, but they will not make any difference to what is said. He may have a new discovery or a new theory to announce, or he may have a general overview of the subject to set forth. A friend in Aachen once described to me an occasion when he was walking along the corridor and heard someone speaking in an apparently empty room. Curious, he paused and looked in. There was the professor of mathematics, writing formulae on the blackboard, and explaining them loudly and clearly, and, sure enough, there was no-one else in the room. That is the pure Platonic ideal of a lecture.

We can make a rough and ready division of lectures into bread and butter lectures and star turns. A lecture series can aim to teach the students what they ought to know: it can take place two or three times a week, make no claim to originality, and set out to cover the ground systematically. As an undergraduate reading History at Cambridge, I went along at nine o'clock of a winter morning, Monday Wednesday and Friday, to listen to Mr Evenett, fellow of Trinity College, telling us about European History in the 16th and 17th centuries. He was neither witty nor eloquent, but he was tremendously thorough, and a couple of hundred students found it worthwhile to get up early (by English standards) and fill their notebooks with his copious information: there cannot have been a religious or political event of any importance in those 200 years that he did not know about and succeed in placing in context. I think I am right in saying that the thousands of sentences he uttered contained only two jokes. One was in an account of the monarchy of one of the smaller (German or Scandinavian?) courts that modelled itself upon Versailles, appointing all the same officials, even a royal mistress — though it was made clear, Mr E added, that the position was purely titular. A slightly better joke concerned Charles of Sweden, who led his country's armies to innumerable bloodthirsty victories (and several defeats) until at Fredricksten in 1718 he put his head above the parapet of a trench and was promptly killed by a bullet. 'He was only 37,' observed Mr E tersely. I have lost the notebook in which I crammed the thick breakfast of facts with which I began three days of every week, but I owe my success in the exam, I'm sure, to the blending of his thoroughness with my butterfly mind.

Mr Evenett must long since have gone to his rest, but for the other kind of lecture I will choose George Steiner, still very much with us (indeed, younger than me), the best lecturer I have ever heard. He came to Sussex to lecture on Freud and Literature some time in the mid-sixties, and to Vanderbilt to lecture on Jephtha's daughter and on modern European philosophy in the nineties, and on each occasion held me spellbound. Perhaps when he compared the threefold structure of the Freudian personality — superego, ego, id — to the three levels of the bourgeois household — bedrooms upstairs, living room and study in the middle, kitchen and servants below stairs — his judgement allowed too much liberty to his fancy (it fits well enough for the two lower levels, but the superego does not thrive in the bedroom — unless we think of it as the room in which you kneel to say your prayers). Perhaps when he began by insisting that psycho-analysis presupposed language, that no analyst is deaf and no patient dumb, he only told us, memorably, what we already knew; but I regarded those points as the enticing prelude to a magisterial and weighty exposition. I even regard his capacity to make enemies as a tribute to his power: to illustrate this I must spend a while on the Jephtha lecture.

It was called 'What's in a name?', and dealt with the story that is briefly told in Judges chapter 11, of Jephtha's vow that if God gave him victory over the Ammonites he would sacrifice whatever came forth from his house to meet him on his return. 'His daughter came out to meet him with timbrels and with dances: and she was his only child; besides her, he had neither son nor daughter.' There was no way he could escape his vow, and after two months of solitude in which she 'bewailed her virginity upon the mountains' she 'returned to her father, who did unto her according to his vow.' This heartbreaking tale is told succinctly and unemotionally, and the first part of Steiner's lecture was devoted to the paratactic narrative style of the Old Testament, its omission of all the connecting explanations and of explicit expressions of emotion, of so much that we consider essentially literary, and how this has somehow increased the resonance of the stories that have echoed down the centuries. He then turned to the daughter, and pointed out that she is never named. Is that also a case of parataxis, or is it an indication that women did not matter in that society? The lecture was about narrative method, and about feminist reading, and Steiner remarked that he had learned a good deal from feminist criticism, and had had to reconsider many of his traditional ideas on reading the Bible. Discussing the lecture afterwards with my friend Z, I was astonished by the virulence of his anger. I can describe Z by saying that though he is a teacher of literature, he cares more about feminism than about literature (I say this with confidence, because when I put the point to him he agreed). He described the lecture as a denigration of feminist scholarship. But, I objected, he told us that he's learned a great deal from it. 'How patronising can you get?' Z replied: 'he didn't name a single feminist scholar.' 'But,' I said, 'that isn't what his lecture was about.' 'Then it should have been,' Z replied: 'what's the good of an airy gesture to feminist scholarship in general?' I think of the occasions when I have objected to recent critical schools that they theorise about poetry or fiction without discussing actual poems and novels: it is clear that the protective insistence I feel about Keats and Milton is felt by Z about his feminist colleagues.

What's in a name? Z had got so sucked into the world of the lecture that he'd taken his angry objection from what he was objecting to; and since he is very intelligent and wide awake, he realised this. The complexities of anonymity explored by Steiner had themselves provided the objection: to Z this was an irony, at Steiner's expense, to me, it meant that the lecture had already replied to his objection. Perhaps that is what distinguishes a brilliant from a good lecture: that its own argument can be used against it, or co-opted for its own defence.

Lectures are not the only form of instruction in a university: there are seminars too, and there are tutorials. The rest of this chapter is about the differences between these forms of teaching, and may therefore be mainly of interest to my fellow teachers (though since there are teachers who have made up their minds, and laymen who are curious, the opposite may equally be the case). Let me first spend a while distinguishing seminars from tutorials. A seminar is a communal activity, in which a question is being discussed: What were the causes of the Crimean War, What is *Hamlet* really about, What is the categorical imperative, How does New Historicism differ from Old? The number of questions is infinite, the ways in which some of them can be answered almost unmeasurable, so we will never run out of seminar topics. In the traditional German method, one student is responsible for giving a paper at each meeting: he prepares this very thoroughly, and it needs to be *wissenschaftlich* (often mistranslated as 'scientific', but the translation is of course 'scholarly'.)

How does one write a seminar paper? I will describe as accurately as I can how the student does it in Vienna, but I need to say first that my students there were intelligent, diligent and enthusiastic, and were being well taught. Why I need to say this will soon become clear.

First, you read the text. If you are a student in your first or second year, the text may be short and minor — a story by Doris Lessing or Kipling, perhaps; or at the most, a short novel. Then you consult the 'secondary literature': great store will be set on completeness, so you dig out every article you can find on that story, every book on Lessing or Kipling. You photocopy these, since you're not allowed to take them out of the library (Austrian students may spend more money on photocopying than on books). Then you produce the outline, which might run: Introduction — Life of Kipling — Summary of the book — Discussion — Footnotes — Bibliography — Index. The bibliography will have two sections, works obtainable in Vienna, and works unobtainable in Vienna, which you will nevertheless make a list of — you never know, someone, sometime might want get hold of them. And yes, an index to your own twenty-page essay. The one thing you're unlikely to do is read anything else by Lessing or Kipling.

I said to one student, 'But this tells me nothing. The only thing that matters is the quality of your discussion. What questions are you asking, and how are you setting about answering them?' She looked surprised: 'I haven't done it that way before, our system is very different, but of course I can try.' She showed willing: they always do, and if you tell them to read an extra book there is no howl of protest. One student asked, nervously, 'Will Professor O be seeing this essay? If he does, and there is no index, he won't be pleased.' I reassured her: 'he won't, and if he does then I'll take the responsibility.' She nodded, a bit nervously, went away, and three weeks later she produced an excellent paper.

'Our system.' Is this a matter of cultural adjustment? There is after all no one way to write a study of a literary text; there's an Austrian system, and there's an English system. In Austria the student might attend a course of lectures called 'From literary text to scholarly paper' (from pupa, say, to butterfly!) What they learn is their own scholarly process: what to do in order to transform the amorphous raw material — the pupa called the 'primary text' — into a butterfly: the patterned structure (introduction — life of author — summary — discussion — bibliography) that they have learned how to manufacture. It is a weird — but revealing — parody of the claim of the cultural materialist that criticism is constitutive of literature. What my nervous Austrian student (she was also learning to be a ski instructor) had in common with Stanley Fish and Terence Hawkes, critics who have put forward this revolutionary claim, was the belief that literature is a rabble of books, fragments, verbal activity wandering through consciousness like the children of Hamelin, until the critic like the Pied Piper calls them to order and leads them in a procession of concepts (readerly competence — textual indeterminacy — sense of an ending — deep structures — ideological function) to the promised land where the critic is in charge: the skiing instructor gets a post in a Gymnasium, the critic an endowed chair. A bit lopsided as rewards, but the distinguished critic is after all much cleverer (or believes he is), and the American system rewards cleverness.

Having written her Seminararbeit, the student reads it to the class — or, as I insisted, presents them with a summary of her main points, and perhaps reads what she considers the most important paragraph: I might have some difficulty persuading her that this should not be an introductory paragraph about method, but one which directly addressed the text. By nudging the system in this way I was, I hoped, improving the students' education, but at the same time I was undermining what was supposed to be its main virtue: the deconstruction of the professor's authority. If the student has followed a standard procedure, and the professor does not know what is coming, then the ensuing discussion can be between equals; and with an independent minded student, this is just what will happen. How equal they are will depend not on rank but on the knowledge or insight each commands. The drawback of course is that each student will interact with the professor as an equal on only one occasion: he may spend all his preparation time on *Hamlet* or the Crimean War, and at the other meetings in the seminar on Shakespearean tragedy or Victorian politics he may simply listen, perhaps not even very actively (or, if the whole seminar is on *Hamlet* or the Crimean War, he may prepare, very thoroughly, only for his own contribution, on the character of Horatio, or the role of the nurses. Of course the professor will urge everyone to prepare for every meeting, but the students are human and busy.

In a more loosely run seminar, therefore, student papers may figure less prominently, even, at the extreme, disappear altogether; very specific reading (one book, or two articles, or three poems) may be prescribed for each meeting, and every student be required to read it. (And if they don't? Some American professors give quizzes, using the first five minutes to check who has done the reading, then marking the answers — or getting their teaching assistant to do so — and devising elaborate systems to determine how much the student's grade will be lowered if he fails one or three or all of the quizzes. The method is no doubt effective, but I could never bring myself to use it; university students are not schoolchildren, and university teaching demands the assumption, even if it is a willing suspension of disbelief, that the student wishes to learn as much as he possibly can, and should be treated as an equal.)

If there is no student paper, the seminar might begin with a short introductory lecture by the professor. Or he might begin by asking a question, or a series of questions, and inviting answers. A method I have often used, if the seminar is not too large, is go round the room inviting everyone to say what they have read, and what they found most interesting about it. This involves everyone, and with a little ingenuity you can, by listening carefully, construct an agenda for the ensuing discussion by grouping various responses together, or contrasting different assumptions, and so making it plain that you are beginning from the students' own interests. Of course this uses up a good deal of time, but I usually felt that it was time not wasted. I tended to ask questions and encouraged others to do so during this preliminary period if they were directed at clarification of what was being said, but once they looked as if an argument was beginning I would say, Let's save that until we've heard everyone's preliminary statement. This is not an easy line to draw, especially if the preliminary statement is obviously producing a lively argument: it might even be best to let it develop immediately, though it is usually not difficult to suspend it by pointing out that there are other students who haven't yet spoken: the student's respect for the rights of his fellow students is usually stronger than his respect for the teacher's protocol.

The skill of the seminar leader consists in two things: getting as many people as possible to participate actively, and deciding on relevance. The first requires not intellectual insights but human skills. There are always several people who say too little (or nothing), and quite often one or two who say too much. Indeed the two phenomena may go together — the talkative student may by his presence discourage the shy student from speaking. I think the best method is always to take the student aside, not during the session, and discuss the problem with him. One might say bluntly (but, of course, privately) 'You really are talking too much,' 'You often talk before you think,' or (no doubt more effectively) 'I want you not to speak for the first hour next time so that X and Y can contribute more fully — you've no doubt noticed that X says nothing, and I need your co-operation to enable me to draw him in.' A little mild flattery might do no harm — 'Just between ourselves, he's not as quick on the up-take as you are.' And to X you can say the obverse: 'I want to bring you into the discussion more.' You can plot with X: tell him to let you know in advance that he expects to have something to say about this or that topic, and you will create a space for him to say it. Sometimes X, if he is a good student, may protest: I pay attention, I get a lot of profit from the class, but I don't like talking: I read, I write the essays, but I'm bad at discussion. That objection should always be treated with respect: if X is happy with that image of himself, it may not be necessary to disturb it. But one must be satisfied that he really is happy with it.

I was once present at a discussion of teaching among Sussex faculty, in which the view was being very strongly expressed that a student had every right to keep quiet in class, if he was attentive and hardworking, and it was not our business to make the shy leopard change his spots. My friend Christophe intervened. 'I've been listening,' he said, 'to all these talkative people insisting that there's nothing wrong with being silent. Now I want you to tell us' — and he turned to the one man present who'd said nothing, a lecturer in Chemistry — 'whether you agree with this.' The chemist then made a thoughtful and quite open statement (which I think he found it difficult to make, but he was quite eloquent), saying that he knew he was shy, that he wished he wasn't, that it had caused him great problems in his private life as well as in his teaching and learning. It was a memorable moment, and reduced the rest of us to silence for a while.

Relevance. A seminar meeting, I believe, should have an agenda. How acceptable is the psycho-analytic reading of *Hamlet?* (Related questions: how do we choose between good and bad psycho-analytic readings? Is a psycho-analytic reading of *Measure for Measure* equally valid? What is psycho-analytic criticism trying to do? Does it matter that Shakespeare had not read Freud? Is there a Lacanian as distinct from a Freudian reading? Are there discrepancies between the good quarto, the bad quarto and the folio that will support or refute our reading? Is there a connexion between psycho-analytic interpretation and treating *Hamlet* as a revenge play? And a hundred others). Or, Does the moral philosophy of Kant involve any rejection of his epistemology? Or, What effect did the Crimean War have on how the British Army was recruited and organised? (Each of those with a whole list of related questions). The aim of the seminar meeting is that each student should understand the implications of the question, decide what would or would not constitute evidence for answering it, be confronted with one or two controversial answers, and begin to develop an answer of his own. This may involve setting aside other and equally interesting questions. Here different teachers will have different policies. At one extreme is the view that whatever any student says must be listened to and pursued: the teacher is there merely to stimulate discussion, never to pre-empt it, for the students know what they want to talk about. At the other extreme is the teacher who always asks questions to which he knows the answer (as Joy says reproachfully to C S Lewis in *Shadowlands*), and runs the seminar as an ingenious way of giving a lecture. At Sussex in the seventies the former method was highly regarded, especially by the sociologists: fellow travellers with the student revolution went so far as to say, 'My students have far more to teach me than I have to teach them.' To me it seems obviously necessary that the seminar leader should say sometimes, 'That's very interesting but not relevant. If you want to discuss it come and talk to me.' Or, 'Let's have a later session about that.' Obviously I think that intellectual rigour must sometimes prevail over the student's interests, that a seminar has an aim, and the teacher's function is to help everyone pursue it. The danger of course is that what the teacher considers irrelevant may to someone else be an urgent challenging of his assumptions. A Marxist teacher may insist that material conditions largely determine the meaning of a text, and firmly put aside consideration of its relation to (comparatively) timeless generic patterns; the Christian humanist, by contrast, may want to deal only with timeless values, and rule out of order the student who insists on talking about the composition of the audience or how Henslow treated his writers.

This now becomes very tricky: it is not necessary for the teacher to abandon his beliefs — or is it? I used sometimes to ask my students at Sussex, usually at the end of the term, a question that ran something like this: if the teacher holds an ideological position very different from the student, which would you prefer, that they engage in fundamental discussion of the clash between their two positions (I cannot accept your Marxist — or deconstructionist, or idealist — position because...) or that he turn chameleon and help the student to write a better Marxist/deconstructionist/idealist essay? To me, in the ideologically charged climate of Sussex in the seventies, this sometimes seemed the most important question about teaching, but the students tended to regard it as a non-issue: of course the teacher's own position will emerge, they said, there's no way that can be prevented. I sometimes answered, Don't underestimate the ingenuity of your teachers: if they want to wear an ideological disguise they may well be able to pull the wool over your eyes. I couldn't do this myself, but I think the reason is a matter of personality, that I'd so dislike the idea, not that it's intellectually impossible.

With this attention to ideological differences, I have begun to move now from seminar to tutorial, for I am now thinking of the position of an individual student. If the lecture is essentially concerned with the lecturer's own intellectual contribution, and the seminar is a communal activity, the tutorial is concerned with the student's views. Nothing the student says or writes can be irrelevant in a tutorial: if it is a wild digression, it might be all the more worth pursuing, to discover and discuss what train of thought set it off. If the student insists on discussing John

Bright instead of Palmerston, *Hamlet* instead of *Measure for Measure,* you want to know whether he simply hasn't read *Measure for Measure,* or has an interesting theory about *Hamlet* which he can't leave alone, whether he admires Bright for his pacifism, or doesn't think foreign secretaries have much influence on how wars are fought anyway. The bee in the student's bonnet may sting, or may make honey, or both. (The student who once wrote me a psycho-analytic discussion of Noddy that I thought full of misplaced ingenuity has gone on to become a successful and highly regarded novelist.) That is why a tutorial must be small. The presence of one other student can be a help, three students is already moving towards a seminar but can be kept individual with luck, four or more will soon cease to be about the thought processes of the individual, and Noddy must be ruled out of order.

My criticism of American universities is that they do not distinguish between different teaching methods, but run them all together under the conception of a course; of French universities that they mount admirable lectures but have no tutorials; of British universities as they used to be when I was a student that there were no seminars, and nowadays that outside Oxford and Cambridge pressure of numbers is causing the tutorial to lose some of its individual qualities.

Don't Look Up

The professor asks a question about the literary text being discussed. Is it really malicious (the author is, say, Pope)? Is it over-adjectival (Spenser, or Keats) or too abstract (Johnson) or too full of clichés (Dickens, or Orwell)? Is it dismissive of women (Pope again, or Milton, or Dickens — or, perhaps, almost anyone)? Does it refute the possibility of its own communication (Beckett, obviously; Marvell, more subtly; all texts, according to some deconstructionists)? Is it moving, brilliant, irrefutable (your favourite author)? What does the student do with his eyes when he answers? He has, we will assume, a copy of the text in front of him: does he look at that, or at the teacher?

First answer: this class is a human situation, participatory, not authoritarian. The student should respond, not meekly submit. We do not want him to bow down obediently, but to engage in dialogue. Eye-contact is essential to genuine interaction, and the good teacher establishes eye-contact with his students because he treats them as equals. Looking down at the book is just looking down at the desk: a form of evasiveness.

Second answer: the most important presence in the room is neither the teacher nor the student, it is *Hamlet* or *Paradise Lost* or *The Rainbow*: these will endure when the others are clay. The teacher's aim is to show the richness of these masterpieces, to help the student respond to their subtlety and profundity; the aim of his questions is to drive the student to the text. If the student listens to and looks at him, she is treating the question as an expression of authority, not as an opportunity. The aim of the class is always, ultimately, to drive the students to the text, for it is a *literature* class; and if it is working well, the student's first response will be to turn to the book.

Third answer: *Hamlet* and *Paradise Lost* have no independent existence. They are constantly reconstituted in the act of being read, and reading is an ideological process. In a patriarchal or liberal-capitalist society, they will be constituted in individualist and patriarchal terms; radical or feminist readers will constitute them differently, decentring or interrogating the structures that traditionalist readers take for granted. To believe that the printed page contains objective meaning that can serve as a court of appeal is precisely the illusion that recent literary theory has destroyed. Of course the student will look at the teacher, because his first task is to understand where the question is coming from, *whose Hamlet* s/he is being asked to constitute. S/he will look at him, if necessary to stare him down.

The journalist, the (fully) retired Professor, the Martian visitor — someone for whom the teaching of literature is an object of curiosity, not an issue on which it is necessary to take a stand — can leave it at that. But the practising teacher needs to choose.

(Of course there might be a fourth answer: the good student knows *Paradise Lost* by heart, and does not need to look down at the book. But we must be realistic.)

I have encountered all these answers in extreme form. The first was especially common during the '1968 years', the time when University teachers were grovelling before the revolution, saying with self-flagellating pride that their students had more to teach them than they had to teach the students. What we might call the Antinomian version of this position would have no text and no subject matter at all. Antinomianism is the logical extreme of Protestantism: if Luther was right in believing that justification came from faith alone, that works, since they are performed by fallen man, must always be tainted with sin and cannot contribute towards salvation, then the sinner who is touched by grace will be preferred to the righteous man who does good deeds (as indeed we are told in the parable of the Pharisee and the Publican). If you really believe this, it would be logical to commit all the sins you can, in order to demonstrate their irrelevance to salvation, and this doctrine was both preached and practised in the doctrinal melting-pot of the England of the mid-seventeenth century. One Laurence Claxton, or Clarkson, wrote in *My Single Eye* (the title suggests, doesn't it, to the 20th century reader, a book of modern poems),

'Sin hath its conception only in the imagination; therefore so long as the act was in God, or nakedly produced by God, it was as holy as God.' As a result, 'No man could be freed from sin, till he had acted that so-called sin, as no sin... And therefore till you can lie with all women as one woman, and not judge it sin, you can do nothing but sin.'

According to Antinomian educational theory, good works are the subject matter that you are teaching; the grace that it is not in your power to compel or resist is the seminar spirit, springing from the uncompelled involvement of the students. The Antinomian of teaching, then, is the one who cares only for setting up the proper group dynamics — or rather, allowing it to set itself up. For the seminar to be *about* anything would simply interfere with the free operation of the Spirit.

Lest you think this is a travesty, I hasten to assure you that I have had colleagues who thought that way. I have (now) to confess that I am falling back on hearsay evidence, since I've never had the fortune to be present at a real Antinomian session. One of my students reported to me that she entered the room at the opening class, sat down at the table, and waited for things to begin. After ten minutes they were still waiting: I don't remember if the teacher was present or absent, but there must have been some mechanism for making it clear that he wasn't just late, that the session had started. After a fair amount of giggling and complaining they would begin to lay out an agenda, and a leader would emerge. By the third or fourth meeting the leader's authority was being challenged; and the teacher (who by then was certainly present) explained to them that this was usual, that initial confusion would be succeeded by the emergence of a leader, and that after a while he would be challenged. By then it would emerge that the seminar was studying itself, and no doubt could enter the curriculum as group dynamics, or (perhaps) patterns of leadership.

I have other examples (also by hearsay): of intending teachers, during their Cert Ed course, receiving a note that instructed them to turn up in such-a-room at (say) 2 pm. They had been divided into three groups. One found the room empty, and a cine-camera whirring at them. The second were ushered in by the Head Porter in his most authoritarian mood: 'Come on now, hurry up, find yourself a seat, not so much chatter, let's have a bit of discipline here.' The third were received by a large and grandmotherly lecturer, with soothing words and affectionate smiles, and invited to sit down. In all three rooms the camera was going. The following week they watched the film of themselves, and discussed their responses. Or there is the tale of the lecturer who announced that she was interested in graphology, and believed she could tell character from handwriting, so invited everyone to hand in a specimen of handwriting; and the following week gave out a rather bland and flattering character-analysis (sense of humour, imagination, interest in people), leaving the class to discover for themselves that everyone had been given the same analysis. Or there is — but we can stop there.

The purpose of all this, in the case of teacher-training, was to disorient them, so that they would later be able to empathise with their pupils. They were, after all, young men and women who had succeeded in life, had done well in exams, knew how to fill in forms, and were, in many cases, going to teach children who had difficulty in even reading a notice-board. Perhaps, then, the first thing was to subject them to some of the confusion and humiliation that for their pupils had always been the nature of the world; so one of the gimmicks consisted in putting up deliberately misleading information on the notice-board, so that the students would get lost.

The colleague who was mainly responsible for this element in the teacher training course (she was the handwriting 'expert') got another job that began in January. I happened to be in the University over the Christmas vacation, and came across her packing up her books and clearing her room. We chatted, and I asked how she felt about leaving, and in particular about leaving in the middle of the academic year. 'The trouble is,' she said, 'the students haven't had time to forgive me yet.'

So much for the Antinomians. The opposite extreme would clearly be the teacher who valued his authority and intended to direct the class. He too of course would want the students to look at him (unless he was so authoritarian that he saw looking as impudence!) Neither the Antinomian nor the authoritarian will be willing to give up his role to the shadowy presence of Milton or Dickens, distilled into the words on the page. For the former, *Paradise Lost* is less important than the group; for the latter, it is less important than himself.

***

Who Needs us?

And how important *is* the teacher? Is he an enabler, an oppressor, or a dispenser of knowledge? Is he needed? I have put this in the third person, but it has often been an urgent first-person question for me. What, I would ask myself from time to time, have I really got to offer my students? When interviewing applicants for Sussex I would sometimes ask them 'Why do you need to come to university to get a knowledge of English literature? After all, Jane Austen, Keats and Dickens don't need me to explain their works — they wrote for you, expecting you to read them without my help.' I never got a really satisfactory reply. 'I'll have the chance to go into it more deeply,' they would say. There were dozens of variations on that theme: more deeply, more thoroughly, really study it properly, get to know English literature really well, learn how to understand it fully. I could always reply (and sometimes did) that the way to understand it more fully, more deeply, more thoroughly, is to read it more carefully, just as I would tell people that the best way to understand a Yeats poem is to read it along with the poems that surround it in the volume. All this can be done without a teacher.

Of course my question was unfair. The students were coming to university to have a good time, to grow up, to enter a rite of passage. By this I don't mean anything cynical: they weren't (most of them) coming to lie in the sun, to go to parties and meet girls (or boys). They hoped to do all that of course, but as extras: they were coming to read Jane Austen and Keats, that was to be the main thing they did. To become an accountant and read Keats in the evenings is all very well, but it doesn't give the same feelings of intensity. They wanted to be told by society: Your function, for three years, is to read Keats; we'll pay you for it — not much, but enough to live on, and we'll demand nothing from you except that you read the books your tutors prescribe, and write the essays they require. The teachers are there to check that they really are reading Keats. So to say to the arriving student 'I have nothing to tell you about Keats that you could not find out for yourself if you had time and opportunity' is to lay an unfair burden on her. Time and opportunity is precisely what she's asking for.

But the teacher does not see his function as that of a mere watchdog. To make sure the student isn't wasting his time, to examine him and check that he really has learnt something about Keats: these are functions that every university performs, but to the individual teacher they are subsidiary. He is not there to examine but to teach. He is writing a book on Jane Austen, or on tragedy, or (nowadays) on power and ideology in the eighteenth century lyric, and it's a book whose points readers could not make for themselves. His self-esteem is at stake: the book is one that only he can write, and by listening to him the students will learn something new about Jane Austen or the eighteenth century lyric.

What hardly any of the interviewees said, but what would have been a good answer, was 'I can read Jane Austen, but I want to learn to write about her.' Reading means absorbing, admiring, listening, but remaining silent; the literary critic has learned to articulate his response. They might have gone further, and said 'I can enjoy listening to a nightingale, or feeling the west wind blow on my face, but it. needs Keats or Shelley to write a poem about it; I can enjoy the *Ode to a Nightingale* or the *Ode to the West Wind,* but only the literary critic can articulate what makes the poem work, and I want to learn to be a literary critic.'

That is a good answer. It would justify the acceptance of a university place and a maintenance grant, but it would of course assume that reading and interpretation, reading and criticism, are distinct activities. If that is so, the reader can ask, Who needs criticism? Is it necessary in order to improve our reading? We are back with my question to the intending students: why not go on reading Jane Austen and Keats, who wrote for readers, not for critics, all by yourself?

We can of course point out that they wrote for educated readers and for their own contemporaries — for readers, that is, who knew things that the modern reader may not know. What is the blushful Hippocrene? What did 'nice' mean in the 18th century, or 'romantic', or 'patriot'? Who was the mother of Hermes? We need people who will tell us these things.

Let me now introduce Meg. She took an English degree at one of the new universities, and now teaches at a Sixth Form college. She is intelligent, enthusiastic, and gets on well with her students. One year the syllabus included the poems of Keats, and the class included Clare, a middle-aged woman who had earlier received an old-fashioned classical education, and now that her children were grown-up, had decided to study for A-level English. Meg knew about levels of irony and women's studies and the metaphoric life of a poem, but Clare knew all the classical and biblical allusions. She knew why Ruth was sick for home and why Marsyas was flayed, she knew the story of Cupid and Psyche. Meg got into the habit of calling on her for explanations, and so did the other students: 'What's Elysium, Clare?' 'Who's Narcissus? Clare will know.' At the end of the term, Meg made an impassioned speech to the class. 'We've been really lucky, having Clare here,' she said. 'I don't know what I'd have done without her. But isn't it a disgrace that I needed her? You can see that I wasn't properly educated: I ought to have known all these allusions, but I'm deprived.' Meg told me that this was the most effective piece of teaching she ever did: her confession, and her obvious sincerity in wanting to know about Greek mythology, fired the students with a zeal she had never quite been able to arouse by herself.

I admire Meg's ability to turn a weakness into a strength, to show the students she was needed through the very process of failing to meet the need. But the literary critic with aspirations is not satisfied to be Clare. She does not believe that her most important function is to elucidate what time or the poet's erudition has rendered obscure. That is the higher lexicography, the function of editors and commentators, useful — necessary, even — but literary criticism is something other and something more. The scholarly commentator has a great deal to say about *Piers Plowman,* the product of a world utterly different from ours, or *Paradise Lost,* with its learned allusions, but he is not needed for 'A Slumber did my spirit seal', or a novel by Margaret Drabble. Literary criticism is equally interested in them all.

So we find ourselves saying that criticism is a very different activity from both reading and scholarship. The poets and the novelists want readers; scholars arise because our knowledge is imperfect; critics arise because any human activity throws up the meta-activity we call criticism. Books are written about chess and cookery, pundits appears on the television to analyse the play of footballers — and the same question arises: are they there to teach us to cook better (yes), or play chess better (usually) or to play football better (no). They are the result of the inevitable self-consciousness of humanity, that whatever we do we have to reflect on it, to understand what it's for and what it's about.

The germ of modern literary theory lies here. Literary theory as it thrives today is a form of philosophy: it derives from the thinker's need to form theories about everything we do. The linguist forms theories about language, not in order to speak better or learn more languages, but in order to theorise; and since poems and novels are in language, it is to be expected that much modern criticism would derive from modern linguistics. Hence structuralism: the attempt (as Barthes declared) to treat all human activities as a language.

Just as Frenchmen go on speaking French whether or not they have read Saussure or Greimas, so readers will go on reading Jane Austen and Dickens whether or not they have read Hillis Miller or Alexander Welsh. Reading and criticism will co-exist, just as speaking a language and studying its deep structures will co-exist, as parallel activities, the one widespread, the other for specialists.

With, however, one difference. Linguistics makes no claim to replace language, indeed could hardly do so without putting itself out of business. But for literary criticism to replace reading is not such an impossibility as might at first seem. Travelling back in the train after a Shelley conference with one of the editors of a new edition of Shelley that would appear on discs, and enable the user to call up all versions of a poem together, in order to see how it had changed, and perceive the artificiality of picking on any one version and calling it 'the poem', I listened fascinated to the exposition of how valuable such an edition would be, how it would revolutionise our concept of text. But, I said, though this edition will be wonderful for the purpose of studying Shelley, it will surely make it impossible to read his poems. My interlocutor shrugged: 'We use words differently' he said. 'For me, that's what reading is.'

He was doing what many textual critics nowadays love to do: deconstructing the signifier. Deconstructing the signified has been with us for longer. As I argued recently with my friend Mark about New Historicist readings of Wordsworth, he observed (it has become a commonplace) that the critical school that the reader belongs to must govern his understanding of the poem. I objected: 'You mean critics, not readers. What about the poetry-lover who reads Wordsworth because he likes to, and is ignorant of modern literary controversies. What governs *his* understanding?' Mark thought for a moment, and answered: 'I don't know anyone who reads Wordsworth, except academics and their students.' For him it was an interesting observation, not a lament.

I revert to our professor who is writing a book on Jane Austen — an old-fashioned book of literary criticism. What has he to offer? Basically — though it's difficult for him to say this too openly — the fact that he's cleverer than other people, and can perceive things in the novels that the rest of us, being slower of study, don't notice. The literary theorist, on the other hand, gives a different answer: he has been trained. He has expertise that amateurs haven't, and that the author could not — would not wish to — expect in his readers. Whereas the older critic must justify his book by claiming to be a better reader and therefore a good critic, the new theorist need not be a better reader, because he knows a method.

Both have problems. The new theorist has to decide what he thinks about reading — not criticism, just reading, the reading done by the common reader with whom Johnson rejoiced to concur (unless, like my Shelley editor, he believes that the activity no longer exists). Sometimes he seems to contemplate its abolition with indifference, even eagerness (Mark, I thought, sounded a bit wistful).

The older critic, on the other hand, has not escaped from my original question: can the students manage without him? Sitting in a colleague's room in Sussex in a moment of gloom, I remarked that perhaps we should all be doing something else, something more useful: the students can read for themselves, I said, why does Keats need us to explain his poems — all the arguments set forth at such length above. 'Oh no,' said Tony, 'I feel I'm very useful to them, I can point out all sorts of things they haven't noticed, and tell them things they don't know.' Tony is the most unpretentious of men, and was clearly saying this not in self-congratulation but as a calmly objective remark. 'Well,' I said, 'You must have stupider students than I have.' One of his students had come into the room during the discussion, in order to raise a point about her next essay, or perhaps just to check something about her reading. She didn't stay long, I remember, but there was a momentary pause before I said, 'Your students must be stupider than mine.' Later it was reported that she had gone away and said to her friends, 'Mr Lerner just insulted me.'

Herein, for me, has always lain one of the attractions of teaching abroad. In Germany or India you possess a skill no-one can dispute, and everyone is grateful for. However brilliant your students — and even your colleagues — may be, they are not native speakers of English, and they are sure to need your help. I once saw Beckett's *Endgame* with a German friend, and realised, as we discussed it afterwards, that he did not know that the title was a technical term in chess. I once discussed Dylan Thomas' poem *The Hunchback in the Park* with German students, and realised that they could not sense the linguistic feel of

And Mister they called Hey Mister
The truant boys from the town
Running when he had heard them clearly
On out of sound

because they did not know that 'out of sight' is normal idiomatic usage, whereas 'out of sound' is a coinage. That at least is one way to feel needed.

***

'Teaching is Therapy'

The one person who can always feel needed is the doctor. When I was a student I had an acquaintance who was studying medicine, and took himself very seriously as a benefactor of mankind. 'You've got no ambition,' he once remarked to me dismissively; 'you just want to be a teacher. Now to be a doctor...'— and his voice trembled with ambition and self-importance.

Thirty years later my friend Derek offered me a way to get my own back. There was a crystalising moment in our long unending argument, stretching over the many decades we were colleagues: 'Teaching is therapy,' he asserted, and leaned back with an amused smile to watch my indignation. Our arguments about teaching had circled constantly round the same question: is the teacher someone with knowledge and insight, at whose feet the fortunate student gets a chance to sit; or is the teacher a helper, an enabler, even a therapist, arousing the student's interest, helping him to circumvent a writing block, providing an ear to listen and even a shoulder to weep on?

December at Sussex, from time to time, produced a discontented visitor from Oxford, often enough for me to see it as a seasonal rite. A student who took a very good degree would go on to graduate work at Oxford, arrive there full of high expectations, and find the first term full of disappointment. When term ended he (or she: it happened to both sexes) would pay a visit to Brighton, to talk to old friends and (often) old teachers, and they would always say the same: 'no-one at Oxford knows who I am, no-one bothers about me.' After three years of careful teaching and pastoral care, they found themselves in the tougher and more anonymous world of competitive scholarship, and they did not like it. Derek, if they spoke to him (they often did) would be wholly sympathetic (as a returning ex-service man, he had given up a place at Cambridge because he did not like the atmosphere), and felt we were being given a glimpse into the less attractive side of Oxford. My response to them was usually to say, 'Universities are full of people who know a lot and have lots of insights. The art of being a student is to extract this from them, even when they lack the talent for passing it on.' I think I could defend this to Derek as a constructive answer, since it aimed to divert the student's disappointment onto the question of what he could do about it (a good therapeutic method, surely). But I did not make this answer for therapeutic reasons; I said it because I believed it. I saw the university teacher's prime responsibility as being to his subject, not, as Derek clearly believed, to his student.

A good test of this difference is the occasion when a student tries hard and does badly. This can come at all levels, and an instance that has remained with me comes from my brief time as a schoolteacher. Pratt was neither able nor hard-working, often got into trouble, and tended to get low marks. Sometimes there was no mark at all, because he hadn't done the work. One day he told me that he'd decided to try really hard, and handed me a piece of work longer than all his previous efforts put together. My delight at this apparent reformation soon evaporated when I began to read it: every sentence contained misspellings and grammatical mistakes, every paragraph galloped from one confused illogicality to another. Pratt's idea of trying hard was to write a lot, not to write better. I gave the essay a low mark (though higher than his usual), and wrote a comment praising him for his effort but saying firmly that the mistakes were as frequent and as serious as ever.

Pratt was furious. 'That's the last time I try hard for him,' he muttered, within my hearing; no doubt he was almost unprintable when out of earshot. It is easy to see, by Derek's principles, where I had gone wrong. I had behaved like an examiner, an upholder of abstract standards, instead of a teacher, looking always for what is positive in the situation. I should have realised that the first thing Pratt would see was the mark, and would feel it as a slap in the face; after that, my carefully pondered remarks would be wasted on him. I had failed to put myself in his position.

There are a host of ingenious devices for getting round this. Why give a mark at all? Why not insist on the separation between teaching and examining that I now so firmly believe in, and respond as a teacher, aiming only to encourage and help? And if it is necessary (because of the school's policy or the pupils' expectation) to give a mark, why not announce it a week later, so that the pupil is first forced to attend only to the comments?

Or take the pupil aside (assuming that time permits — as it always does, if one cares enough) and ask him to explain some of his sentences, leading him to discover for himself what is wrong with them. A host of devices.

But there is a limit to what can be done by devices. What Pratt wanted was praise — unqualified praise. If I gave him that, he would be spurred on to future efforts: so what sort of pedantry prevented me from saying what was needed, instead of what I felt was truthful?

In 1982 I spent a week at Lumb Bank in Yorkshire taking part in an interactive workshop between poets and actors, organised by the Arvon Foundation; and one of the things I learnt was that actors believe it is most important to be supportive of one another. One of the actors performed a one-man show he was about to do on the fringe of the Edinburgh Festival. It was disjointed, overacted, and in grotesquely bad taste, and as I listened to the other actors wishing him luck, and praising his performance, I felt astonished at how uncritical they all were. Travelling home with one of them, I remarked on this: 'I thought Nick's show was dreadful,' I said, and began to criticise it. 'Poor Nick,' said my friend, 'I'm afraid he's due for a flop.' 'But you told him how good it was,' I objected — 'I heard you.' 'Of course,' said Bruce. 'There's no point in saying anything else, is there?' I realised that during the whole week, I had never heard any of the actors say anything derogatory about the others. 'Actors are always supportive,' said Bruce. 'If you go into someone's dressing room just before the show, it's not much use to him if you tell him all the things he's been doing wrong, is it?' I thought for a while. 'You know,' I said, 'I earn my living by pulling students' essays to pieces. It's my job to tell them what's wrong with their work.'

David Holbrook's educational writings were very influential in Britain in the sixties, and they made the case for a totally non-judgemental approach to elementary teaching. In *English for the Rejected* he described how he would give back a pupil's semi-literate essay and tell him it was very good; he would not tell him what mistakes he'd made, since his overwhelming aim was to strengthen the pupil's confidence. As confidence grew, the mistakes would right themselves. If even the teaching of spelling and grammar should be open and non-judgemental, how much more so for the discussion of ideas and arguments.

Or should we draw the opposite conclusion? Because there is universal agreement on what is correct spelling, there is no need to teach them normatively: for the rest of the student's life, educated society will constantly correct his mistakes, and the task of the teacher should be to give him the confidence to enter into dialogue with the educated. But students of literature are already in that dialogue, and here, perhaps, the task of the teacher is to improve the quality of their contribution.

There is no way of settling whether Derek and Holbrook are right, or whether they are right in the elementary school but wrong in the university; we need both kinds of teacher, perhaps we even need both kinds to co-exist in the same person. Perhaps it is necessary to observe that Pratt had chosen the easy way: praise must be earned and Pratt was not willing to pay the price. It must be earned not by writing a lot but by writing better.

Many years later, at Sussex, came a similar case with even wider implications. The seminar that Anthea belonged to had been asked not only to do some advance reading, but to write a preliminary essay. Most of them wrote half a dozen pages: Anthea wrote forty. But delight at such diligence soon evaporated in the reading. No doubt Anthea's essay was better than Pratt's, since she was a 20 year old who had been admitted to University, not a 14 year old who might never pass a public exam; but as I read it with my professorial eye I grew ever gloomier. Along with the grammatical errors and the confused sentences, there was a shrill hostility to the historians she had chosen to discuss because of their lack of revolutionary zeal, their pedantic insistence on evidence. Indeed, as the seminar proceeded, I discovered just how deep was Anthea's loathing of scholarship. Once she denounced a historian for supporting the 'official line' instead of starting from the way the people saw things. I don't remember who the historian was (E P Thompson? George Rudé?), but I pointed out that he considered himself a radical, and had indeed been much criticised for the reliance he placed on popular tradition; whereupon she burst out, 'Well, if that's all you can say, that he's not as reactionary as most of the others, that's not saying much, is it?' By that time, relations between us were bad: she had never forgiven me for my comments on her preliminary essay. Of course I had praised her for devoting so much effort to it, but she had dismissed that as a sop. And she was right, really: I had criticised both its confusions and its grammar very strongly, and had wanted to begin with a sop.

A few years earlier, I had been on the university admissions committee, and had put forward what I thought was a bright idea: that we should 'adopt' a few inner city comprehensive schools. The linking of an Oxford or Cambridge college to individual public schools had a long tradition behind it: I know a classics teacher who had studied Latin and Greek at Eton and then effortlessly acquired a place at King's College, Cambridge to read classics, as his own teacher had done before him — a chain that could, in principle, go on for ever, though my friend broke the mould to become a lecturer in English. This system — corrupt in the eyes of some, warm and human to others — meant that the process of admission was not merely a matter of examination results and interviews by strangers; why, I thought, should it not retain the humanity, but linked to a different ideology? If the university adopted a school where the pupils were underprivileged, and offered a few places to pupils selected by the school, whatever their A-level results, would it not be striking a valuable blow for democracy?

I only spent one year on the committee, and when I left it the scheme was still being discussed; but others took it up (including Derek, who was a tower of strength), and a year or two later it reached the senate as an official proposal, and was accepted. For some reason I missed that senate meeting, and first learnt about the proposal from my rather conservative friend John. 'Another well meaning liberal scheme,' he said: 'just like Sussex. No-one has thought it through. Do you reveal the identity of these guinea pigs,' he asked, 'or do you keep it secret? Do they know it themselves? What happens if they do badly?' (he may even have said 'when they do badly'). 'So many questions unanswered — even unasked.'

What I discovered — but only later — was that Anthea was one of the guinea pigs. She had come from an inner-London comprehensive on the adopted schools scheme. There may have been others, but she was the only one I was aware of. I was told, at the same time, that she was pregnant and had left the university. Hoist with my own petard? I felt guilty — at least momentarily. But does it matter what I felt? What matters is Anthea and the tangle she had, with my help, got herself into. I wish she could read this, and tell me what she now thinks.

Who is assessing who?

Who is assessing who? Perhaps the question betrays its answer. Students write 'Who assesses who?' their teachers write (or used to) 'whom'. So it is clearly a student who asks this question, and he asks it in order to proffer his answer, which will be, Why shouldn't I assess you as well?

Which, in America, he does. Well, in a sense, students anywhere do: how can you sit at the feet of a masterful figure, with power over you, without forming an opinion about him? Teachers are judged by their students all the time: they are seen as brilliant or dull, conscientious or lazy, bullying or kind, dogmatic or open, rigorous or slovenly and (no doubt) sexy or frigid. But judging is not the same as assessing. When the comments and conversations about teachers are promoted from the refectory and the bedroom to something that is recorded and handed in, the process becomes institutionalised and official, it can then be called assessment, and people turn out to have strong views about it.

If students are given the right to assess their teachers, they are, at least to a modest extent, being empowered. The empowering of students came in 1969, as part of the revolution (more about this revolution in the final chapter): failing to change society, to turn the army pacifist or the factory socialist, the revolution addressed itself to the university, and there it had slightly more success. Student representatives sat on decision making bodies, in most countries; and in the United States large numbers of universities gave them forms at the end of each course, and required (or at least invited) them to grade their teachers. It could be argued that this was long overdue, that there was — and had always been — a very ordinary and nonrevolutionary argument for it. We all believe that teachers should teach well, and who knows better how well they teach than their pupils? Appointment and promotion committees had for decades recognised the importance of good teaching, and striven to reward it; and in order to do so, had to rely on hearsay: He must be a good/bad teacher because... What came after the 'because'? Because my nephew is in his class and tells me... Because his students seem so lively/dull when they come to me. Because I've argued with him about teaching and he said... That committee must often have sounded like a meeting of ancient historians, struggling to draw important conclusions from fragmentary and trivial documents: how can you decide if Publius Scaevola Maro was a good consul if you re not even sure what his real name was, whether he was consul in 485 or 495 BC, or even whether he was ever consul. The difference is that in the case of the teaching committee the real evidence is available. Why not ask those who know?

'Those who *know*?' cries out the traditionalist in horror. *We* are the ones who know, our students are the ones who are learning They are not competent to judge our teaching; if they were, then they would be the teachers. In Sussex in the seventies this conservative argument was joined by a parallel argument in the mouth of the radicals whose thinking was — shall I say? — trade union oriented: that the career structure of the academic was arranged by negotiation between his union and his employers, and was not to be tampered with by anyone not party to the negotiation. This alliance — plus, no doubt, other arguments, plus a good sprinkling of natural inertia, has kept British universities as they are, while America has gone far down the road to student assessment of their teachers.

Let us put our cards on the table. Here is Vanderbilt University's form, as handed out at the end of every semester by each teacher to the members of his class. He then explains the procedure, asks one member of the class to volunteer to gather in the forms and take them to the Department secretary, and leaves the room. If he is self-confident and tenured, he might forget about it, or simply look at the forms at the beginning of the next semester, when he has handed in his grades; if he is nervous and untenured, he may have built up a good deal of anxiety by then.

It is the policy of the College of Arts and Science that: (1) the responses to these questionaires shall be anonymous; (2) these completed forms will not be read by the instructor until after he has turned in the grades for this course; (3) the responses will be used to improve the quality of the course; (4) the responses will be considered when making personnel decisions.

Use only pencil to fill out this form

Do not mark on this side of form except in the scoring column and in the information boxes at the top of the form.

1) Rate the effectiveness of the instructor in communicating with the class.
   1. poor   2. marginal   3. average   4. very good   5. excellent

2. Rate the helpfulness of the instructor outside of the class.
   1. poor   2. marginal   3. average   4. very good   5. excellent

3. Rate the effectiveness of the instructor in stimulating your interest in the subject.
   1. poor   2. marginal   3. average   4. very good   5. excellent

4. Give an overall rating of the instructor.
   1. poor   2. marginal   3. average   4. very good   5. excellent

5. Rate the grading standard of this course compared to others you have taken at Vanderbilt.
   1. very easy   2. easier than average   3. average   4. more rigorous   5. most rigorous

6. Rate the course requirements compared to others you have taken at Vanderbilt.
   1. very easy   2. easier than average   3. average   4. more rigorous   5. most rigorous

7. Estimate how much you learned in the course.
   1. almost nothing   2. a little   3. average amount   4. above average   5. considerably above average

8. Rate the effectiveness of this course in challenging you intellectually.
   1. poor   2. marginal   3. average   4. very good   5. excellent

9. Give an overall rating of the course.
   1. poor   2. marginal   3. average   4. very good   5. excellent

10. General comments about the course and instructor:
   (Please use back of the evaluation form for general comments)

11. My gender is: 1. female   2. male

12. My classification is:
   1. graduate   2. senior   3. junior   4. sophomore   5. freshman

13. I took the course to satisfy:
   1. major or minor field requirements   2. other specific degree

requirements   3. elective credits required for degree   4. non-degree requirements   5. no requirements

14. Before taking the course my interest in the subject was
    1. very low   2. low   3. average   4. high   5. very high

15. On average, how many hours per week did you spend on this course outside of class?
    1. fewer than 2   2. 2–4   3. 4–6   4. 6–8   5. more than 8.

When I was at Sussex I was in favour of a system something like this — but failed to persuade my colleagues. I therefore designed my own form, and gave it out to some of my students. Often they didn't return them; just as often, I forgot to give them out; so I ended up with a mere handful of replies out of the hundreds of students I had taught. Here is my form:

Now that our course is nearly over, I'd be glad if you'd let me have any comments (favourable or unfavourable) that may have occurred to you during the term. Such remarks will be helpful to me in considering how to teach this course in future. You may do this either by answering the following questions, or simply by recording your reactions in your own words.

Laurence Lerner

1. How successful did you find the system of weekly seminars and fortnightly individual tutorials? Would you have preferred the conventional system of tutorial pairs?

2. Did we cover too much material during the term, or too little?

3. In every course there is a tension between seeing the whole course as a unity into which individual texts are fitted, so that one is asking the same set of questions all the time; and allowing each book or author to shape our discussion in a way that will be appropriate to him, even if that makes the term's work rather miscellaneous. Did we err by leaning too much in either direction?

4. Did you feel the tutor controlled the seminar discussions too much, and should have allowed them to range more freely?

5. How important is it that the tutor read your essay before a tutorial?

6. Do you feel a tutor's main job is to present his ideas on the subject-matter of the course, or to comment on yours? And in this course, did you think the tutor erred in either direction?

7. Would you pick out any of our meetings as particularly helpful or particularly unhelpful; and can you indicate why?

8. If a tutor thinks a student is not working very hard, should he
    i) do nothing   ii) mention it casually   iii) take a strong line
    iv) tell the Dean or   v) invite the student to discuss his
    problems?

9. Do you feel that a tutor should make his own ideological posi-
    tion plain, or concentrate on treating the texts on their own
    terms? If there is an ideological difference between tutor and
    student, do you prefer the tutor to emphasise and discuss the
    fundamental questions on which they differ, or to try as much
    as possible to get on the student's wavelength in order to help
    him express his (or her) ideas? Did you in this course feel your
    tutor erred in either direction? (This question is particularly
    relevant to the Modern European Mind, but you may feel it
    worth answering even if you did a primarily literary course
    with me).

10. Any other observations?

It doesn't take much insight to see that this form would be totally useless for any official purpose. It contains nothing
quantified, and its questions are elaborate and controversial.
Obviously I will defend this — I will even say that good teaching is elaborate, unquantifiable and controversial, and though
I would expect colleagues to argue with the wording of my
questions and suggest their own, I would argue back, and
defend them. What I would not, of course, expect, is the right
to impose my wording on them.

***

And now that I have been on the receiving end of the process
for ten years, have I grown less enthusiastic — the reformer
subjected to his own reforms, and rediscovering the case for
leaving well alone? Resisting the lure of self-immolation, I reply,
Not much. I still favour such assessment, for all the good un-
revolutionary arguments set out above, but realise now that
even the tenured and the (apparently) self-confident may get
surprisingly upset by what the forms contain. And I realise too
how much I dislike anonymity.

One student wrote on the back of his (her?) form: 'Mr Lerner
has a lot of prejudice against Catholics. How dare he insult me
because of my religion?' The remark is distressing, of course, but

above all it is puzzling: it leads one to ask, What on earth did I say? It leads one want to get hold of the student, no doubt to express regret, but even more than that, to *ask,* to clear up the misunderstanding. But of course I never could, because of anonymity — necessary anonymity, the Dean's office will maintain, to protect the student. She who fought and ran away lives to fight another day.

I remember, at this stage, my friend Anthony. He taught French at Queens University Belfast in the early sixties: I don't think we overlapped by more than a year, two at the most, but we were good friends, and he told me about the trouble he got into. He too had insulted Catholic students, and his trouble was, potentially, more serious. Lecturing on French society in the seventeenth century, he had spoken about monasteries and convents, and described the nuns (in perhaps one particular convent) as dancing girls for the monks. He received a note from the Catholic chaplain (a powerful man in an Irish university), saying that a number of students had complained about this insult to their church. The situation was ironic, because Anthony is a devout Anglo-Catholic, and probably had more sympathy with the Catholic students' beliefs than most of his colleagues; it was also rather dangerous, because Queen's University then had (and perhaps still has) an assurance which every faculty member was required to sign, that he would not say anything that would stir up religious controversy. The chaplain's note concluded: 'Have you anything to say to me before I take this matter to the Vice-chancellor?'

Anthony went to see the chaplain, remarked on the irony (which the chaplain was already aware of) and declined to retract. 'After all,' he said to me, 'it's true.' This was well before the Jesting Pilates of the 1970s had removed our confidence that there could be such a thing as historical truth, but my response was, I now see, a kind of unwitting anticipation of post-structuralism, though I intended it only as the basest kind of prudence. 'You should,' I remarked to Anthony, 'have simply read them the contemporary documents, that made the accusation, and observed, That is what a contemporary wrote about monastic life.'

That wounded Catholic (how I wish she could be reading

this) caused me more puzzlement and, I suppose, more distress, than any other student evaluator; and for symmetry I should set against this the one who gave me most pleasure : that was the student who said 'At first you think Mr Lerner is too dogmatic, then you realise that what he wants is to make you think.' We have all had comments like this but it's nice to feel they are just about oneself. Everything that affects us strongly has a context, a fuller and richer context than the outsider can realise, and I know why this remark meant so much to me: it was because of my experience teaching the Introduction to Poetry.

***

'That's what it means to me'

American students are very sensitive to what they see as dogmatism: the teacher who tries to impose his own opinions on them. And when the evaluation forms are handed out at the end of the course they get their chance to answer back. For the teacher of literature, this will be a particularly tricky issue, since reading a poem is — or can be — such an intensely personal experience and teaching is the attempt to pass on objective knowledge. Both these statements look like truisms, and when one truism meets another, the result sometime. looks like the unstoppable projectile and the immovable obstacle. As happened, sometimes, when I taught English 112, the Introduction to Poetry.

This was a course we all enjoyed teaching, since we all enjoyed talking about poems, but it was impossible to avoid the question of subjectivity. How can you introduce students to a poem without talking about what it means?

Uphill

Does the road wind uphill all the way?
  Yes, to the very end.
Will the day's journey take the whole long day?
  From morn till night, my friend.

But is there for the night a resting place?
  A roof for when the slow dark hours begin.

May not the darkness hide it from my face?
    You cannot miss that inn.

Shall I meet other wayfarers at night?
    Those who have gone before.
Then must I knock, or call when just in sight?
    They will not keep you waiting at that door.

Shall I find comfort, travel-sore and weak?
    Of labour you shall find the sum.
Will there be beds for me and all who seek?
    Yea, beds for all who come.

Christina Rossetti

I ask the students to write an essay on this poem, or to compare it with other religious poems or other poems about death. A great variety of interpretations ensues. One says that it's a conversation between a man and God, another says between a man and his priest, another suggests a ghost, or a dead father, or even a sarcastic commentator showing how smug the Christians are; one says there is only one speaker, answering himself. One claims the inn is Heaven, one says it's the grave, one doesn't see it as being about death at all. Several say it's about the dangers of sin, the need to avoid sin so that you will be rewarded by God after death. Many find it a Christian poem, some find it pagan, one or two are puzzled or wonder if it's by an atheist.

We start from their suggested interpretations, and I try and sort them out. Are some clearly wrong, are any certainly correct? But first I ask them if they want to know about the author (no-one actually knows anything about her). That divides the class to begin with: most want to, some (who have been told about the intentional fallacy) dismiss it as irrelevant or distracting. So I tell them (or don't) that Christina Rossetti was a devout Anglican who wrote a great deal of religious poetry. Those who claimed that the inn is Heaven, or that the poem is about the necessity to lead a virtuous life in order to attain peace afterwards feel they are vindicated. But are they? I then point out that there is no hint in the poem that some are being received at the inn, and some turned away: on the contrary there are 'beds for all who come.' If this is Christianity, it is

Christianity without any division into sheep and goats, indeed, without any concept of sin. And what is promised at this longed-for inn? The answer is, surely, only rest. So what does the inn represent? Someone, I hope, will say the grave: if not, I'll say it. But, someone will then object, you said she was a Christian. That's right, she was; but she seems to have written a pagan poem. Why did she do that? someone is sure to ask, and I have to say I don't know, and am as puzzled as they are, but I can't misread the poem in order to fit it to what we know of the author. I do not say, with the New Critics, that we must ignore what we know of the author; I say that it would be fascinating to know what she thought she was doing, but we don't.

Next we turn (or perhaps we began there) to the fact of dialogue. Who are these two speakers? I don't think this poem is a riddle, I say: there's no guessing game required. What's clear is that the second speaker knows the answers to the questions of the first, that's all. Of course he could be a priest, talking to a parishioner; or Christ, or God, talking to a worried human; or two parts of the same person (why not?), reassuring herself. There don't seem to be many wrong answers, and quite a lot of right ones.

Throughout the discussion (which may last a long time, if they get argumentative) I am concerned to separate the questions to which there are right and wrong answers from the questions which are left open. Suppose we read 'Crossing the Bar' along with 'Uphill'. Tennyson too was a Christian; and he hopes to see his Pilot face to face when he has crossed the bar: God is present in this poem as he was not present in the first. And what can we say about how Tennyson's poem represents death? It is a setting forth, it is the beginning of a journey: not to see that, is not to understand the poem. And what is the voyage going to be like? We are told very little but we are told that the setting forth will be peaceful That still leaves plenty of uncertainty, which can be filled in to taste, or according to belief. And the detail they need to understand is, of course, the bar: there will be some who think it' a legal term, there may even be some who think it's where you buy drinks (have I really had anyone who thought *that?* Never underestimate). There will be some who are puzzled. So I explain that it's a sandbar, at the entrance to the harbour, only traversable at high tide; it's not hard to convince them that this is right, but harder to convince them that they could be expected to know.

We might, then, go on to read Donne's sonnet 'Death, be not proud.'

Death, be not proud, though some have called thee
Mighty and dreadful for thou art not so
And those whom thou think'st thou dost overthrow
Die not, poor Death, nor yet canst thou kill me.
From rest and sleep, which but thy pictures be
Much pleasure, then from thee much more must flow,
And soonest our best men with thee do go,
Rest of their bones, and soul's delivery.
Thou art slave to fate, chance, kings, and desperate men,
And dost with poison, war and sickness dwell,
And poppy or charms can make us sleep as well
And better than thy stroke; why swell'st thou then?
One short sleep past, we wake eternally
And death shall be no more; Death, thou shalt die.

By now we have got into the habit of asking of each poem about death, Is this Christian, so the question proposes itself more or less automatically. Again, I might ask if they want to know the poet's beliefs: by now they are used to the fact that I will reserve the possibility that the poem does not contain them. Are there any incontrovertibly Christian touches? There is one, of course: 'One short sleep past, we wake eternally.' There can't be any doubt about that, surely, but it doesn't come until the end of the poem. Before that we have 'From rest and sleep, which but thy pictures be, Much pleasure, then from thee much more must flow'. If we hope to go to Heaven, then it is clear that much pleasure flows from Death, but is it not odd to introduce this by a comparison with rest and sleep? It sounds as if the pleasure will be the pleasure of repose: is there some kind of substratum, whatever one is saying about death, that values it simply because it brings oblivion? Would you expect a Christian poem to mention that? I ask: what is clear is that a number of Christian poems do. In this sonnet, could it be a rhetorical strategy, as if the Christian message is being deliberately withheld until the end? Someone may remark that we know perfectly well that it's a Christian poem, especially if they have got me to tell them who Donne was. Then I might remark that the reading experience is a progression: we are not intended to know everything until we reach the end.

One question has run through all this like a red thread: the question of latitude in interpretation. What can we say with certainty is the meaning of a poem? What readings will be clearly mistaken? And what is left open, for different readers to fill in according to their tastes or prejudices? I might discuss all this at some length, and lay great stress on the openness, even saying that the pleasure of filling out the open meanings from our own experience is one of the central experiences in reading poetry, but I can be sure of one thing: when they come to fill in their evaluations at the end of the semester, one or two will say that I'm constricting them, that I want everyone to interpret the poem the same way as I do, that I don't realise that what makes literature so exciting is the fact that we can all interpret a poem differently. Of course this is disappointing: I don't want to be called dogmatic. And if don't, how would I avoid it? By not teaching them anything, perhaps.

I've discussed this with American colleagues, and there is one thing they often say. They describe the high school education they have all had, and I haven't. The English teacher at their school, they tell me, will have made a great issue of free interpretation: he will have told them that he wants *their* reading of a poem, that they don't need to be told by anyone else what it means, because it's written for them to respond to, and personal response is everything. If the teacher is well read in the latest critical theory, he will have plenty of support for his view of a poem as open-ended; but he may not need that, he may simply get it from the ethos of the American High School, from the theory that education is the chance for the young to develop as themselves, that they are not pitchers but seeds, that we are pouring water on the soil to enable them to grow, not water into the pitcher for them to acquire. Coming to college with the habit of saying 'That's what the poem says to *me*: how can you tell me it doesn't?', the aspiring literary students do not want to be told that any of their readings are wrong.

Their readings may be their own, but facts are objective: that the poem was written by Donne in the early 17th century is not, surely, a subjective question. Or so I thought, until I met Anne. Anne was an exchange student at the University of Sussex, and she brought to the tutorial system a little preliminary taste of America. 'As Donne makes clear in love poems like "To his Coy Mistress" she would write in an essay; and I would say to her, 'Anne, who wrote "To his Coy Mistress"?' Anne did not go in for one word answers. 'Oh, you mean Donne's poem about having world enough and time. Not really much like Donne is it, with those couplets. There are all those interesting poets, Donne, and Jonson and Marvell, not always easy to sort out. Questions of authorship are often so difficult to settle, aren't they? I mean, that carpe diem stuff is more typical of Marvell really. I guess you could say Marvell wrote "To his Coy Mistress" couldn't you?' Anne was a splendid advertisement for American teaching styles: facts were never dull to her.

It is no accident, surely, that the system which sees education as the drawing out of the student has institutionalised student assessment: if the teacher's main function is to help his students develop, who will know better than they how well he has succeeded?

A colleague at Sussex once consoled me for the fact that I was having difficulty with an American graduate student because I was 'treating him like a sixth-grader' (i.e. I was pulling his drafts to pieces), by offering a smiling description of the way that student had, so far, been 'taught'. The professor will listen politely to the student's contribution to the discussion, perhaps puffing on his pipe (this was before the no-smoking days), and then when he has finished will say, 'Thanks Joe. Very interesting. Now my view has always been...'

Perhaps the reason for arguing with students instead of puffing tolerantly on one's pipe cannot be based on educational theory. Whether it improves the quality of their reasoning, or merely makes them angry, can perhaps never be established: the situation is too complex for controlled experiments. It must depend on the conviction of the teacher, that arguments must be confronted, not evaded, that a good teaching relationship is one in which you can tear an argument to tatters. Some will like it, some will hate it. And some, of course, will relate it to the

130

revolution in English studies, since criticising an argument may be seen as resisting its ideological premises. Reading the student responses to a graduate course I had taught, I came across one which complained that I constantly misunderstood his (or her) arguments so that she (I suspected it was a she) was having to defend positions she didn't hold against irrelevant objections, and another which complained that I was not sufficiently receptive to new ideas. In the same batch were forms which remarked that Prof Lerner's comments are always incisive and he does not allow shallow observation, which I appreciate; that Prof Lerner's chief skill is his rigorous analysis of those arguments with which he is presented: because he rigorously interrogates I find myself clarifying my own claims. Of one thing I feel sure: that these contrasting assessments are responding to the same thing. One student's gratitude for rigorous probing is another student's grievance at being misunderstood.

Ought I not to be grateful that reading my students' assessments has taught me all this?

The Kiss of Death

What's in a Name?

Juliet was deeply wrong. It is true that a name is not part of our physical being: 'It is not hand, not foot, Not arm, nor face, nor any other part Belonging to a man.' But it is part of our social being, which is quite as important. Perhaps Mr Bohun was nearer the truth. Sorting out the family tangle in the last act of Shaw's *You Never Can Tell,* he begins with the question of what name each person is to be known by, dismissing the suggestion that they should 'dispose of the important questions first'. 'There will be no difficulty about the important questions,' he states. 'There never is. It is the trifles that will wreck you at the harbour mouth.' As Juliet bitterly discovered.

How should we name the author of *Aurora Leigh*? She used to be called 'Mrs Browning'. But it is only minor writers (Mrs Henry Wood, Mrs Humphrey Ward) who shelter behind their marriage lines: Mrs Gaskell's growing reputation in our time has promoted her to being 'Elizabeth Gaskell'. So, 'Elizabeth Browning'? But it's part of the feminist reform of language that women should not be designated differently from men: if Henry Fielding is known as 'Fielding', Jane Austen should be known as 'Austen' — and Elizabeth Gaskell therefore is now 'Gaskell'. So, 'Browning'? Not unless you want hopeless confusion. 'Do you prefer Browning's poetry to Browning's?' What of 'Barrett Browning'? That is ingenious — a form of her surname that distinguishes her from her husband. But it won't work for the Shelleys — Mary is never known as Godwin Shelley, and most readers, seeing 'Godwin Shelley', would wonder if an 'and' had dropped out. Furthermore, 'Barrett Browning' would have seemed odd and probably improper to the author herself. Is that important? If we are rehabilitating the women ill-treated in their time and neglected by history, does it not seem right to pay attention to their wishes? But if we do, we can't say 'Austen' either, which would certainly have seemed as ill-bred to that lady as it was ill-bred of Mrs Elton to refer to Mr Knightley as 'Knightley'. So do we just say 'Elizabeth'? That, surely, would be the most patronising form of all — acceptable, perhaps, if we also refer to her husband as 'Robert', but suppose we are not speaking of her husband? The assumption that we always will when discussing her is, after all, even more deeply offensive. There is, we have to admit, no solution that will satisfy everyone, and fit all occasions.

That was the sort of paragraph that academics love to write; and it shows why academics do not make good reformers. The reformer, disliking existing arrangements (such as naming) proposes something better, and leaves the subsequent difficulties to get ironed out later. The academic looks for the difficulties and enjoys exploring their complications, so much so that he forgets the reforming impulse. I confess that I love names and their complications, and I believe, with Mr Bohun, that they tell us a lot about our social selves.

Suppose Elizabeth Barrett, living in our time, goes to university: how should her teachers address her? When I was a student there was no doubt: they all called her 'Miss Barrett'. My wife has told me how delighted she was, as a first year student, to be called 'Miss Winch': a sign that she had become an adult. But this may date her. Whenever I have asked a group of students how they wished to be addressed, they have invariably preferred Christian names ('much less formal'; 'much more friendly'). Perhaps their enthusiasm was not completely genuine: the young person who declares for formality in the later 20th century risks ridicule; but they were at least expressing their culture, and so I now always call students by their first name. An Oxford professor of my acquaintance informed me that he always addressed his students as 'Miss Brown' and 'Mr Jones', since that meant he only needed to learn one name, not two. He was an Oxford Professor, and probably did not mind being thought rather stuffy. I sympathise with anyone struggling to learn the names of fifty students before the term is over, and my policy, I realise, had the same advantage as his. I knew Andrew and Judy and Liz, but often had no idea of their surnames. This turned out to be surprisingly unimportant: who was this Elizabeth Barrett whose essay I had just read and thought so brilliant? Realising that she was Ba, the quietly incisive girl with dark ringlets who sat in the front row, gave the experience of joining two kinds of intellectual styles together and creating a person. If there is also a Tony Barrett in the class I could be puzzled when I looked at the class register and had to sort out A C Barrett and E B M Barrett, but fortunately I have never mixed up one student's A with another's C–, and I had the satisfaction of knowing that my high opinion of Ba's essay was formed without prejudice, since I'd assumed it was by the lively Liz who sits at the back (and who actually wrote a rather conventional essay).

I call her, then, Elizabeth, or Barrett, according to her preference. What does she call me? Two generations ago this was even clearer: she calls me 'Mr Lerner'. If I have been elevated, she calls me 'Professor Lerner'. In America she calls me 'Dr Lerner'. There is a complication here if (like me) the professor hasn't actually got a doctorate: apart from our resident poet and resident novelist, I was the only member of the department in Vanderbilt without a Ph D, and I soon had to give up trying to prevent the students bestowing an honorary doctorate on me — it is no doubt a quirky system that had me supervising and examining Ph D theses, but what would universities be without their quirks?

What, however, does Elizabeth call me today? 'I don't like this fake cameraderie,' my Sussex colleague Charles complained to me once: 'Good morning Jenny — Good morning, Professor Smith'. I don't know whether Charles succeeded in getting his students to call him Charles (or even Charlie?), and if he did, how would he set about it? 'Do call me Charlie'? 'Call me Charlie if you wish'? 'Feel free to …'? Should he even force the issue, refuse to answer or make a fuss when called Dr Jones?

In Richard Hughes' novel *A High Wind in Jamaica* the ten-year-old Emily develops an intense friendship with the grown-up Miss Dawson, whom she adores. One day Miss Dawson kissed Emily three times, and told her in future to call her Lulu.

> Emily jumped as if shot. Call this goddess by her Christian name? She burnt a glowing vermilion at the very thought… For Miss Dawson to tell her to do so was as embarrassing as if she had seen written up in church, PLEASE SPIT.

And so she ends up avoiding Miss Dawson, who is puzzled and hurt. The theme of Hughes' novel is the incomprehensibility of the intense world of childhood, which adults constantly misunderstand. But Mr Bohun was dealing with adults, when he claimed that the details can wreck us at the harbour mouth. The hierarchical relationship between Jenny and Professor Smith may not have the intensity of childhood adoration, but if he said to her 'Please call me Cecil', she might well respond by calling him 'you', and then, when the effect had worn off, reverting to 'Professor Smith'. If she stays on as a graduate student, perhaps even writing a thesis under his direction, there will probably be a moment of transition to Christian names, and it will be her decision, not his. I have had graduate students who stayed with 'you', others who found the transition effortless. One addressed me as 'Professor Lerner' and 'Larry' in alternate letters and on alternate meetings. Many manage the transition more easily in writing. One began a letter (after he'd left the country) 'Dear Larry (I finally made it)'. One middle-age woman never left off saying 'Mr Lerner' and clearly never wished to, but when she introduced a cousin who called me 'Laurence' she corrected her, saying 'He usually goes by Larry' — establishing, as I read the situation, that she was the guardian of the Christian name she preferred not to use, the guide to those who, knowing me less well, moved more easily to familiarity.

Visiting Stephen

What your graduate student calls you is the tip of a huge iceberg, one in which human relationship and academic function are inextricably merged; for that reason, supervising graduate students can be seen as the kernel of academic life — and of this book. This chapter will explore the iceberg.

The relationship between graduate student and supervisor is very close — and, often, intense. The supervisor reads what the student writes, and is often the only person who does so until the thesis is finished. For some, this is precisely what is wrong with being a graduate student in the humanities: that it is so solitary and unsupportive. Paddy, my best graduate student ever, and now a good friend, explained the situation to me:

you have to be married, he said; you ought to cycle out to the university; and you ought to give yourself a task that's related to your thesis but very different from it (his was learning ancient Greek): then you'll survive. Reformers have often suggested that research in science would provide a better model : students work together as part of a team, exchange ideas, show one another their results, and are spared the isolation that has caused talented literary scholars to give up their research sometimes in near-despair. Sceptics reply that isolation is in the very nature of graduate work in the humanities; when the atmosphere is good, graduate students form a supportive community, especially in America where they all have teaching assignments and can compare notes on how to handle a freshman composition class; but for the thesis itself you are alone with the library your supervisor and God (the temptation to confuse the last two needs to be resisted).

'When I began on my dissertation,' said Stephen wryly, 'Professor Lerner informed me that he was the kiss of death to doctoral students.' Stephen was the student who, after returning to America, began a letter 'Dear Larry (I finally made it)'. Now I was spending a semester at the University of Ottawa, and Stephen had arranged for me to come and give a lecture at the small upstate campus in New York where he was teaching. This turned out to be more complicated than either of us had realised, because of the problem of getting into the country. When I produced my British passport, Stephen smiled at the immigration officer and remarked proudly, 'He's my old professor. He's coming to give a visiting lecture.' That turned out to be a big mistake. Was I being paid for this lecture, the official inquired. 'Well', I said lamely, 'not very much.' Had I got, or had the college got for me, the appropriate visa? Of course I hadn't. 'You know,' said Stephen patronisingly, 'universities like to invite distinguished scholars to come and lecture.' That was his second mistake. The officer had no doubt this was common practice, but even universities have to obey the law, and it was necessary to apply to an office in North (or was it South?) Dakota for the correct form, which they clearly had not done; he shook his head sternly, and went to fetch his superior officer. We got another lecture on how rules were rules and universities were not privileged institutions It was not until the senior man smiled and said, 'I suppose they're all sitting there, waiting for the lecture,' that it was clear they were going to let us through. 'We'll have to parole him,' said the one officer to the other. This meant they were letting me in without a visa, and I would have to report back to them on my way out. 'Sorry I can't make the lecture myself,' was his parting remark.

Stephen raised a good audience for the lecture (visitors were not all that common at that remote campus), and his introduction, naturally enough, was largely about the experience of being my graduate student. He was warm and appreciative, but he felt impelled to quote what I'd said to him when he began. Most of the theses I had supervised had run into trouble when examined; most of those I'd examined had seemed to me unsatisfactory. Driven by insensitive honesty, I said this to Stephen, and he never forgot it. His thesis did in fact run into trouble, though it passed in the end. He felt lively resentment at the examiners, and an angry but forgiving amusement at the accuracy of my prediction.

Ali's Doctorate

Ali too survived the kiss of death. His story stretches over several years, since his government, wanting to do the job properly, had given him a long scholarship to acquire an English doctorate. He began at Sussex, then went off to Edinburgh for a year of applied linguistics, then came back to Sussex to write his thesis. There seemed to be no time limit to his scholarship (another African, a few years later, remarked to me that his bargaining position with his own country was very strong — 'they've invested so much in me they can't afford not to let me finish'); and by the time he finished he had begun to feel like a fixture. I knew him well, and liked him, and since I had not been his supervisor I was appointed as the internal examiner. The bulky thesis arrived, and as I read it my heart sank: as I ploughed through its pedestrian account of Lawrence's career and his overdiscussed novels, I did not recognise the sceptical, often shrewd student I knew and admired. He had sat alone in the library and gone astray; perhaps he had not spent enough time sitting there or perhaps he had not trusted his supervisor enough. The longest and the worst chapter was the last, which summarised the plot of *Lady Chatterley's Lover,* at great length, quoting abundantly, sometimes several pages at a time with little or no comment. I sought out the colleague who had supervised him: why on earth did you let him put in that last chapter, I asked. What last chapter? was his reply: it turned out that the chapter had been added at the last minute, without ever being shown to his supervisor. But worse was to come.

The external examiner was Arnold Kettle who in the fifties and early sixties (òu sont les neiges d'antan?) enjoyed renown as our only Marxist critic. He came to Brighton on the day arranged for the oral, and we had lunch together. To my surprise, he declared that the thesis was fine. He had recently spent a year in East Africa, and was clearly aware of (and, I thought, indulgent to) the situation of the young African academic dealing with English literature. He was pleased that Ali had written on Lawrence (Kettle's Marxism, in a very English way, was combined with the influence of Leavis) and was satisfied that he showed a good understanding of the novels. He agreed that the final chapter was rather long.

I was a little surprised that I hadn't seen Ali during the last few days: I'd half expected him to drop in to my room and ask for guidance on how to conduct himself in the oral or at least to tell me that he'd be there. As we moved to my room surprise turned to worry, and we waited: no Ali appeared. Once it was clear that he was not going to turn up, there was nothing to do but put Kettle on his train and say, shamefacedly, that we'd get in touch with him.

It turned out that Ali was in Sweden, I never discovered why: a girl friend, perhaps, or a political contact. Everyone had been inefficient: he most of all, for not sending the graduate school an address, but they too for sending a letter to his Brighton lodgings and leaving it at that. The person who came out of it best was Arnold Kettle, who uttered no word of complaint, and even defended Ali against my indignation: he was sure it was just a misunderstanding, rearranging the oral would not be a problem. I didn't know whether to admire his magnanimity or shake my head at his indulgence, the same indulgence he'd shown to the thesis.

In the end we got hold of Ali, he acquitted himself well in the oral, and returned to his university with a doctorate; before long he became head of the English Department. How and whether he has survived the political unpheavals in his country I do not know: he has now passed out of my life, in the way that former graduate students so often do (òu est la très sage Helois? Et Jehanne la bonne Lorraine?). I have told Ali's story not just for its own interest, but in order to ask about examining doctorates.

Doctor: a learned man, a person qualified to teach others, a recipient of a higher degree from a university. The word goes back to the 14th century at least, and these are the original meanings. It was, naturally enough, associated with the three medieval professions, divinity, law and medicine. Used absolutely, 'doctor' could refer to a divine ('the doctors of the church') or a lawyer (Bellario recommends Portia to the court of Venice as 'a young doctor of Rome'), or a physician: all three uses are old. What is absent from earlier uses is the idea that a doctor must be someone who advances knowledge or does original research. I do not know if we owe that idea to Romantic notions of the value of originality (seeping from the arts into scholarship), or to the influence of the natural sciences, to which research is central. Whatever the reason, it became part of the requirement for a doctoral degree at British universities that the thesis should contain new research, or be an original contribution to knowledge.

This requirement is reasonable in the sciences, where tiny discoveries (often as part of a larger but still very specialised collaborative project) can be made by very young scientists. But as the number of doctoral candidates in the Humanities multiplied, it began to look more and more unreasonable that each should be expected to contribute something new. Was there *anything* new to say about Dickens or Thackeray? Especially by a young man or woman who had not yet got around to reading Trollope, or Smollett — let alone Balzac or Gogol?

The late Terence Spencer, who was director of the Shakespeare Institute at Stratford-on-Avon in the sixties, once told me a story of an American research student who wrote a thesis under his supervision at London university on (I think) Ben Jonson. At the end of the first term she disappeared for

Christmas, and when she came back in January he made the usual polite inquiry about whether she'd had a good vacation. 'Lovely,' she said, 'I've been reading Shakespeare.' 'Ah yes,' said Terence, who could summon up a soupy donnish rhetoric when he chose, 'we can never return too often to the works of our great bard.' 'Oh no,' she replied, 'don't misunderstand me. I wasn't rereading Shakespeare, I was *reading* him.' It turned out that as an undergraduate she had taken great pains to avoid all knowledge of Shakespeare, feeling that she was too young to appreciate him; now that she was a graduate student, she felt the moment had come. For 37 days she had read one play each morning.

'This was the moment I had waited for all my life,' said Terence melodramatically. 'Breathless, I leaned over towards her and asked, "What did you think of them?"' To his delight — and relief — she replied that she thought they were marvellous. He breathed again.

This story has two morals, which contradict each other. On the one hand, I feel that young woman had it in her to write a splendid thesis on Jonson: how could so much shrewdness and strength of character fail to have something valuable to say about *Volpone?* But on the other hand it is clearly absurd to set out to make an original contribution to the study of Jonson, or any other Elizabethan dramatist, with such a sketchy knowledge of Shakespeare. Her way of spending her first vacation was an indictment of the academic system she had entered.

My experience of research students is mainly English and American, since I never taught in other countries long enough to be truly involved in doctoral work; but the differences between these two systems are striking enough to detain us a while. The English practice of separating teaching from examining, always under pressure but always more or less surviving, is found at all levels, right up to the doctorate; whereas it is virtually unknown in America. At my American university, the student chose the person she (or he) wished to work with, and was from then on that professor's protégée; much later she would discuss with this supervisor (or director, as the Americans say) who else should be on her committee. Not only would the committee be chosen by the student; its other members would usually be reluctant to put a spanner in the works. When I remarked at a Department meeting that if I were asked to join a student's committee when the dissertation was submitted, I would consider myself an examiner, and exercise my right to criticise and even if necessary fail the dissertation, my colleague Walter burst out laughing. 'Well, I can tell you,' he guffawed, 'that I'll see you never get on any committee I'm concerned with.' Since Walter teaches creative writing, and so is never involved with dissertations, the threat was symbolic, but the attitude revealed was real enough.

The argument for the English system is that teaching and examining, both necessary functions, are best kept apart. The teacher's function is to encourage, to tease, to help the student formulate his views, and this is best done as an ally, not a judge, as a helper collaborating with the student against the examiner (even if the examiner is the same person: the role is different). True of undergraduate teaching, this is even more true in the case of a thesis, where the collaboration will be so close, the student's dependence so intense, that it becomes virtually impossible for the supervisor to step back and declare that the work will not do. Christian theology has had trouble with the idea of a God who is both loving advocate and judge, and has solved the problem brilliantly by declaring that God consists of three persons but one substance, so that we can think of the Son as the advocate and the Father as the judge; but the supervisor is not God, and judging will come hard to him. Examiners are needed for that. They will keep up standards and protect scholarship.

But this argument can easily be turned on its head. Just because the relationship is so close, is it not futile to try and dismantle it? The director is the person who does everything for the student: guides and encourages her, makes sure the dissertation gets written, makes sure it is acceptable — and accepted; and helps the student get her first job. The German term Doktorvater, apart from its assumption that the director will be male, sums up the situation. If there are directors who sleep with the student (as there surely are), the term can remind us that it is a form of incest.

Doctoral examiners in Britain are offered several recommendations to choose between. They can recommend that the degree be awarded: this clearly is what everyone hopes for, and it is arguable that after the student has worked for three years it should be the norm (as it is in America). They can ask for revisions, minor or major — the latter carry no guarantee that the revised thesis will be accepted. They can recommend that an inferior degree be awarded, usually known as an M Litt or M Phil (since it is possible to enter for an M Litt direct by studying for a year less than for a doctorate, it is never clear whether this degree should be considered a kind of stigma or not). And they can recommend failure, which clearly is a stigma. If the regulations of that particular university include a statement (as many still do) about original research or contribution to knowledge being required, they will presumably have to satisfy themselves that that is what they have got.

A contribution to knowledge, in the narrow sense, would give us a particular piece of information which we didn't know before. My colleague James, a classical scholar who wrote his thesis on Boethius, informed me that he could state very succinctly what it had contributed to scholarship. Boethius was known to have used certain Greek philosophical texts, and James showed that he had read them not in Greek but in Latin translations. A small piece of knowledge, but his own. If a thesis tells us who was the typesetter of the Quarto *King Lear,* or that several passages in a Conrad novel are virtually translated from Flaubert, or discovers a hitherto unknown story by Sheridan Lefanu, then it has made a contribution to knowledge and the author will get a doctorate. I have never read such a thesis — or discovered such a piece of knowledge myself — but I like to know that such activity takes place. For most theses, the idea of making a contribution to knowledge must be interpreted more widely. Since Sussex prided itself on inter-disciplinary study, a thesis which identified a point where the methods of one subject could throw light on another was clearly acceptable: to write on George Eliot and 19th century science, and show the presence of scientific concepts in what may look like purely literary strategies in her fiction, or to write about poems of faith and doubt in a way that correlates particular poetic techniques with particular theological positions, is to earn a doctorate, even if it is imperfectly done. But not every thesis is interdisciplinary, so it must also be possible to award a doctorate for the sheer intellectual quality of what the student writes: in a literary thesis, this would be the ability to make us gasp (or even just nod) in admiration for the intelligence and insight of its interpretations.

In the last two decades a new possibility has arisen. Now that there are so many new schools of criticism, the student may hope to be the first to apply structuralism, or deconstruction, or New Historicism, to *Pride and Prejudice* or *The Spanish Tragedy*. That pioneering possibility may not last long (the army of students is large, the list of works limited), but it will be with us for a while yet, and there can always be yet newer critical schools arising (gay and lesbian studies has already been tried on an astonishing range of works). There are not all that many first books of literary criticism published in America today which do not claim allegiance to deconstruction, new historicism, feminism or psycho-analysis. 'All these theses,' a colleague remarked, 'on Derrida or Foucault or Lacan, dressed up to look as if they were about the seventeenth century.' More of all this in a later chapter: here I simply observe that it has given a new range of possibility to the requirement that a thesis contain new knowledge.

I sometimes dream of the archetypal thesis that will emerge from the womb of the future, perhaps in 2001, written by Anne Dante Cuntabile. It will be about Barrett Browning. The word 'Elizabeth' will not appear in it, except in a long footnote explaining that calling her Elizabeth is part of the patriarchal plot to patronise her. It will have discovered that she was a candidate for putting on the British £5 note, but lost out to George Stephenson, not only a man, but inventor of the very phallic steam-engine. It will claim that Aurora Leigh, deciding to live the solitary life of a poet instead of marrying her cousin Romney, has opted for masturbation instead of heterosexuality; that Marian Earle's decision to bring up her illegitimate child by herself is a blow on behalf of one-parent families; and that the fact that Romney (like Rochester in *Jane Eyre*) is blinded before being allowed to marry the heroine, shows the symbolic castration of the hero by female authors in the nineteenth century. It will raise the possibility that Barrett Browning's relationship with her father was incestuous, and that Aurora's affection for Marian Erle is a Lesbian attraction. Most of these points can be found in recent criticism, so the claim of this thesis to be an original contribution to knowledge may be rather weak.

There will also be a section on names. 'If the pen is a metaphorical penis, with what organ can females generate texts?' This now famous question opens Gilbert and Gubar's huge study of nineteenth century women's writing, *The Madwoman in the Attic*. Anne Dante will address this question through a discussion of the Brownings' son Pen. This is said to have resulted from the child's own attempt to pronounce his given name Widerman, which he reduced first to Penini, then to Pen. This may be factually true but it is mere fact; entering into the symbolic importance of the name, the thesis hesitates between two explanations: that he represents his father's penis, and that he represents the implement with which Barrett Browning inscribed herself on the world. If the two are combined, she can be seen to have provided an answer to the Gilbert and Gubar question.

A final question, perhaps the most important of all, can return us to sobriety. Are we examining the thesis, or the candidate? In the case of those who find new facts, it is clear that we are examining the thesis: patience and industry might suffice to spot Conrad's thefts from Flaubert, as they certainly suffice for many a piece of research in Physics or Chemistry; even if the candidate is brilliant (as, in his quirky way, my friend James undoubtedly is), the brilliance may not find its way into the laborious scrutiny of the Latinisms of Boethius. In the case of the third criterion, however, it is clearly the candidate we are judging. Her intelligent interpretation of a Hopkins' sonnet is not a piece of knowledge we needed (we can interpret the sonnet for ourselves), but it is evidence that Ms X is an interpreter of high quality whom we'd be happy to let loose on the most able students at Oxford, or Harvard, or Munich.

If our function is to judge the candidate, then I wanted Ali to pass. He would do a good job when he returned to Africa, wiser for his five or six years in England. Suppose he had a colleague who had stayed home, cultivated the right people, perhaps picked up a doctorate from the local university, perhaps even stagnated intellectually: if Ali came back without his D Phil, would not Mustafa become head of department instead? We surely don't want a situation where studying overseas becomes a disadvantage? But this was not a train of thought I wanted to pursue too far: was I suggesting a lower standard for foreign students? If so, which foreign students? Was there to be a ranking of countries? And would it only apply to those who intended to return home? Suppose Ali decided to stay in Britain — suppose he were female, and married an Englishman, and, quite understandably, started looking for teaching jobs in a British university. Was I to say in a letter of recommendation, 'No, she hasn't really got a Sussex doctorate, she's only got the less rigorous degree we give to people from her country'? Why, it could produce headlines in *The Times!*

What a lot of heart-searching Professor Kettle saved me, by deciding that he thought Ali's thesis was fine. He was the one who applied the kiss of life.

Two Heads are Better than One?

Two teachers to one class? What extravagance! You don't call in two plumbers to mend the cistern, or go to two doctors when you' re ill (or rather, if you do, it means that you haven't confidence in the first, or at least that he's afraid you mightn't have). If we lose confidence in a teacher, so that an extra one needs to be brought in, why not get rid of him and hand over the class to the new one? It is very difficult, surely, for an administrator or a finance officer to resist the obvious commonsense of this argument.

Why then is university teaching so different from plumbing and (even) from medicine? The reason is that it does not go in for clearcut answers Both nature and humanity behave in such a complicated way that what we find out about them depends on our method of inquiry; when methods intersect, we can learn things that neither could have found out alone So an art historian and a political historian, a philosopher and a psychologist, an intellectual historian and a literary scholar, coming from their different departments, can conduct a dialogue in front of the students that will open up intellectual possibilities beyond the reach of either. That at any rate was the theory behind the Sussex curriculum in the 1960s, which institutionalised jointly taught seminars in literature and history. These were the most exciting teaching I did in my twenty-two years there. Three of these dealt with nineteenth century England, and I taught all of them several times: the Industrial Revolution and English Literature, the English Romantics and their Society, and the 'Late Victorian Revolt' in politics religion and culture — elaborate and even pretentious titles showing some uncertainty over just what the course was about, but announcing clearly that it was about lots of different things, that it would be unlocking the doors between one subject and another. Counting them up, I find I taught — ominously? — with thirteen different historians, whom I got to know well, as colleagues and as friends, and (in one or two cases) almost as enemies.

The literary scholar (let's call him L) asks his students to read, say, *Bleak House.* He hopes they will be delighted, as he is, by the famous opening description of the London fog (if he is a good old-fashioned literary scholar he knows it by heart), and moved, as he is, by the description of Tom-all-Alone's, the London slum:

> As, on the ruined human wretch, vermin parasites appear, so these ruined shelters have bred a crowd of foul existence that crawls in and out of gaps in walls and boards; and coils itself to sleep, in maggot numbers, where the rain drips in; and comes and goes, fetching and carrying fever, and showing more evil in its every footprint than Lord Coodle, and Sir Thomas Doodle, and the Duke of Foodle, and all the fine gentlemen in office, down to Zoodle, shall set right in five hundred years…

There are plenty of things L. knows about *Bleak House* and is competent to expound. He knows that it was originally to be called 'Nobody's Fault'. He can compare it with other novels by Dickens, and quote descriptions of slum landscapes from *Dombey and Son* or *The Old Curiosity Shop.* When discussing the alternation between Esther telling her own story and Dickens' omniscient narrative, he can offer some technical observations about point of view to provide a more impressive terminology (if he has read Genette he may even call it 'focalisation'). He knows there were articles on the slums, on the law, on reform movements, in Dickens' periodical *Household Words,* and if he's done his homework he will know how likely it is that Dickens wrote them himself; he can ask how much of their reformist indignation has spilled over into the fiction (there is clearly a good deal of it in the passage above). He can discuss the complicated plot of *Bleak House,* and point out that Tom-all-Alone's may be part of the estate which the endless Jarndyce v Jarndyce case is about. When Jo the crossing sweeper, neglected and ignorant, sits down to breakfast on the doorstep of the society for the propagation of the Gospel in Foreign Parts, L. will obviously say something about irony, and remind the students of Mrs Jellyby, who neglects her family to organise the conversion of the natives in Borrioboola-Gha. Nowadays he will probably add that this is a cheap sneer at feminism, and remark that John Stuart Mill was very angry about it.

And at the other end of the table sits his colleague, who teaches history. We'll call him John (most of the historians I've known seem to be called John). He wants his say too: what otherwise is the point of his being there? What can he talk about?

John can point out that poverty in London is different from poverty in the industrial north. It is not a new phenomenon in London, and not necessarily connected with industrialisation. London the great Wen had been there for centuries, whereas the slums of Manchester, so unforgettably anatomised by Engels, belong with the new class structure of expanding capitalism. He can contrast the casual labour of London with the factory labour of the north: London was a city of small masters, where seasonal fluctuation was enormously important, and where there was a chronic glut of unskilled labour. He can describe the displacement of population from central London, and the street clearance schemes that often made things worse for the very poor. He can move forward a little in time and describe the work of the Charity Organisation Society, which, although it was set up to help the poor, was so hostile to indiscriminate alms, to relief funds and to outdoor relief, so keen on laissez faire solutions to housing, that it was more and more perceived as the enemy of the poor. L. is panting to keep up with all this, remarking every now and then, Yes, Dickens thought that, or No, he didn't think that. John asks how seriously we can take Dickens as a social reformer. If L. is an old-fashioned literary scholar, he believes, as Dickens himself did, that he was a powerful force for social improvement; if he is more hard-headed, he knows that there was nothing of the pioneer in Dickens' interventions into political arguments, and may quote Fitzjames Stephen, who wrote in 1857 that Dickens 'seems to get his first notions of an abuse from the discussions which accompany its removal'; and if he is really up-to-date he may quote D A Miller's brilliant reading of *Bleak House,* which claims that it is written in two different voices, that of Chancery and the law's delays, in which every question is evaded, individuals can never be identified as responsible for actions, and closure is impossible; and that of the detective story, in which mysteries are solved by individuals who act decisively; and to John's objection that this is all very well as an account of what goes on within the text of the novel but does not tell us about the impact it had on society, he may reply that society itself is a series of texts, and the historian's search for 'facts' is simply a matter of learning to read what each social text can and can't say. At which point the tables have been turned, and it is John who is panting to keep up.

The danger of such an enterprise is obvious: the two teachers get more and more interested in their intellectual exchange, and forget about the students. Ideas are flung from one end of the table to the other, and the students turn their heads from side to side like the spectators at Wimbledon. Sussex was a tutorial university, where students were accustomed to a great deal of individual attention and concern from their tutors, and they did not like being brushed aside. I was often aware of this, and never more vividly than in a letter from an American visiting student, who attended the seminar on the Late Victorian Revolt when I taught it with my admirable colleague N, a polymath who as well as being professor of Education had written a book on dream theory, a lively life of Dickens, and was one of the leading authorities on the Webbs and on the history of socialism. N always had a great deal to say, and I learnt something at every meeting; and so I'm sure did Alex, our visiting American. But when it was all over Alex wrote me a long letter of complaint: N talked too much, did not listen to the students, and treated the seminar as an occasion to show off. Alex was going back to California, and I would never see him again, but I thought it important to answer this. So I wrote back saying that yes, N did talk a great deal, and did not make a lot of space for the students. I told him that he had plenty of other opportunities (some of them at Sussex) to be taught by caring tutors who treated him with respect and were careful to elicit his views, but the chance to hear N on Victorian England was unrepeatable: his ideas on Shaw and Wells and the Webbs, on Ibsen in England, on the workings of Parliament and the arguments about poverty, opened a hundred doors to those who were listening and who cared about the subject. I told him that I had learned something from N at every meeting; and I claimed that there was no need for every educational experience to be the same, and that N showing off was a small price to pay for N's knowledge. I sent off the letter and hoped it would at least be read.

It turned out to be the most successful letter I've ever written. A reply came in which Alex capitulated completely. He claimed that he'd now been able to see the seminar in a totally different light, and realised how valuable it had been. He probably added some words of apology, but it was not the apology which mattered (N had anyway not seen his letter), it was the realisation. I have no difficulty in believing that a valuable educational experience had been able to disguise itself as an annoying one, and that once one looked at it differently the duck changed into a rabbit.

Thought, Felt, Did

The English Romantics and their Society I taught with the most interesting of my Johns, John Burrow, professor of intellectual history. I sometimes described our teamwork by saying, 'John knows what people thought between 1789 and 1830, I know what they felt, but we're both a bit vague on what they did.' The last was much truer of me than of him: I remained vague to the end on the differences between the National, the Constituent and the Legislative Assemblies in the French Revolution, or about which of the radicals in the British treason trials were acquitted, and which were convicted. John modestly disclaimed any ability to talk in detail about the Odes of Keats or Wordsworth's self-exploration in *The Prelude* (that, I suppose, was what people felt); I listened fascinated to his account of *The Wealth of Nations* (what people thought).

We found ourselves in almost complete agreement on everything. We would often look back on a seminar meeting and reflect that virtually everything each of us had said could have been said by the other. Was this an advantage, or a limitation? I had had virtually the opposite experience teaching the Industrial Revolution and English Literature with another John, John M. M could not take anything in the poets or the novelists seriously as analysis of their society: he thought Elizabeth Gaskell offered only genteel nostalgic idealisation, that Wordsworth was only really interested in himself — and though he was too polite to say so directly, he thought much the same about me. He set out to subvert all my historical assertions (often with a wealth of evidence that I'd have found fascinating if I could have looked at it calmly), since my economic history, in his view, was just as half-baked and gullible as Gaskell's. Not surprisingly, I enjoyed this much less than my teaching with John Burrow; and the students' response to our seminar, I learnt from a colleague, was that we didn't seem to like each other. Yet I didn't really want to conclude from this that one should teach with those one agreed with (I didn't in fact dislike John M personally; but I could understand that the students had perceived the intellectual gulf between us as personal abrasiveness). If John and I were so close in our ideas, why have two of us? Joint teaching, surely, must require some kind of contrast.

It was not until after leaving Sussex that I devised a strict protocol for joint teaching. In order to make sure that the students weren't excluded, I proposed to the colleague that each meeting should be in the charge of one of us, and that the other not be allowed to speak for the first hour. That hour could then be run as a discussion, and the teacher would not be distracted from what the students were saying by arguing with the colleague. This turned out not only to be better pedagogy, but to improve the quality of the discussion: the intervention of the second teacher, when it came, often had a dramatic effect on the discussion, either by questioning something everyone had taken for granted, or by introducing fresh material. Inevitably, there were comic moments. When I taught with Jean, our eminent professor of political theory, she took charge of the first meeting, and halfway through the first hour asked me a question. I replied, 'I'm not allowed to speak yet,' and she gasped in astonishment. 'You really mean it then?' she said. Something very similar happened two years later with Jim: this time the intervention by the silent partner at the first meeting produced waves of mirth from the students, who had obviously been speculating beforehand. 'I knew it,' said one. They had not

believed either of us would be able to keep quiet for an hour —
though at the remaining meetings we more or less did.

***

Political Trials and Trial Narratives

Jim is Jim Epstein, who teaches History at Vanderbilt, and
with whom in 1993 I taught a joint seminar on Political Trials
and the Literary Representation of Trials. We had as it happened both been at the University of Sussex in the 1960s: I
was on the faculty and Jim was a student, and though we
ended up with very similar interests, we did not meet until
we both came to Vanderbilt two decades later: he took the
course on the late Victorian revolt in a year when I wasn't
teaching it.

For our joint seminar we had fifteen graduate students
whom we were able to choose from about twice as many applicants. Six of them came from the English Department, four
from History, two from comparative literature, one from German and two from law. One of the students of English also had
a law degree, and one of the lawyers had majored in political
science. Clearly a true inter-disciplinary group, since the most
obvious definition of inter-disciplinary study is that the
teachers, and if possible the students too, should come from different departments. The most obvious but not perhaps the most
interesting, as we can see if we reflect that the great inter-disciplinary movement of the later 20th century has been
structuralism — the search for deep structures that link
together disparate social and intellectual activities, as in Levi-
Strauss's comparison between the exchange of women in
marriage customs and the exchange of goods, or Chomsky's
search for deep structures of grammar that speakers of a language use but cannot formulate. The structuralist who explains
social action through the analogy of language is automatically
inter-disciplinary — as is the post-structuralist, seeing deep
structures as inherently unstable, or as political strategies that
ought to be destabilised. The difference between the traditional
literary historian and the post-structuralist, both operating in
the same department, may be more profound than between the

former and the political historian, or the latter and the deconstructive philosopher. We arrive, in other words, at a more interesting conception of the interdisciplinary if we look at what actually goes on.

When the same text is examined by two scholars who ask different questions, or when the same question is asked by both of them but answered through different kinds of text, then interdisciplinary study is at its most interesting. In our seminar, we looked at the execution of Charles I, and read a contemporary account of his trial. 'Remember,' he said to the court, 'I am your King — your lawful King — and what sins you bring upon your heads ... Let me know by what lawful authority I am seated here and I shall not be unwilling to answer ... I have a trust committed to me by God, by old and lawful descent ... I will not betray it.' Charles' sympathisers referred to him as the royal martyr: this is not a legal expression, so by using it the royalists were themselves taking what we can call an interdisciplinary step, moving from one form of discourse to another: by refusing to recognise the authority of the court Charles was making it virtually certain that he would be condemned, and was in that sense making himself a martyr. Then after observing the obstinate, legalistic integrity with which Charles refused even to plead we turned to Marvell's *Horatian Ode upon Cromwell's Return from Ireland,* in which Cromwell is compared to a force of nature ('Then burning through the air he went, And palaces and temples rent') and Charles upon the scaffold to an actor playing his part flawlessly among a crowd of real-life groundlings:

That thence the royal actor born
The tragic scaffold might adorn
    While round the armed bands
    Did clap their bloody hands.

In the midst of a poem about Cromwell's greatness and the fact that he was inspired ('Tis madness to resist or blame The force of angry Heaven's flame') Charles is praised for his dignity, for the polish of his performance: 'He nothing common did or mean Upon that memorable scene'. This seemed to me a perfect opportunity to see what poetry can and cannot do: it can compress a complex political argument into a balanced sentence, carefully not taking sides in a life-and-death struggle; and beyond that it can show us the interconnections between action and contemplation. I have even tried to reproduce some of this by putting the lines about Cromwell in parentheses (we take him for granted, like Nature), and highlighting those about Charles: we pause to contemplate him, like art.

And then, putting together the account of the trial and the Horatian Ode (and noticing that although this term, for Marvell, probably referred primarily to the metre, Horace did write Odes in which Roman virtue and Stoical courage are praised with tight-lipped understatement) we can ask if the Charles of the legal record is the same as the Charles of the poem; and the answer seems to be, no, not quite. The Charles of the official record is not performing a part, he is stating a political philosophy — yet, alerted by Marvell, we contrast the dignity of his bearing with the occasional bluster from the kangaroo court that was trying him. How far, we then ask, are we looking at two versions of Charles which can be directly compared, and how far at two different kinds of text? That seems to be a question that goes to the heart of interdisciplinary study.

What is there to learn by studying political trials from the past — what, that is, besides satisfying our curiosity (which ought to be insatiable) about what human beings have done to one another in the course of history? No doubt we all learned different things, depending not only on our disciplinary training but also on who we were. Jim and I had decided to contrast the trial of Charles with the almost exactly contemporary trial of John Lilburne, the Leveller: trying the king and trying the subject. Lilburne had always been one of my heroes: a believer in democracy two hundred years ahead of his time, a fiery but non-violent radical, a believer in the Inner Light (he became a Quaker at the end of his life). Reading the transcript of his trial, I found myself deeply thankful that we didn't have Lilburne in our class: his constant legal quibbles, accompanied by fulsome insistences that he was no lawyer, his questioning of the authority of the court, not with Charles' quiet dignity but with hectoring interruptions, and on the most trivial pretexts, all reminded me of the worst moments with rebellious students in the heady days of 1969. I found myself identifying with the judges (I'm getting old, I thought), realising how infuriating they must have found his readiness to identify himself with Christ, and his constant insistence on the Inner Light, until finally one of them burst out, 'Never talk of that which is within you; God is in us, as well as you.'

A good deal of the future (that is, of our present) can be found in Lilburne: proto-Marxism (property is antecedent to magistracy, he claimed), or Hobbesian views of the state of nature ('if you take away the law, all things will fall into confusion'). I have often thought that the English civil war can be seen as the womb of the future: the sudden outburst of pamphlets in the 1640s that questioned every human and divine institution seems to throw up the entire political philosophy of the ensuing three centuries. The students were not as surprised at this fit of mass prophecy as I'd have expected; and they turned out to have more sympathy than I had with Lilburne's legal quibbles. But then they were Americans: they had — and believed in — a written constitution, and were used to watching the Supreme Court tie itself into knots interpreting it!

After Charles and Lilburne, we moved to the treason trials of the 1790s (this being a subject on which Jim was expert). John Frost, tried for sedition in 1793, was defended by Thomas Erskine, one of the leading lawyers of the day. Erskine dealt only with the law, not with politics: he ignored the arguments for and against Frost's egalitarianism and republicanism, and confined himself to showing that some of these opinions had been held by Pitt before he became Prime Minister, or that when Frost declared, 'I am for equality, I am for no kings,' it could not be proved that he was speaking about the king of England. Joseph Gerrald, tried the following year, conducted his own defence, stating his political opinions and defending them at length: 'Every nation has a right, not only to preserve the form of government which is actually established; but also, by the peaceful and calm operation of reason, to improve that form of government, whatever it may be.' Gerrald's reasoned statement of the case for democracy make him seem a heroic figure in the history of political controversy, especially when he

said to his obviously hostile judges, 'Reason alone and not assertion can convert me.' Here then were, in sharp contrast, the two
ways to defend yourself at a political trial: get a lawyer to push
hard on all the legal quibbles, or state what you believe, with no
equivocations, no attempt to guess what will be most acceptable
to the judges. Which is better? Frost and Gerrald were both
found guilty.

Gerrald offered us an example of a radical who believed passionately in reason, and in his own freedom to think
independently. 'The great and distinguishing mark of man is
reason,' he declared; and, later, 'moral light is as irresistible by
the mind as physical by the eye. All attempts to impede its
progress are vain.' Here is an assertion of the freedom and
autonomy of the reasoning subject, precisely the doctrine that
in the age of Barthes and Foucault has come under severe post-
modernist attack. I cannot place next to Gerrald a ringing
denial of what he so eloquently asserts, since post-structuralism does not go in for ringing denials — or assertions; but
I can quote Foucault's claim that the subject is 'not the speaking
consciousness, not the author of the formulation, but a position
that may be filled in certain conditions by various individuals.'
And since post-structuralism belongs on the left in politics, it
has become common to claim that asserting one's belief in
reason simply conceals the degree to which we are socially con-
structed, that liberalism is a way of upholding the status quo,
and that true radicalism will involve the subverting of the social
codes themselves. For the subject, according to a now very
fashionable piece of word-play, is not only the one who thinks
and acts, but is also the one who submits to the authority of a
ruler: the subject who thinks and acts is also the subject of King
George. As a good liberal I have never accepted this argument;
and as I read Gerrald and his fellow radical Daniel Eaton, and
saw how strongly their belief in reason and individual
autonomy was being used *against* the status quo, I felt confirmed in my scepticism about post-structuralist radicalism.
The true conservative position, after all, does not respect the
subject, but dismisses the possibility of serious criticism from
the 'swinish multitude'; we got that from Gerrald's judges, who
after all his careful arguments simply said 'all that you have

been saying is sedition.' 'I cannot sit here, as a judge,' asserted Lord Henderland (who, now, is Lord Henderland?) 'and as a man, without saying that is a most indecent defence.' If authority is to be subverted, then belief in the possibility of free judgement is not self-deception but the necessary basis for criticism.

The students, naturally enough, had strong views on this point. Our most committed post-structuralist was a literary student, eager to deconstruct the individual into the social pressures exerted on him or her, and of which he or she might not even be aware. One of the historians expressed himself passionately on the other side. 'You are the only one,' he declared, 'who can constitute your own subjectivity.' Existential authenticity, he claimed, is so important that it must not be 'objectified into an idea.' His vocabulary bore the stamp of the post-structuralists, but the thrust of his argument was directed against them. Here we have a small but fascinating irony: the discipline which has traditionally thought in terms of movements and tendencies is of course history, whereas literary scholars, reading poetry about the growth of the individual mind, used to be the ones who believed most strongly in the importance of subjectivity and the autonomy of the creative individual. Yet these two students were typical, for on the question of the autonomous subject, the two disciplines have changed places.

All the more reason, then, for both of them to be represented in the same seminar.

WRITING

The History of a Poem

'He became his admirers,' wrote Auden in his elegy on Yeats. To a modern school of reader-response criticism, this is a tautology. If the meaning of a text is constituted in the act of reading, if it has no intrinsic or objective meaning but only that which is attributed to it by those who interpret, then to say of Yeats' poems 'The words of a dead man Are modified in the guts of the living' is not going far enough: the words of the dead man come into being in the consciousness of the living. If the poet returned from the dead to say 'That is not what I meant; that is not what I meant at all' he would, like poor Prufrock, be condemned to frustration. After the death of the author, the critics come and go, talking of Michaelangelo, talking of T S Eliot, and creating the meaning of the texts they talk about.

It is not even necessary for the author to be dead. To his friends and the census taker he may be alive, but in the Barthesian sense he will be dead, as all authors are dead in order that (according to Barthes) their readers may be born. The extreme of this is the *scriptible* (or 'writerly') text, replacing the old idea of the *lisible* (or 'readerly') text. The obvious objection to this, that in that case any text could mean anything according to the whims of the individual reader, is met by Stanley Fish's concept of 'interpretive communities': the rules of interpretation are as rigid as for any old-fashioned historical scholar, but they derive from the reading practices of the community to which the reader belongs (and the writer, presumably, doesn't, or didn't). The prime example of an interpretive community today is obviously a university English Department. The words of Yeats are modified in their well-trained and orderly — and powerful — guts.

The story I am about to tell can be seen as a way of putting this theory to the test. It is the story of how my words were 'wholly given over to unfamiliar affections'. The author in this

161

case is not dead — indeed, he obviously could not tell the story if he were. He is merely, shall we say, 'dead'.

My poem 'A Wish' was published in *The Listener* in 1964, and appeared in my book *Selves* in 1969.

Often I've wished that I'd been born a woman.
It seems the one sure way to be fully human.
Think of the trouble — keeping the children fed,
Keeping your skirt down and your lips red,
Watching the calendar and the last bus home,
Being nice to all the dozens of guests in the room;
Having to change your hairstyle and your name
At least once; learning to take the blame;
Keeping your husband faithful and your char.
And all the things you're supposed to be grateful for
Votes and proposals, chocolates and seats in the train —
Or expert with — typewriter, powderpuff, pen,
Diaphragm, needle, chequebook, casserole, bed.
It seems the one sure way to be driven mad.

So why would anyone want to be a woman?
Would you rather be the hero or the victim?
Would you rather win, seduce and read the paper,
Or be beaten, pregnant, and have to lay the table?
Nothing is free. In order to pay the price
Isn't it simpler, really, to have no choice?
Only ill-health, recurring, inevitable,
Can teach the taste of what it is to be well.
No man has ever felt his daughter tear
The flesh he had earlier torn to plant her there.
Men know the pain of birth by a kind of theory;
No man has been a protagonist in the story,
Lying back bleeding, exhausted and in pain,
Waiting for stitches and sleep and to be alone,
And listened with tender breasts to the hesitant croak
At the bedside growing continuous as you wake.
That is the price. That is what love is worth.

It will go on twisting your heart like an afterbirth.
Whether you choose to or not you will pay and pay
Your whole life long. Nothing on earth is free.

Although it is now more than thirty years since I wrote this poem, I still cannot see it (as I can see much of what I then wrote) with the cool eye of a stranger. There are details that please me about it (the ambiguity of 'beaten', for instance, or the bit beginning 'Men know the pain of birth by a kind of theory') but I fear that my liking for them is not the objective assessment of a critical reader, but the affection of an author. The poem had a modest success in the sixties, and was included in several anthologies, including Philip Larkin's *Oxford Book of Twentieth Century Verse.* Large numbers of women told me how much they liked it, often adding that they were touched to find that a man had understood them so well. No-one, to my memory, singled out any details in its technique — their favourable response was vague, warm and intense: perhaps that should have warned me.

Twenty years ago I began to realise how much a new generation of women disliked the poem. The sharpest shock came when I gave a poetry reading to one of the many sixth forms I used to go and read to. I said, as I often did, to the teacher who had invited me that I thought everyone would get more out of the occasion if they had read some of my poems beforehand. He replied that they had read *A Wish* and that the girls were very angry about it. When Philip Larkin received a letter from 'a girl in Ramsgate' telling him how disgusting his poems were, he responded 'Whoops. The only ones she cited were *very* mild. Thank God she's in Ramsgate.' Well these girls weren't in Ramsgate, and Larkin's ironic detachment was out of my range, so I would have to read the poem — but how? Should I simply read it, without any comment, and then invite responses; or should I introduce it with some explanation? Clearly I ought to do the first, since that is the way to learn something about your poem and its readers, but in this case cowardice prevailed, and I spoke about it first. I read them a short poem about a little girl who is frightened by soldiers when a demonstration is taking place, and explained that I was fascinated by victims — by the temptation they must feel to dramatise their situation, and by the way they are often the ones who see things most truly, because they have nothing more to lose. I said that the fact that life had treated me so well made me profoundly grateful that I was not a victim, and yet gave me a kind of envy too. Then I read the poem. The girls listened fascinated, and in the ensuing discussion some of them apologised; they had disliked the poem when they read it, but they now realised that they had misunderstood it.

This was, no doubt, a kind of triumph, yet it also left me with the feeling that I had cheated. I had used my skill and experience as a teacher to give a boost to the poem, the kind of boost that no poem is entitled to, at any rate from the author. In that sense the author is dead, and should lie down.

Since the poem was written in 1963, is it fair to judge it by the standards of the 1980s? The question is an obvious one, and perhaps the answer seems obvious too, but it is not an answer I want to hear. Any literary academic is familiar with the argument about timelessness: do poems belong to the time when they were written, or are they for all time? The argument has taken on a more strongly ideological quality since new historicists and cultural materialists have begun attacking the doctrine of the timelessness of great literature as a way of enlisting past literature to defend the status quo. I have taken part in this argument as a professor, writing against what seem to me the cruder forms of historicism, but it is quite a different experience to find oneself not a participant but the very subject of the dispute. The academic discussion tends to see the past as remote and difficult to understand — according to the extreme historicist position, impossible to understand fully. In this case, however, the past in question is recent, perfectly easy to understand, and politically unacceptable.

What happens to the poem in such a situation? Above all, I felt I didn't want it condescended to. The facts that men no longer stand up in the train for women, that married women no longer have to change their name, do not really matter. The issue is politically charged, but my poem was not merely about politics. (Do I hear a cultural materialist sniffing at the word 'merely'?) The well-meaning friends who have remarked, in what seem to me the innumerable discussions the poem has provoked, that I could hardly have been expected, in 1963, to foresee the future, were offering the wrong kind of defence. If the poem is read in the 1980s, I wished it to be treated as if it had been written in the 1980s.

Easier said than done: as I learned when I received from Alison Leonard, a Quaker, whom I did not know, a poem written in reply to mine. She assumed, rightly, that I would wish to see it, both because of our common membership of the Society of Friends, and because poets, while they are only 'dead', not dead, ought to be shown such things. The poem was called 'Another Wish', and was written in the same loose couplets as mine. It was a plea for marriage as true equality, in which the partners would 'share, work and love', and it asserted 'I don't need/to paint my lips, or practise tricks in bed'; here is the last section:

This knotty thing of being fully human,
it's not a question of whether you're man or woman.
it's about feelings, bearings, — about pain,
yes — about who has babies, and who's alone.
But more than that, Professor. It's about
Who has the final word, who has the clout.
Surely you can be protagonist
when I give birth — don't stay below and waste
your energies in pacing up and down —
come near, and stay beside — let life detain
you from your busy-ness — mop my blood
my breastmilk and my tears. Oh look! — you shed
tears of your own to mix with mine! That
is the price: to pause, to weep, to plead, to knit
your steadfast backbone with the guts of life —
of life and death. Both you and I must give
way to the sharp necessity of time:
there's no easier way to end this game.

But for the moment, back in the world of power —
I'll be the Prof, and you can be my char.

My children were born in the fifties, when husbands were not allowed to be present during birth. I envy my sons the fact that they have been participants (though not, I must insist, protagonists) in the story; and I love my eldest daughter-in-law for saying that she felt sorry for what her husband had endured watching her in labour, as if that was more important than her own pain. That is not the only thing that has changed, but it is the most important. Do I want it to be ignored, when the poem is read? Obviously, the answer is Yes and No. Can we read the poem as if it was written yesterday, and at the same time refrain from castigating it for its outmoded patriarchal assumptions? I have long claimed, speaking as an academic, that when Portia says to the man she loves and whom she now knows she can marry

> But now I was the lord
> Of this fair mansion, master of my servants,
> Queen o'er myself; and even now, but now,
> This house, these servants, and this same myself
> Are yours, my lord's. I give them with this ring.

— we have to read with a double awareness, that on the one hand she is telling us that there was no married women's property act in the 16th century, that a woman lost her fair mansion when she married; and on the other hand that Portia is not complaining, but rejoicing that her love can offer so rich a gift. We read as feminists, and we read as the world that loves a lover, and it must be possible to do both. It is not my place, speaking as a poet, to make the same claim for myself, but I hold to my belief in double reading.

I replied to the author of 'Another Wish', and we exchanged letters with a fair bit of Quaker frankness. I told her that her lines were hostile to what she had found in my poem, and she agreed. Interestingly, she said that the word which had really sparked off her hostility was the word 'char'. 'You want to be a woman,' she wrote, 'but you don't want to be a humble cleaning woman.' I suspect that she disliked the very word 'char' ('cleaning woman' is more politically correct), and she admitted that this introduced questions of class power as well as gender power. If it now becomes a political argument, I then make the obvious rejoinder that the two do not always coincide, that plenty of women who employ chars do not want to be humble cleaning women either. But I have been saying that I do not want to engage in the purely political argument, because poems are not merely political gestures. My correspondent revealed her ideological position most clearly when she wrote: 'The question of power seems to me crucial at every level of experience. My feeling is that the deepest kind of sharing *will never take place* while unequal power relations exist.' This is an ideological statement that must, surely, permeate one's whole way of seeing human relations. It is not merely political, it is the unavoidable overlap between the political and the poetic.

I can now state the difference between us succinctly. It is true that the question of power is crucial, but it is not overriding. It is true that much humanist writing has been marred by its reluctance to recognise the importance of power, but it is equally true that radical discourse can be marred by utopianism. To claim that the deepest kind of sharing *will never take place* while unequal power relations exist (the italics bring the utopianism to the surface) is in one sense irrefutable: that perfect future which has not yet happened may well contain new dimensions of experience. We cannot yet know this, and will probably never know it. But to dismiss the love and the sharing we have because it is all tainted by power is to ignore the distinctions that matter in our imperfect human lives. There is selfish love, there is selfishness disguised as love, and there is comparatively unselfish love, and they all exist while unequal power relations are still with us; to distinguish between them is our most necessary task. And my correspondent, rising above her ideological limitations, knew this, and said it in her poem. Her vision of the husband mopping her blood and mixing his tears with hers does not have to wait for the future when unequal power relations have been abolished.

My poem does not say all this, and in springing to its defence so abrasively I feel I have bruised it. And am I glad or sorry that I was shown how my words were modified in the guts of the living?

***

We're Reading Lerner

I may have been the first visiting lecturer at the University of Regensburg, at any rate in the English Department. When I arrived the buildings had just been put up, the students had begun their studies, and not all the professors had been appointed, so that I was greeted in the lobby by a petition from the students of (I think) psychology, complaining that they had no professor, that conditions of study were unsatisfactory, and that the Ministry (always, in Germany, it's the Ministry) must do something. There may have been further complaints (it was, after all, 1968). I said, very politely, that I was a stranger, and didn't think it was appropriate for me to sign a petition; they replied, also politely (it was early in 1968), that surely I must agree that students should be allowed to study properly (perhaps they were complaining about the library too), and that an eminent visiting lecturer would be a great addition to their signatures: 'eminent visiting lecturer' was of course a tautology. I don't remember whether I signed or not: I may have been rescued by the Professor of English. I sometimes wonder if the Professor of Psychology, when he arrived, was treated as a hero or an oppressor by the then no doubt more militant students.

Professor G had an advanced seminar going: the Oberseminar is one of the first things a German professor sets up. There will be flocks of undergraduates, and he'll accept them with a sigh or a shrug, but first of all there must be a scholarly nucleus. He will have brought his assistants with him, and no doubt a few doctoral candidates, and from out of the air a few advanced students will appear and cling to the flypaper. There must have been 25 people in the room. I was to give a formal lecture later; first of all I was invited to meet the seminar. What are you reading? I asked. Lerner, he replied.

And indeed they were. Knowing that I was a poet as well as an academic, they had got hold of some of my poems, and distributed copies (quite rightly assuming that vanity would mean more to me than copyright). It was the first, and almost the last, time I had sat and listened to a formal academic discussion of poems I'd written, without being the person in charge. But my heart sank when I saw the poems. I am not a much-anthologised poet (whether through neglect or intrinsic unimportance is a digression it would be impertinent to indulge in), and they had got hold of *New Lines* 2, a kind of aftermath of the 'Movement' of the 1950s, in which I was represented by a few poems which I'd now be glad enough to forget about (my third book of poems, *Selves,* so much better than what had gone before that I see it as my beginning, was then in the press). It would have been impolite (and imprudent) to tell them they were wasting their time, and anyway how could I resist the seductive pleasure of being the fly on the wall — a highly visible fly, not without influence on what took place.

The discussion was mostly of 'This Poem', which now needs to be quoted:

This poem is a personable mask
  Worn by the author to conceal his thoughts;
The metre sets his muscles into lines,
  The rhymes, like sticking plaster, hide his warts;
The fiction it imposes on the reader
  Like a false nose disfigures and distorts.

As for myself (my real self, that is)
  I stroll at evening through the fading light,
And spin sick fancies from my musing heart,
  And watch the faded moon bemuse the night.
My sickly lusts are like the candied clouds
  That billow like spun sugar in my sight.

I dabble, you perceive, in poetry
  (The reason is, that I indulge in life).
Eaten with lust, and eager to escape
  From his true self, a man might take a wife,
And wedding nights recur like rhymes until
  His wanton choice subdues his wantonness.
My verses rhyme and echo: pleasing as
  A husband's kiss, and just as passionless.

Yet marriage grows on one — like poetry.
  Indulged by life, one has to learn one's place.
The pose you wore becomes the self you fled;
  The cure succeeds — by altering the case.
Made honest by deceit, made known by stealth,
  I wear this mask that all may see my face.

This is the sort of poem that academics wrote in the 1950s: it may be no worse than lots of others. That I was a lover of

Donne is perhaps evident, as is the fact that I used to explain to students that it was misleading to ask whether Donne's love poetry was 'sincere' (which they all did, in those days), because that was a biographical question for which we had no evidence. If you thought it was proved by the quality of the poem you were arguing in a circle: good poem — therefore sincere: how do you know?: because sincerity produces good poetry. Donne strikes postures, and knew he was striking postures, and expected the reader to enjoy it:

> If ever any beauty I did see
> Which I desired, and got, 'twas but a dream of thee.

'And got': a wink at the reader, followed immediately by an extravagant compliment in an extravagant rhythm. What an act I can put on as a lover, it says. What do you want in a lover? it leads us to ask: someone who only tells the literal truth, or someone who can pay magnificent compliments, who can make you feel flattered, and knows that he is performing?

That was how I spoke to my students about Donne, and perhaps I should have stuck to Donne and not tried to turn the point into a poem of my own. But I did, and enjoyed writing it, and enjoyed the feel of playing with the paradoxes. I was a true New Critic, or thought I was. As a person I was a romantic, and believed in sincerity, but as a poet I found it was fun to mock at it. (The current belief that New Criticism derived from Romanticism is grossly misleading). So I listened to Professor G's students batting my paradoxes to one another, and smiled and nodded and felt pleased they were not native speakers so would not notice all the awkwardnesses. The discussion was intelligent, and I didn't intervene much. I felt grateful that it was the kind of poem I could discuss without embarrassment, a witty academic exercise. I may even have said, 'That's not really the kind of poem I'm most interested in writing', or (more truthfully) 'I'm fascinated by writing that sort of thing, but what I really want to write is poems charged with intense experience' (but still, I would insist, not 'sincere': the biographical basis is of interest only to me.) They had translated the poem into German, and if I had not been there the discussion might well have been in German. Someone proposed 'gefällig' for 'personable' and asked if it was correct. I didn't then know much German, and had never heard the word, but I realised it must come from 'gefallen' and I smiled and nodded: he had seen the word-play. Afterwards someone said to me 'We couldn't decide if you know German, or if you were making inspired guesses. Poets are supposed to be inspired, aren't they?' I didn't know either.

It's rather humiliating to realise that I remember that session vividly, and have completely forgotten what my ensuing lecture was about.

To hear one's work discussed is the privilege — and the pain — of poets. The eminent could no doubt hear this almost endlessly if they wished, which they wisely don't; for those who are comparatively little known, the experience can be rare enough not to have lost its interest. Of course any writer sees reviews of his work, and the advantage of a review is that you can read adverse criticism. From members of the audience at poetry readings you get compliments and occasional praise: those who disliked what they heard don't say so — or not to the poet. From your friends you might get suggestions, and perhaps advice on which poems to throw away, or suggestions like the one that came from my friend Tony: 'this poem needs one strong new idea to finish it off,' he observed. Doubtless true, but what can one do? I took what seemed the best detail in the middle and shifted it to the end, and the poem ended better, but grafting a piece of skin from one's buttock onto one's wounded face does not improve the overall skin quality.

Reviewers, however, who do not know you and do not have to speak to you face to face, can devote themselves to systematic statements of what's wrong with your book. Only the eminent are treated to lengthy carve-ups of their books, but even a casual dismissal might teach the author something (as well as the obvious fact that the world is unfair). For the poet who is also an academic one extra experience is available, at any rate if he is in an American university: student responses. I gave a reading in my own university in 1994, and several of my colleagues teaching introductions to poetry encouraged (in one case required) their students to come, and asked them to write half a page describing their reaction; and one friendly colleague sent them to me. He no doubt thought I would be pleased, since they were highly favourable: 'my reaction to the reading was very positive,' wrote one student, and added with charming honesty, 'I am glad that it was mandatory, because otherwise I would not have gone.' What he may not have thought about is that the compliments may be more disappointing than insults. In my case, the commonest disappointment is to be praised for how one reads. 'His great control of his voice, his animated and very facial expression and his accent all make him a very pleasing speaker to hear.' And supposing I had read from the telephone directory with my English accent and my very facial expression, would that hearer have been just as impressed?

A rather more pleasing way of praising my manner of reading came from someone who began by complaining that I had not, as he expected, given a 'behind the scenes' look at the poems and an insight into the poet's mind, but was concerned more with the audience's understanding of the words; then went on to remark that 'as the reading progressed I realised that through the writer's tone and facial expressions I am also able to see into the poet.' Reassuring, but all the same making one long for a comment that will complain of the clumsy and misleading reading, behind which he was able to glimpse some really good poems. This hearer went on to remark that he had left the room with incomplete notes: 'I was so engulfed in the poet's words I had failed to note some of the titles of the works from which he read (and the titles I had scribbled down on paper were eligible). I do remember the contents of the poems, one in particular. A poem drawing a link between poetry and science is incredible. As an engineering major I tend to look at the concrete aspects of poems and many times I want to point out grammatical or punctuation errors and incomplete sentences. This poem, read the way the author intended for it to be heard, the way he read it Monday night, is now one of my favourite poems!'

How satisfying to know that there are engineers who care strongly about grammar and punctuation, and since they do all their writing on computers their notes can be as eligible as we might wish. I would like to pass on his remark to the poem, but alas, he omitted to mention which one it was. Since I haven't written many poems about science, I think it might have been 'Faustus, from Hell', which I have already quoted, in an earlier chapter; but I would like to think it was 'Raspberries', my most anthologised poem:

Once, as a child, I ate raspberries. And forgot.
And then, years later,
A raspberry flowered on my palate, and the past
Burst in unfolding layers within me.
It tasted of grass and honey.
You were there, watching and smiling.
Our love unfolded in the taste of raspberries.

More years have passed; and you are far, and ill;
And I, unable to reach you, eating raspberries.
Their dark damp red, their cool and fragile fur
On the always edge of decay, on the edge of bitter,
Bring a hush of taste to the mouth

Tasting of earth and of crushed leaves
Tasting of summer's insecurity,
Tasting of crimson, dark with the smell of honey

Tasting of childhood and of remembered childhood,
And now, now first, the darker taste of dread.

Sap and imprisoned sunlight and crushed grass
Lie on my tongue like a shadow,
Burst like impending news on my aching palate

Tasting not only of death (I could bear that)
But of death and of you together,
The folded layers of love and the sudden future,
Tasting of earth and the thought of you as earth

As I go on eating, waiting for the news.

ACTING

Amateur Theatricals

Student theatre is both peripheral and central to the professional theatre. Who wants to see an amateur *Hamlet* when he
could see Gielgud or Redgrave, Jacoby or Rylance? Who wants
to watch Shaw or Chekhov in a clumsily adapted school hall
when he could be at the National Theatre or the Barbican?
Student theatre, however, could be considered important because so many of our leading directors, and some of our actors,
came from universities and not from drama schools; or, and
this is the view that underlies this chapter, it could be important because productions that are technically incompetent
might be interestingly conceived; or because they are part of a
learning process; or even because of the choice of plays.

This chapter is about three productions I directed, in three
countries. In 1951, while I was teaching at what was then the
University College of the Gold Coast, I directed an open-air
production of the *The Tempest,* in African dress. In 1957, my
music colleague Denis Arnold and I produced Milton's *Comus,*
also (astonishing for Belfast) in the open air. And in 1965, with
my colleague Gamini Salgado, I produced *The Changeling,* by
Middleton and Rowley, at the university of Sussex. Each of
them taught me a lot, none of them was much good as a production, and each of them (I believe) brought something valuable
and even unique to the audience.

The Tempest

I arrived in the Gold Cast with an untrained, unskilled enthusiasm for drama, and a determination to produce some
Shakespeare in an African setting. There was no suitable
theatre, but that did not matter, since the West African climate
guaranteed several months without rain, and by good fortune I
discovered the Hill House, a concrete platform with a thatched
roof and no walls, which could be used as an open air stage. It
had been built by Quakers as an open air meeting house, and

since there were no longer any Quakers around, nobody was sure who it belonged to (I did not dream that in future years I would myself become a Quaker). So we simply took possession of it, and in my first year I produced *The Merchant of Venice,* with Shylock dressed as a Hausa trader, the Prince of Morocco in tuxedo and fez, and the Duke of Venice an Akan chief accompanied by talking drums.

'Much better than I expected,' said my sceptical head of department, and there was enough enthusiasm for me to do another play the following year. This time it was *The Tempest;* once more the costumes, like the cast, would be African, but with the non-human creatures white: I played Caliban, and the teenage daughter of our finance officer played Ariel. Once again Mr Amu, the music teacher from the Teacher Training College next door, brought his drums to provide the thunder and the magical music. Mr Amu was a gentle enthusiast who lived only for indigenous music. He wore nothing but locally woven cloth, and never played an instrument that he had not made, or could not have made, himself. (Later I learnt some of the complications of cultural nationalism when he acquired a colleague, newly returned from studying in England, who wore a navy blue suit with collar and tie, and confided to me one day, 'Poor Amu, his music is riddled with European influences.')

Stiff as the acting was, amateurish as the directing was, the play was a cultural event. Students and faculty and faculty wives paid to sit in basket chairs on the awkward upward slope in front of the Hill House, and as the production went on and the news spread they were surrounded by an ever thickening band of locals — servants, local villagers, nursemaids (including, I noticed, our own nursemaid, with our baby in her arms) — who had not paid, who can have understood little of the play, but who knew that what was taking place was the culture of the colonisers on show. This gave an extra dimension to the irony of our casting, which had reversed the colonial theme by using white people to play the parts of the indigenous inhabitants of the island.

Again the production was a success; and we decided to take it to Accra. Only the university and its hangers on had seen it, and there, just a few miles away, was the capital of the Gold Coast, filled with literate people who got no chance to see a Shakespeare play. Accra had a splendid new community centre, with a very suitable stage; we would be their very first production, and we arranged to give three performances there. This time we'd have to act indoors, in the evening, so we would need lighting: the community centre had just been opened (perhaps it wasn't yet officially open) and had no stage lights. Sensible people think of all the difficulties first, solve them, and then decide to go ahead; but what sensible person would ever have taken that untrained cast to perform in an unequipped theatre? At the age of 25 I jumped in first, then wondered if I could swim.

I wrote articles in all the local papers, telling the story of the play and singing its praises; and I drove round Accra for days, consulting electricians, then, when I realised we would have to provide our own power, hunting for a dynamo — which, miraculously, I found somewhere, begged or borrowed or hired (or even bought) it, and persuaded a colleague from Physics to help me refurbish it. I must have got floodlights from somewhere, and our stage was lit. We got a small audience the first night, but as word spread (Accra functioned like a big village) the hall began to fill up. We had begun a pattern, and the following year (or was it the year after?) we brought a double bill — *Everyman* and *Dr Faustus* — to the Community Centre. After that I returned to Britain, and that was it.

As I look back on what I did and try to describe it, I find two formulations. One says that it was a learning experience: I learnt about production, about working with people, and about *The Tempest.* I learnt that although Caliban is the son of the foul witch Sycorax and the devil, he is not a mere villain: his simple lusts (to rape Miranda, to slit Prospero's throat) are almost healthy compared with the sophisticated wickedness of Antonio and Sebastian, the real villains. Genetically, Caliban is human and diabolic, but his nature is that of an animal: hence his doglike devotion to Stephano, the drunken butler who gives him liquor to drink, and hence his love of the island, where he knows every stream, every food source. 'Be not afeard: the isle is full of noises, Sounds and sweet airs, that give delight, and hurt not': Caliban has the most beautiful speech in the play, reassuring Stephano and Trinculo, the frightened humans, that the supernatural music is part of nature after all, in the same way that dreaming is part of reality. Ariel is there to tell us that poetry is of air, Caliban that it is of earth.

Even when I did not find the answer, the production was a learning experience. Why does Prospero interrupt himself three times, when telling his story to his daughter, to accuse her of not listening? There could be two explanations, one located in her, the other in him. Is she really not attending, because she is already aware of Ferdinand's impending presence — love at first sight, when engendered by a magician, turning even more magically into love that precedes sight? When pleading with her father to save the ship, she calls it a brave vessel, That hath no doubt some noble creature in her: 'creature' in the singular, because she is not merely observing that it looks like a royal boat, but mysteriously aware that it contains her own destiny. Or is Prospero uneasy because he feels guilty? He did after all neglect his dukedom in order to study, and it is very understandable that Antonio, who had done the work of governing, should want the title too, so that Prospero's querulous insistence that Miranda must listen is an inarticulate plea for her approval. I never found the answer, and the text will sustain either interpretation; and as I got to know the play better and better I extended this ambivalence to include the whole character of Prospero: is he in control of everything, like the Duke in *Measure for Measure,* watching his plans unfold as the author watches the play grow (the magician, then, being a figure for the author)? Or is he tormented, more like Lear — or even Leontes — than the Duke, uneasy about his daughter's sexuality, jealous of the young man he gives her to, whom he keeps accusing of wanting to seduce her before marriage, whom he threatens with startlingly real venom: 'I'll manacle thy hands and feet together, Sea-water shalt thou drink...' Is that just his plan to make the wooing uneasy 'Lest too light winning Make the prize light' — or is this 'explanation' the rationalisation of a real wish to torment the young man who is stealing his daughter? Ambivalences are everywhere in the part of Prospero. In the last act, when all is being wrapped up, he declares to his brother: 'You, brother mine, that entertained ambition, Expell'd remorse and nature... I do forgive thee, Un-natural though thou art.' The actor must choose, when he speaks these lines, whether to sound godlike and definitive, adding the reminders of Antonio's guilt so that he will appreciate the forgiveness, or whether to use a voice that betrays the hatred rankling beneath the surface, so that the crucial words are not 'I forgive thee' but 'unnatural though thou art'.

For our production there was little choice. The stage, the drums, the simple setting, all conveyed straightforward dignity rather than inner complications. If I wanted to insert some signs of inner conflict, I had to reckon with the handsome, imposing young man who played Prospero; he made a splendidly commanding figure as he lifted his arm, wearing the locally made magic garment I had borrowed from an art teacher, and bade Ariel make herself like a nymph of the sea, or boasted how 'the strong-based promontory Have I made shake', but he did not have the talent to convey twisted hatred or inner torment.

Although I could not decide between the two interpretations, this did not make it any the less of a learning experience: I was learning about the central ambiguity of Prospero, and indeed of the play, and how to formulate it. Even today I could still give a lecture on the play without a single note, indicating which details can be used to support each reading. Though it made no mention of me, it would be a lecture about my own inner life, so thoroughly am I impregnated with the poetry of *The Tempest*, not Shakespeare's greatest play, but the one that is most deeply in my bones.

That is what I learnt; but once you have learnt what it had to teach you, a learning experience can fade from memory without loss. The fact that I once directed *The Tempest* becomes a rung on the ladder that gets kicked away. But the other way of regarding the experience sees it not as a means but an end, and its value consists in the fact that it endures. This is the memory of timeless moments whole sole function is to be. Prospero's deep voice, drawing out the first word of 'Graves at my command, Have waked their sleepers, oped, and let 'em forth', bestowing on the magic of an opening grave a mystery that inheres in the sound of the dark lengthened vowel; or the moment when I announced, as Caliban, 'No more dams I'll make for fish,

Nor fetch in firing At requiring', while in the auditorium of the community centre a child began to cry, not interrupting, not spoiling the defiance, but offering a setting for that moment of liberation, and for the bringing of Shakespeare to a culture where women carry their babies everywhere; or sitting in a basket chair during rehearsal, while Ariel sang 'Of his bones are coral made', and the crystalline words were carried towards me through the sunlight. These moments lead to nothing, and teach nothing, but in some realm of existence they are *The Tempest,* and last for ever.

***

The Historical Imagination

On 29 September 1634 the Earl of Bridgwater, who had been appointed Lord President of Wales, had just taken possession of his official residence at Ludlow Castle. To celebrate the event, a musical entertainment was arranged, under the care of Mr Henry Lawes. Lawes invited his friend John Milton, a young scholar and poet, to write a masque, for which he supplied the music. Milton chose a story which would serve as a compliment to the Earl's three youngest children, the Lady Alice Egerton and her two younger brothers, who took part in the performance, representing themselves on a journey through a wood to join their father.

Denis said to me one day, 'Have you ever thought of producing a masque?' I never had, but I knew immediately that I wanted to, that it would have to be *Comus,* and that he was just the right person to do it with. He was a musicologist specialising in the seventeenth century, an authority on Gabrielli and Monteverdi (he subsequently became professor of music at Oxford), and also an enthusiastic conductor and organiser.

To revive a masque today is impossible. The court masque was a favourite — and very expensive — form of entertainment in Tudor and Stuart times, a mixture of elaborate scenery, music, dance and allegorical story: the celebrated combination of Ben Jonson and Inigo Jones produced masques for the court of James I, to celebrate weddings, birthdays, and other occasions deemed important by the monarch. They were not just entertainments, but state occasions, and their purpose was the assertion of hierarchy and royal splendour. Protocol — and elaborate arguments — governed the seating arrangements, the most prominent place, visible to everyone, always going to the monarch. As Stephen Orgel observes, the audience 'watched not a play but the Queen (or King) at a play.' The content of the masque would be a compliment to some member of the royal family: riot, disorder and vulgarity (the parts played by professional actors) would be quelled and reduced to order by the prince, who played the part of himself, and the performance would end with a dance in which the audience, including the monarch, would join, thus finally abolishing whatever barrier had existed between the represented world and the world of the watchers.

Here for instance is Jonson's *Masque of Beauty,* performed on the Sunday after Twelfth Night, 1609. Boreas, one of the winds, and January began with 'horrors as sharp as death,' which were swept aside when a curtain was drawn, revealing 'an island floating on a calm water. In the midst thereof was a seat of state, called the Throne of Beauty, erected: divided into eight squares, and distinguished by so many Ionic pilasters. In these squares the sixteen masquers were placed by couples: behind them in the centre of the throne was a tralucent pillar, shining with several coloured lights…' and so on. To recreate these elaborate effects today would be easy in a well-equipped professional theatre, though far beyond the resources of any university production; but the reason that a modern revival could not be genuine is that the social context is missing. The sixteen masquers were the Queen and a no doubt carefully selected group of gentlewomen: that is, the figures who dominated the performance were also those who mattered in the world outside. The masque was topical (the text specially written for the occasion) and political (an assertion of hierarchy and royal power). No revival can recapture this situation: our interest today has to be not immediate but historical, an attempt to enter into an event firmly located in the past.

In comparison with court performances, the masque at Ludlow Castle was a modest provincial affair, but for this very reason it may be easier to bring it alive today. It must have been a much less elaborate production (the Earl of Bridgwater could hardly afford Inigo Jones), and partly because of this it has a much fuller and richer text; and the text, if powerful enough, can break free of the occasion as the representation clearly cannot. It is the one masque that has survived into modern consciousness, the one which is still read and occasionally performed. It is a text suffused with the genius of our great anti-puritan puritan poet.

The text was published in 1637, without Milton's name and without a title, simply called 'A Masque', but since the eighteenth century it has been called after the principal figure. Comus is the son of Bacchus and Circe: the name means 'revelry' and he represents the temptation to a life of riot and dissipation which the lady, with stern puritan morality, resists. As in all masques, the story is very simple: the children are lost in the wood, the lady is separated from her brothers, and she is met by Comus, who invites her, in a wonderfully eloquent speech, to join his revels ('Wherefore did Nature pour her bounties forth, With such a full and unwithdrawing hand...But all to please and sate the curious taste?'); Comus can be seen as a figure for the very idea of 'masque' and the Lady's very prim rejection ('I had not thought to have unlocked my lips In this unhallow'd air') is a kind of rejection of the production of which she is part. The children are protected by an Attendant Spirit, played by Henry Lawes, who arrives on the scene with the lady's brothers; Comus flees, but the Spirit cannot release her until he invokes the aid of the river goddess, Sabrina: an excuse for another singer, and a genuflection to local pride. The masque ends with the triumph of virtue and the return of the Attendant Spirit to 'those happy climes that lie Where day never shuts his eye, Up in the broad fields of the sky', and the children are reunited with their father, symbolised by the dance in which, in accordance with the custom at the conclusion of a masque, the Earl and the rest of the audience no doubt joined.

Denis chose and arranged the seventeenth century music (not all of it by Lawes, who he said was rather a dull composer), and he found the musicians. We hunted for a suitable stage, and fixed on the garden of the Psychology Department: they were in an old house with trees all round and a slope at the back, leading down to a large lawn on which the audience could sit. It was a perfect setting: the Attendant Spirit could descend from Heaven at the beginning (but he would not come out of the house: we did not want to suggest that the Psychology Department was Heaven), the children could be lost among the trees, and there was even a gardener's hut out of which Comus could burst with his rout, to the blaring of trombones ('Meanwhile welcome joy and feast, Midnight shout and revelry, Tipsy dance and jollity'). The great snag of course was that we were in Northern Ireland, land of wet weather. We would just have to keep the splendid hall of the university in reserve, and move in there if it rained. If we had done this, the result would have been disastrous: a hurried rehearsal on the afternoon of the performance would never have sufficed to readjust our movements, and the loss of the pastoral setting would have removed all the magic. We chose two days in early June for the production, and then (I forget why) moved it back to the 21st and 22nd. On the day we'd originally chosen it rained steadily from morning to night. I stared at the downpour and tried to decide whether that was a good or a bad omen, whether on midsummer day Nature would pour her bounties forth with such a full and unwithdrawing hand.

That June was warm and dry and sunny; the constant question was whether it would last. Never before or since have I been so conscious of weather, listening to the forecast every day, watching and even counting every cloud in the sky. It did last, but only just: all was well at the dress rehearsal, then on the opening night a breeze sprang up, and the noise of the leaves threatened to drown the performance. I stood at the back and willed Comus and the Lady to speak louder, and the audience to listen harder, but I was as helpless as a football manager on the touchline. Not everyone heard everything, but one of the local papers, in its review headed 'Milton Work to the Rustle of Leaves', assured us, in almost Miltonic diction, that 'If the rustling of leaves put audibility at a higher premium than usual, this was more than compensated by the atmospheric appositeness of the scenery.'

Norman Stevenson, who played the Attendant Spirit, was the best amateur actor I have ever seen. He understood every nuance of a line of poetry, and he controlled every vibration of his own voice; but his attention was always on what he was saying, never on how well he was saying it. I have, alas, long since lost touch with him, as with the rest of the cast (and Denis is now dead). James Park, an art student, who subsequently taught art in Brighton (and taught my niece) played Comus, and designed the costumes and the wonderfully effective half-masks worn by his followers. I had far more luck with the cast than I had a right to expect, and the result was a triumph for Milton. Everyone who came enjoyed the production, and the professor of Biochemistry came back on the second night. We had to turn people away on both evenings, and we still let in more than we had seats for (the well-bred Public School boys from Campbell College stood up and offered their seats without a murmur). Twenty-five years later I met a professor of English who came from Belfast, and who had been at the performance; he may have been one of those who had no seat, but his memory of it was vivid and appreciative.

My feeling for drama is deeply verbal. For those who truly think in theatrical terms, the text is only one element in a complex experience, where movement and grouping, scenery and lighting, music and audience response, combine to produce a new experience, that of theatre — a world in which a crucial, non-verbal detail (an embrace, a musical note produced by a cable snapping in a distant mine, two hands appearing over the edge of a dustbin) can be as eloquent as a long speech. I understand this view, but I cannot lose my belief that the words of a play *are* the play, that everything else is there to serve them. I loved to produce or act in plays, in order to hear them over and over, to savour the words, to play with their meaning, to listen to their resonance. I would repeat the speeches of Comus and the Attendant Spirit as I went to sleep, and think of them when I woke up. When the Spirit tells us that the children are coming to join their father and their way

Lies through the perplexed paths of this drear wood,
The nodding horror of whose shady brows
Threats the forlorn and wandering passenger,

I felt the hesitation between the drear wood as a metaphor for life (like the opening of Dante's *Inferno*) and as a real wood outside Ludlow (or behind the psychology Department): I felt it as a physical sensation. My body tensed with the transaction between literal and figurative. I would repeat the words over and over, or just think about them, and felt a deep joy every time I heard Norman's voice speaking them.

Milton's poetry cannot have meant much to most of that audience: if they had sat down to read it, they would have found it remote and difficult. To appreciate *Comus* required from them an act of historical imagination, and as I thought about the experience I realised how powerful, and how complex, are its workings. The spectators were being offered a chance to recreate the occasion that took place at Ludlow Castle on Michaelmas Night 1634, and they seized it eagerly: but in what sense could they be said to have returned to 1634? They cared nothing for the Earl of Bridgwater; whether he turned out to be a good or bad governor of Wales did not matter to them. They could not take seriously the world of natural magic, both wicked and benevolent, which informs the play, a world where the stars were hung out by a Nature who 'filled their lamps With ever-lasting oil to give due light To the misled and lonely traveller'. It was a quaint conceit to describe the stars as lamps filled with oil, but it fitted onto a belief in Providence and in benevolent Nature; today all that is left is the conceit. Belief in the magical power of chastity, belief that 'no evil thing that walks by night…Hath hateful power o'er true virginity' is even harder for us to credit — though it might have seemed slightly more acceptable to the Belfast culture of 1957 than to the England of the 1990s.

I learned from the production how powerful a sense of history can be, and how complicated its operations. The world of 1634 and the world of 1957 had somehow met and modified each other in the awareness of a few hundred people: the audience had returned to the past without leaving the present, they had changed but not distorted a text that could come to life only in the minds of those prepared to open themselves to it. It was not a timeless experience, for it was a reliving of something that belonged completely in its own time, but that had also been lifted into ours. Perhaps I did not understand the historical imagination any better than before, but I had experienced it, and helped others to do so.

The Changeling

In 1965 Gamini Salgado and I produced *The Changeling* in the courtyard outside the Physics building at the University of Sussex. That all three productions described in this chapter were in the open air is worth at most a passing mention; more interesting is that all three were in spaces not designed as theatres. In every case, it was necessary to decide where the audience would sit, what the main acting area would be, and what spatial effects, what appearances and disappearances, were possible. If the space is complicated, these decisions become difficult but potentially enriching for the play. We were reverting to what was the normal situation for drama before Elizabethan times. When Burbage built the first permanent theatre in England in 1576 (calling it, revealingly, simply 'The Theatre'), he instituted a far greater revolution than he can have realised: from now on, plays could be performed in a building exclusively designed for producing plays. It would no longer be necessary to look at a street corner, the steps in front of a church, a great hall, or an innyard, and ponder how best to turn it into theatrical space. But I was, though I did not pause to think about it in these terms, back in the pre-Burbage world, imposing theatrical possibility onto ordinary space.

In the Physics courtyard we had half a dozen long shallow steps leading down in two directions from the acting area: this meant the demarcation between stage and audience would not be very clear cut, but this could be an advantage as well as a weakness. The Physics building looming behind us enabled Piracquo's ghost (most Elizabethan tragedies of blood have their ghost) to appear on the roof — a sensational effect, which it seemed a pity to squander on what is unfortunately a very minor detail in this play. A long wall ran along the side of the audience: actors could wait unseen behind it, and we hinted that the lunatic asylum lay there: madmen could peer round it, and any of them willing to risk a broken leg (and falling onto the audience) could caper along the top of the wall. In the end I was the one who did this: once the play has opened, the director is, after all, expendable — but fortunately I remained unhurt.

The Changeling is probably, after *King Lear,* the most brilliant use of the double plot in Jacobean drama. The main story tells how Beatrice-Joanna, plighted to Piracquo by her father, falls in love with Alsemero. She is pestered by a gentleman of her father's household, called De Flores, whom she cannot abide, and it is actually her violent aversion that gives her the idea of making use of him to get rid of Piracquo: when Alsemero suggests challenging Piracquo to a duel she rejects the suggestion with horror, since even if he isn't killed, he will be judged guilty, and 'blood-guiltiness becomes a fouler visage' — and immediately she thinks of the foul visage of De Flores. Only after De Flores has killed Piracquo for her does he name his price, which is of course her virtue; he brushes aside her moral indignation, and her social superiority, with 'Push, fly not to your birth, but settle you In what the act has made you...Y're the deed's creature'.

The sub-plot is set in the private lunatic asylum of Alibius. Two young men disguise themselves as lunatics in order to seduce his handsome wife Isabella, but though she despises her husband's foolish jealousy, she is virtuous and resists. The links between the two plots are almost endless: the two disguised young men are suspected of Piracquo's murder, a dance of lunatics provides the entertainment at Beatrice's wedding, Isabella's virtue resists but Beatrice's succumbs. Who is the changeling? Explicitly, it is the man disguised as a lunatic, but it is also Beatrice ('I am that of your blood was taken from you,' she tells her father at the end), and in another sense De Flores, who from being loathed becomes for Beatrice 'a wondrous necessary man'. Madness is central to this play, and what we think about lunatics is crucial. The Jacobeans were callous enough to regard madness as comic — deplorable, obviously, but opening up a series of terrifying parallels. 'The effect of the vulgar asylum scenes,' wrote William Empson, memorably, 'is to surround the characters with a herd of lunatics, howling outside in the night, one step into whose company is irretrievable.' When Richard Eyre directed the play at the National Theatre in 1988, he surrounded the stage with staircases where the madmen haunted, and surrounded the text with dumb-shows in half-light in which the main characters parodied the plot. We had not the resources for such grotesque brilliance in our courtyard, and we set out to make our madmen as comic as their limited talent could manage. In particular, we used them to parody the virginity test.

Alsemero, as the well-equipped Spanish gentleman, has an apparatus for testing whether a woman is a maid or not. 'Give the party you suspect the quantity of a spoonful of the water in the glass M, which upon her that is a maid makes three several effects: 'twill make her incontinently gape, then fall into a sudden sneezing, last into a violent laughing; else, dull, heavy and lumpish.' Beatrice has to trick her way through the test by feigning the symptoms, and in the next scene we brought in the lunatics with glasses marked M, who incontinently yawned, sneezed and laughed all over the stage. Though we have lost their reverential attitude to virginity, the Jacobeans may have found this test as ridiculous as we do, if not for quite the same reasons; and perhaps the same may be said for the bed-trick.

Shakespeare uses the bed-trick twice, in *Measure for Measure* and *All's Well that Ends Well;* clearly it obsessed the age. In this play it is used by Beatrice to prevent, once more, Alsemero discovering that she is not a virgin. Pretending that her modesty requires darkness for the wedding night, she sends her maid Diaphanta (who had passed the glass M test) in her place. The trick assumes a particularly unpleasant view of male sexuality: that a man will not notice the identity of the woman he has intercourse with, but will notice whether she is a virgin. In *The Changeling* there is a further twist, based on the medieval view of the voracious sexual appetite of women: Diaphanta finds she is enjoying it so much that she doesn't want to stop, and threatens to reveal everything by staying in Alsemero's bed till morning. De Flores, a 'wondrous necessary man' for this as for so much else, has to find a way of getting rid of her. When Beatrice calls on him for help his comments on Diaphanta are full of male nastiness:

> Sure the devil
> Hath sowed his itch within her; who'd trust
> A waiting woman?…They are termagants,
> Especially when they fall upon their masters,
> And have their ladies' first-fruits; th'are mad whelps,
> You cannot stave 'em off from game royal.

We had had some difficulty in choosing our De Flores. It is the most important part, and though there were plenty of competent candidates, no-one seemed inevitably right. One evening I was chatting in the student bar to one Mike F, newly returned from his year in France: he was sophisticated, intense, ugly in a handsome way, and vaguely corrupt: his long hair and full beard framed a blotchy red complexion. As I was leaving, Gamini accosted me: 'Who was that?' he asked. I told him. 'Get him for Dr Flores,' he said; 'he's perfect.' And he was.

I liked Mike, but had never been wholly at ease with him: his sophisticated understanding of films made me feel naive, his sexual freedom made me feel staid, his mild contempt for art that wasn't modernist made me feel outmoded. We approached Middleton from different directions, but we both responded intensely to De Flores' poetry. Mike, a man of progressive views, could hardly have responded with sympathy to the misogyny, but I could sense in him the radical's contempt for traditional pieties (in the way so many of our students warmed intuitively to Nietzsche, whose actual opinions they can hardly have approved, because he was an iconoclast and a tablet-breaker). Should I have found it disconcerting that Mike was such a good De Flores? But why was I too so attracted to the part? Was it the same kind of attraction as Mike's?

This is a question about acting; and also, I realise, a question about drama itself. The ambivalence of the actor's art is a kind of parallel to the ambivalence of the dramatist's. Is Middleton, writing those lines about the waiting woman's itch, expressing social contempt and misogyny, or is he showing us how misogynists think? We can ask the question about all the brilliant nasties in drama: did Shakespeare share Leontes' violent contempt for sexual hypocrisy, or Goneril's impatience with her father? And in what sense must the actor share it, in order to perform the part convincingly? Not only is the question unanswerable: if there were a clear yes or no, then drama would lose its power.

Beatrice has a good deal to say about De Flores' complexion. She calls him an 'ominous ill-fac'd fellow'; when she changes her mood in order to coax him to the murder, he remarks 'Tis the same physnomy, to a hair and pimple, Which she call'd scurvy scarce an hour ago'; now she promises to make a water that will cleanse it. Just how scabrous and pimply should De Flores be (no-one except Beatrice remarks on his complexion)? We did not use any make-up to make Mike more gruesome (performing by daylight, in mid-June, we did not use make-up at all), but his blotchy complexion, with its hairy surround, already looked sinister enough (as Gamini had sensed). When I saw the play at the National Theatre twenty years later, there was a shock in store: De Flores was a black man. George Harris was big, good-looking, with tribal markings, and splendidly dressed in cream: he smiled a lot, stiffly and rather grotesquely, and there was a strong suggestion of suppressed violence about him.

It is now the policy of our leading companies to use colour-blind casting — for admirably liberal reasons, since it gives more opportunities to black actors; but it is difficult to ignore the problem it raises. One expects an actor to use every element of his or her person — height, shape, beauty, timbre of voice, all physical features — and if the audience is asked to ignore one of the most striking features, then the theatrical effect may he weakened or confused. If you can ignore colour, can you also ignore sex, so that gender-blind casting should come next, to give more opportunities to female actors? Which may not be as silly as it sounds, since it is exactly what the Elizabethans did — except that they used it to give more opportunities to males.

Casting George Harris as De Flores, however, was not colour-blind: it was giving a particular interpretation to Beatrice's remarks. What now were we meant to think about Beatrice's dislike of his complexion, and her change of heart and promise to 'make a water for you shall cleanse this Within a fortnight'? Is this a sign of Beatrice's self-deception? Or of her colour-prejudice? Or of Middleton's? Or ours? Was the production being politically incorrect (blackness is a blemish) or politically very correct (skin disease is no more of a stigma than colour)? The director, surely, had lost control of the meanings he wished to convey.

Control of meaning: this is a highly charged issue nowadays. The radicals of literary theory accuse old-fashioned scholars of controlling meaning as a form of political control: the subject of a sentence, in Roland Barthes' notorious formulation, rules over the predicate with fascist authoritarianism. Discussing drama in a small seminar once, when I was in Würzburg, I remarked that the relation between Hamlet and Polonius, in the fish-monger scene, was like that between comedian and straight man. The young colleague who specialised in drama leapt at the idea: the obvious first thing to do, he pointed out, was to reverse things: try making Polonius the person in control, and Hamlet the straight man. It was no use asking him why. The answer would have been in terms of opening up the text, subverting our assumptions, and if he had read Barthes, could have led to a preference for the scriptible over the lisible text. I have no idea whether Richard Eyre had read Barthes, or any radical theory, but if I had told him that he was no longer in complete control over the meaning of what he was doing, I presume he would not have minded.

***

The Changeling was not quite the end of my amateur dramatics. Eight years later Gamini and I produced Ben Jonson's *Sejanus* in what we thought might be the first produc-tion since the 17th century (it wasn't: we discovered there had been a Sunday evening performance by professional actors in 1928, and we kept hearing (unconfirmed) rumours of other universities having put it on). We confirmed, to our satisfaction, our view that the play does not deserve its reputation as pedan-tic and unactable, but is a brilliant dramatisation of political corruption, tyranny, and liberal nostalgia. Producing it was a learning experience that taught us about ancient Rome (Jonson was extremely accurate), about Jacobean political ideology, and about politics itself; seeing it was, for a few hundred people, an experience they will almost certainly never be able to repeat. But like all dramatic productions it has now disappeared into the grave of time.

After that, academic duties and middle age took over, and I produced no more plays.

POLITICS

Memories of Revolution

Disruption of lectures is as old as lectures. Put a large number of 19-year old males in a hall, and make them sit still and listen to improving sentiments from their elders, and the result will not always be peaceful. In Belfast in the 1950s there was a university lecture once a term, on a subject which it was felt would be of general interest: the future of Africa, the morality of scientific research, Shakespeare today. The lecturers were distinguished, often good, but sometimes prosy or moralising or dull, and some of the young men in the audience had come to enjoy themselves. A nervous joke, a pause, a slip of the tongue, could produce catcalls and stamping, and once or twice the noise threatened to get out of control. Some of my colleagues were furious, and felt such behaviour must be punished; I could not blame their anger, but wondered what you could do to punish a mob. I wondered too about another question. Suppose, I said to colleagues, this was Eastern Europe or a fascist state somewhere; suppose disrupting required courage and was morally and politically admirable — world it be the same students who would disrupt then? Of course not was the usual answer; these rowdies are not being heroic, or doing it out of political principle, they're just indulging themselves, making trouble.

Making trouble. The students in Tiananmin Square were making trouble, the Vietnam protesters were making trouble, the French Resistance in 1943 were making trouble. We all know that one man's freedom fighter is another's terrorist, one man's undisciplined teenager is another's heroic protester. I felt my colleagues were a bit too sure of their answer; but I did not realise how urgent the question would, in another decade or so, turn out to be.

I can remember the day, in March of 1968, on which I first realised that student revolution was a phenomenon in its own right. A leaflet was thrust into my hand inviting me to a protest meeting about oppression in Eastern Europe: nothing unusual in that. But there was something odd about it, all the same:

Student Freedom!

DEMONSTRATION

in sympathy with students in WARSAW & PRAGUE

CONDEMNING   BRUTALITY of Militia
              IMPRISONMENT of hundreds of students,
              Political CENSORSHIP of the Press & Theatre
              DENIAL of human rights

What was odd, of course, was that there was no mention of Communism, no suggestion that the oppression of students in Warsaw and Prague was any different from what might happen in San Francisco or Paris.

This protest meeting was not to be about how totalitarian regimes differed from democratic — clearly a superficial matter — but about how 'the authorities', whoever they were, treated students. The international student movement had been born.

***

Political Files

'You ought to hear Müller-Seidel before you leave Munich,' said my friend Werner. 'He's the most famous person in the German Department. Personally, I can't stand him, but it would be a pity to miss him altogether.' So I turned up the following Wednesday morning to hear one of his lectures on — I've quite forgotten what, but it was no doubt Fontane und der Eheroman, or Goethe and narratology, or even (since it was 1969) a defence of Germanistik as a subject. And since it was 1969, I didn't hear the lecture. The room was full when I arrived, and so was the dais: waves of students broke and swirled around the lectern, and used the microphone to announce that there would be a general meeting to discuss the presuppositions of the study of Germanistik, and how it could be turned to revolutionary purposes. Müller-Seidel, when he arrived (for some reason accompanied by a colleague) never had a chance. He was only fitfully able to reach the microphone, swept aside periodically by the surging wave of bodies, and when he was audible he offered only moral indignation: 'Never have I encountered such shameless interference — I wish merely to state that this amounts to the use of force to prevent —' The breaking sentences scattered their foam over the front rows of the audience. People were leaving in large numbers, convinced (before the lecturer himself was) that there would be no lecture; eventually the colleague looked at Müller-Seidel, shrugged, and said 'Abbrechen', and everyone except the revolutionaries streamed out.

The following year — or perhaps the year after — I witnessed a comparable scene at Sussex. It was the year of the political files. When the students at Warwick University occupied the administration building they began breaking into filing cabinets, and found a letter from a director of Rootes Motors to the Vice-chancellor about what a visiting lecturer from America said to a local Labour Party meeting, together with other correspondence about the political activities of faculty and students. Jubilantly interpreting this as political interference with academic freedom, they published the documents and unleashed a controversy that swept the nation's universities. Thousands of students who had never before thought about the contents of their confidential files were suddenly convinced that these contained information about their political activities and even beliefs, whether hostile ('he is a active supporter of the occupation') or well-meant ('he hasn't done himself justice this term because he's spent so much time on student politics'); and they began to demand access to their files. For a few months this was the main issue in student protests, then it died down, not as suddenly as it had arisen, but suddenly all the same.

Here I pause for a few comments on the political files issue. It was shot into national prominence by E P Thompson's book *Warick University Ltd,* a narrative of Warwick's student occupation, and a very interesting attack on the attempt to make Warwick a 'business university' at (Thompson felt) the expense of academic freedom and democracy. I found it difficult, after reading Thompson's book, to feel that the Vice-chancellor had done anything very sinister. It is true that he had from the first seen the university as closely tied to local industry, not as a way of openly supporting capitalism, but as a way of avoiding an ivory-tower mentality, encouraging scientists to address themselves to practical issues, and seek outside support for their research (anticipating, in the latter, a growing tendency of the later 20th century). He also saw it as a way of avoiding town v gown hostility. His contacts with industry, in the early sixties, were with management rather than with workers, and this naturally lost him the sympathy of left-wing students. In the particular cases revealed by the examination of his files, he did not seem to me to be guilty of much more than opening his letters in the morning and answering them politely.

But once the rumour began that there were political files on students (and even on faculty), it became impossible to refute: how do you prove the non-existence of anything? The only method of refuting the charge would obviously be to open the files, and the one beneficial effect of the controversy was to make everyone think about confidentiality. Would you write the same report on a student you had taught if it was going to be made accessible? Would you, for instance, write: 'Be gentle with her, she tries hard, but really the work is too difficult for her' if the student would be reading it? Should you write such things anyway? Are such well-meant remarks patronising, do they reveal a sense in which the student is not really being treated as an equal? And *is* the student an equal?

Back, now, to the lecture at Sussex. It was not an ordinary teaching situation but a public lecture to which students and colleagues and outsiders had been invited. The Department of Continuing Education planned a series of centenary lectures, and the first one was to be given by Asa Briggs, the Vice-chancellor. It was 1970, and he spoke on the Education Act a hundred years earlier. The hall was filled to overflowing, not, alas, because of the interest of the subject or the fame of the lecturer, but because the radical students perceived this as an opportunity to raise the issue of political files. From the first moment it was clear that trouble was brewing. Before the session began a student representative called out loud and clear: 'Vice-chancellor, we have come along to ask about political files. We have reason to think that confidential information on students' political opinions is kept in their files, and we wish to know the university's policy on this matter. We also wish to have access to our files in order to see what they contain.' There was thunderous applause and stamping.

The Director of Continuing Education was in the chair. I watched him pause and then, I presumed, make up his mind. He walked to the microphone and began, 'Ladies and Gentlemen, I am delighted to welcome you to the first of our centenary lectures; I am particularly pleased to welcome those who have come from outside the university to hear our distinguished Vice-chancellor, who as you all know is perhaps the greatest living authority on Victorian England...' He had decided to ignore the invading students and proceed as planned, presumably hoping that they would submit or go away.

But of course they didn't. They were still streaming in, and determined to turn the meeting into a discussion of political files. Several students had got onto the platform, and one burly young man kept saying, 'You answer our questions and then we'll let you give your lecture: it's as simple as that.' As simple as that. I found myself thinking, 'So that's what a politicised university is like. No more complexity.'

The two constituencies in the hall — those who had come to hear the lecture and those who had come to disrupt it — fought their battle with applause. A student announced that they insisted on having their questions answered, and his supporters clapped long and loud. Briggs' ironic response, 'Thank you for that ovation', gave him a moment of triumph, but did not endear him to the disrupters. The lecturer or the chairman remarked that there were visitors present who had come to hear the lecture, and that must come first; and their supporters clapped longer and louder. I had never heard so much applause in a lecture hall; no contest is simple, and the students then tried the trick of joining in their opponents' applause and converting it to something nearer mere noise. Neither side really won the applause battle.

Briggs made his position quite clear: 'I'll talk about political files as long as you like,' he kept saying. 'I'll stay here till midnight to answer all your questions, after I've given the lecture. But the lecture must come first.' He had by then taken over from the Continuing Education Director as the man in charge — or trying to be in charge. This was no doubt inevitable, since he was the man the revolutionaries had come to challenge, and they addressed their remarks to him; but it was also, it seemed to me, unfortunate. The role of command and the role of lecturing did not go well together. To the burly and persistent young man on the platform (I never found out who he was, or if he was really a student) he said at one point, 'and I say to that student there that I will not hesitate to use disciplinary measures against those who disrupt university activities.' The fact that he clearly did not know the student's name made the threat sound hollow; worse still was the thought that he was threatening punishment for those who wouldn't listen to *him.* The separation of discipline and teaching, I now saw clearly, (the legend of the Jesuits having one to teach and one to beat) had much to be said for it. As Briggs for the umpteenth time repeated his proposal he said, 'If you listen to the lecture — which will do you all good — then I'll be perfectly happy to stay on and discuss political files.' The touch of irony in his invoking of the morality of the teacher gave — momentarily — a human dimension to the struggle for control, but once again did not endear him to the disrupters.

And in the end it worked: the lecture did take place. It was (what else would one expect from Asa Briggs on social history?) an excellent lecture, and the revolutionary students more or less listened. No explicit bargain was struck, but a silent pact began to emerge, that they would let him lecture and then he would stay and listen to them. A sizable minority of the disrupters clearly did not listen very hard (what did they care about 1870? They were interested in the future), and there was a good deal of whispering and giggling of a quite unpolitical kind, but he did give the lecture, and everyone heard it. After that the one constituency (including me) left, but I later learned that the subsequent discussion had been inconclusive, and the students had stated that they were not satisfied with his answers. Presumably he failed to prove a negative.

***

Anna and Alienation

The revolution was most obvious in lectures. In a tutorial, the student is meant to argue back, in a lecture he is meant to sit quiet and listen, so a refusal to accept the teacher's authority will in the one case be seen in words, in the other in disruptive action: the larger the audience, the more lurid the disruption. Yet the effect of the revolution on tutorials was perhaps more disturbing. Take for instance the case of Anna, the only student who to my knowledge ever lodged a formal complaint against my teaching.

The Sussex course called the Modern European Mind was taken by large numbers of students, and in the early seventies it was to be expected that my group would contain a few fiery radicals. This was the high point of ideological resistance, a moment when a significant number of students, instead of assuming that what a teacher said was true, were more likely to believe the opposite. University teachers in the seventies, who had for their whole careers longed for lively students who argued back, were now complaining that their students rejected everything they said. To the radicals, this showed their hypocrisy, that they didn't really want students who answered back, they wanted a token resistance issuing in comfortable acquiescence; to the teachers, there was an obvious difference between genuine, open-minded argument, and what they felt they were too often getting, the replacement of automatic acceptance by automatic rejection. The trouble of course is that if you really want disagreement you will not be able to dictate the terms, so that this dispute may be inevitable. As it was with Anna.

What does teaching a Marxist student entail, for a non-Marxist teacher? Should you bombard the student with awkward questions, or give her texts to expound? In the Modern European Mind course I'd had plenty of essays on the Economic and Political Manuscripts from students who gave me back what Marx said, reverently reproducing all his abstract nouns, but never applying them to concrete examples, never even translating them into other abstractions, or asking if there were potential contradictions in the position, never asking what it all *meant*. By the time Anna arrived I'd decided that such bland paraphrase would not do, and had worked out a series of questions to put to the text. One of my favourite questions was, Are the bourgeoisie alienated?

When asked what alienation actually referred to, in terms of human experience, the students liked to illustrate from their own situation. Having to sit exams was a favourite example: knowledge which should be acquired for its own sake was degraded into a means towards passing the exam and so qualifying oneself for a place in bourgeois society. It was after all a characteristic of the revolutionaries of the 1968 generation that they saw themselves as victims. I once heard Stephen Spender lecture on what it was like to be a revolutionary student in the thirties, and he remarked that they all assumed that when the revolution came they would be worse off than they had been, even that it would be a personal disaster for them. The revolutionaries of the seventies, however, did not see themselves as the privileged who would be dispossessed: they intended to do the dispossessing. But, of course, they were not the proletariat : most of them were the children of bourgeois parents; even those from working-class backgrounds were, arguably, in the process of embourgeoisement. If they denied this, indignantly, as they often did, and pointed to their opposition to the capitalist system, to whose overthrow they were dedicated, then they were being deeply idealist: to classify themselves according to their opinions rather than their social and economic situation could never be called materialist. So if they were alienated, then alienation was as common to the bourgeoisie as to the workers, and in that case what did it have to do with class exploitation? So I would press the question.

The question goaded Anna to fury. She grew more and more impatient as I insisted that her examples of the necessary alienation of capitalism all seemed to be taken from bourgeois experiences, until she burst out impatiently, 'Why do you keep going on about the bourgeoisie? Who cares about them, they're doomed anyway!' As soon as that class was over she marched into the Dean's office and lodged her formal complaint, saying she had been subjected to anti-Marxist diatribes. The Dean was my friend Michael, and he was careful to behave with official propriety. When he informed me what had happened there was a twinkle in his eye. He explained that he had told the student what the appropriate procedures were, that she should bring him a written statement in which she described what had happened and made her objections, and he would then interview me, and decide whether and how to proceed. I said I hoped she would do this, and that a public confrontation would, in the present climate, be good for the university. In reality, I felt more ambivalent. If a student lodged an official complaint against my teaching today I would be very distressed, but in 1971 I was younger and more resilient, and believed strongly that there were issues which needed airing: if there was an official inquiry arising out of her complaint, I would describe what I thought a tutorial was for. I would have the advantage that I had been thinking about it for longer than Anna. I hoped she would use the word 'diatribe', so that could point out that I had bombarded her with a series of *questions,* and what had irritated her was her inability to answer them.

No doubt there was a touch of vindictiveness in my reaction. A caring and paternalist tutor, like my friend Derek, would surely have reproached me for being more concerned to defend myself than to help Anna. Yet I felt I was defending the university as much as myself; and by Anna's own criteria was I not behaving rightly? I was treating her as an equal, not probing into why she wanted to confront me, but accepting the confrontation. In the end, however, it never took place. Anna never returned to the Dean and never made a written statement, having presumably calmed down and thought better of it. But there is an epilogue.

The following year it was my turn to be one of the Modern European Mind examiners. I was paired with Christophe, who taught French, and Anna's paper happened to be one of those we marked. Normally one had no idea who the candidates were, since they were identified only by a number, and in the case of the MEM course, which was compulsory for so many students, it was not even likely that one would have taught those one examined. Occasionally you might recognise a handwriting or a favourite idea, and think, that must be Z or Y, but without considering this important. But Anna's paper riveted me, and I had no doubt it was hers: everything we had argued about in tutorials was there, sometimes even in the very words we had used. A week or so after her 'complaint' Anna had attended my lecture on Brecht: we had studied some of Brecht's plays in the tutorial, as examples of Marxism in literary practice, and as I noticed her taking notes when I said something controversial, I even wondered if she was gathering material for her complaint. My lecture discussed how far Brecht should be called a Marxist dramatist, and I claimed that the view of history informing *The Life of Galileo* could best be described as the common element between liberal and Marxist theories of the rise of modern science. Since Anna had insisted to the Dean that I was 'misrepresenting' Marxist authors, I was not surprised to see her writing eagerly at that point, and I even added a further sentence or two to explain just what I meant, and how I would support it from other plays.

In the exam, Anna answered a question on Brecht, and there was my lecture, lucidly expounded, with exactly the examples I had used, from *Galileo* and *Puntila* and *The Good Woman of Setzuan,* accurately remembered and reproduced. Christophe gave the paper a higher mark than I did. When I suggested that some of its views were obvious and could even be called Marxist clichés, he replied that they were based on accurate knowledge of the texts, and enriched with apt illustrations. When I told him that all this account of Brecht came from me, he smiled and remarked that that was what teaching is for. Only after I had accepted his high mark did I confess that not only had I recognised the student, but that she had lodged a complaint against my teaching, and indeed against the very ideas that she had then used so effectively in the exam. He thought she would have no difficulty in fitting her views on Brecht into her Marxist framework, and added that our aim as teachers was to educate our students, not to demand their gratitude Of course it was easy for Christophe to be more mature than me on an issue he was not involved in. And we both of us realised that we had demonstrated the value of having two examiners for each paper.

***

My poem *Student Unrest* was published in *Critical Quarterly* in 1970, and reprinted in my volume *The Man I Killed* ten years later:

> Good morning, ladies and gentlemen, students, children,
> Guitar-players, dogs, and — surely I'm not mistaken? —
> Giraffes.
> Our subject today is tenses: a difficult topic.
> The English tenses, as you have doubtless noticed,
> Have never really accommodated themselves
> To either convenience, reason,
> Or class interests. Never.
>
> I am beginning. I usually begin
> At the beginning. In five minutes
> I will (shall) have begun. The beginning
> Will have ended. But the end
> Will not yet have begun. Not yet.
>
> I beg your pardon? The end has begun? What end?
> There are ends and ends; and the end of my lecture
> Has not yet begun, and nothing has ended. I hope
> You are paying attention. I hope
> That you always pay attention. I hope
> That you paid attention last time. If you have paid —
>
> Yes, paid. Paid. Does that express
> An ideology? Yes.
> I mean, No. I mean, What? Explain what you mean.
> 'Paid' is the usual word, and this is English.
> And now the beginning has ended —
>
> Now ladies and gentlemen, all of you,
> Those wearing ties and those wearing trousers,
> Those who are singing those exquisite four-letter words,
> Those taking notes, and the gentlemen playing football,
> I beg you to note this example:

If you had not done this
He would not have had to do that.
If you, for example, had paid attention —
All right, if you had lent attention: yes, lent,
Yes, with interest — NO! If you had given attention —
I take another example: if you had not fed the dogs
They would not have done *that*. If you controlled the giraffes
— PLEASE control the giraffes!

Now gentlemen — goal!
I mean, no goal — I mean, in my lecture!
No goals in my lectures. Example:
If the goalie hadn't been listening
The goal would not have been scored.
That's passive. The passive tomorrow.

Tomorrow? Well, so far tomorrow
Has always arrived. Intervention
Would surely be needed, quite drastic
Intervention be needed in order
To stop tomorrow from coming.
If tomorrow comes I shall lecture tomorrow. If not
Then I shall lecture
On what comes instead.

If the gentleman on the giraffe
(On the fourth spot from the shoulder)
If the gentleman isn't careful —
Ah: since the gentleman wasn't careful,
Since care was not taken (that's passive)
Goal!

I began at the beginning. The beginning is ended,
The end has begun. The end will soon be ending.
Perhaps I ought to mention to the couple
In the back row that I know of no other examples
Of children begotten in lectures
(No doubt he will turn out a scholar).

We have spoken of tenses: the past,
The expanded present, the perfect,
And the future perfect. The past

208

Has a certain desperate charm.
The present is always expanding,
(Would the giraffes bend down
As they pass through the door.) The lecture
Has more or less ended. The future
Is seldom perfect. Tomorrow
The passive will be considered,
The past will have been abolished,
The lecturer won't be present.

If I hadn't gone to Munich, I'd no doubt never have written this, or at any rate not in the same way. I'd have chosen a lecture on Shakespeare or on social biology, but the setting of the teaching of English grammar to foreigners was too tempting to neglect. I often used to read this poem at poetry readings, where it would go down very well, but later I gave up doing so. My friend Alan, principal of an Adult Education centre in Brighton, who was himself a student of the revolutionary generation, said to me once that he wished I would stop reading it. He found it offensive, and said I had stooped to easy sneers at the student revolutionaries. It was said more in sorrow than in anger, and didn't damage my warm feelings towards Alan, but it did make me decide not to read it any more. Suddenly I saw the poem from below, and the jokes took on quite a different feel. I give fewer readings nowadays, but I might one day use it again, and tell the audience about Alan's objections, to see how they now feel.

One ripple which it produced has remained unforgettable. In the early seventies I lectured in Dublin to a very large audience of schoolteachers: every English teacher in the city seemed to be there. In the chair was a nun, with the sharp wit that Irish nuns sometimes possess. 'I knew that Mr Lerner likes to have a giraffe in the audience,' she said, 'so I went along to the zoo and hired one. You don't realise just how bad the traffic is in Dublin till you've tried to get a giraffe through the city centre. Giraffes don't of course understand red lights, and there were one or two unfortunate incidents. So in the end I had to dismount, and sent him back to the zoo with Sister Angela, who I hope will get back in time to hear what I'm sure will be a fascinating lecture…'

Political Correctness

(i) in 1704

During the European war against the French, the allied forces were led by John Churchill, first Duke of Marlborough; through his famous victories, beginning with the battle of Blenheim in 1704, he acquired probably the greatest military reputation of any general in English history. Immediately after the battle, Joseph Addison published a poem to celebrate it, called *The Campaign,* filled with uplifting descriptions of England's hero defeating the haughty household troops of France. As befitted an eighteenth century poet, Addison wrote in heroic couplets, the normal metre at the time, and in poetic diction. Poetic diction in the 18th century meant that there were certain words and locutions you were not supposed to use because they were not dignified enough for poetry: you must say 'finny tribe' for 'fish', 'feathered choristers' for 'birds', and so on. Its purpose was of course not purely aesthetic but also social: by excluding even ordinary words on the grounds of vulgarity, it established that poetry was a gentleman's occupation. To the modern linguistic theorist, this would be an example of register: the choice between different words and expressions which have the same meaning on the grounds of their suitability to the social situation. 'Shit' and 'excrement' mean the same, and the choice between them is made according to who you are speaking to, and on what occasion.

Poetic diction was like an elegant game, and one can see both why it seemed such fun, and why poets and readers eventually grew tired of it. Though it was a reduction of language it was not a reduction of thought, because awareness of what is excluded was part of the effect: everyone knew that the usual word was 'fish', and if they paused they could hear it knocking at the gate of the poem as the finny tribe swam by. Such reductiveness can be very stimulating when it forces the act of excluding into our awareness. To define man as a featherless biped is to remind us of all the other ways we are not birds.

Addison's poem mentions Britannia's graceful sons in arms, the mighty schemes of godlike leaders, generous Britons meeting their doom, along with an angel that rides in the whirlwind and directs the storm, in language that glorifies and uplifts. It is full of praise for 'Marlborough's mighty soul' which

> Inspired repulsed battalions to engage,
> And taught the doubtful battle where to rage.

Its ringing phrases must have pleased the Duke, and certainly did Addison's career no harm.

ii) in 1852

Among the British soldiers in the battle was a colonel named Henry Esmond, a friend of Addison's who happened to call on him when he was writing the poem. He admired Addison's talent, but was not altogether satisfied with the way he described war. His description of the campaign is neither in heroic couplets nor in poetic diction, and is very different from Addison's:

> We found places garrisoned by invalids, and children and women: poor as they were, and as the costs of this miserable war had made them, our commission was to rob these almost starving wretches — to tear the food out of their granaries and strip them of their rags. 'Twas an expedition of rapine and murder we were sent on: our soldiers did deeds such as an honest man must blush to remember.

Esmond wanted to know why all this got left out of the poem. 'Why does the stately Muse of History,' he asked, 'that delights in describing the valour of heroes and the grandeur of conquest, leave out these scenes, so brutal, mean and degrading, that yet form by far the greater part of the drama of war?' Addison replied by describing the practice of earlier poets: the horrors take place offstage in Greek tragedy. His public, he insists, expects the great Duke to be painted 'not as a man, which he no doubt is, with weaknesses like the rest of us, but as a hero.' That is to say, the poet must follow literary conventions, and these depend on precedent; public taste governs poetry; and poetry must avoid the tediousness of long lists.

When Esmond asked what poet there is to sing the fate of the ordinary men, Addison replied 'with a smile' 'Would you celebrate them all?'

This conversation took place only in fiction. Henry Esmond, hero of Thackeray's historical novel of that name, never lived; and Thackeray was following a common practice in historical novels, when he made his hero the friend of someone who really did live. His novel sets out to make History pull off her periwig, and to show the ordinary man under the ceremonies of kingship, the realities of war under the flattering diction of heroic poetry; and though by twentieth century standards his frankness may seem rather limited, it does at least point to the horrors that the dignified language of *The Campaign* excludes completely.

The tediousness of long lists: Addison, in Thackeray's novel, ventures to criticise the divine Homer by suggesting that the catalogue of ships in the *Iliad* is 'somewhat wearisome', and adds 'what had the poem been, supposing the writer had chronicled the names of captains, lieutenants, rank and file?' Is this an aesthetic matter (it would bore the reader) or a political matter (ordinary people aren't worth chronicling)? Thackeray seems to be suggesting that the poetic conventions have a concealed political function. Neither he nor Addison lived to see the Vietnam memorial in Washington, which consists of nothing but a list of the names of the sixty thousand who were killed, with no embellishments, no epic similes, no leaders' grief swayed by generous pity, not even any leaders mentioned. Addison would no doubt have found such a list even more tedious than the catalogue of ships — not merely wearisome but actually unreadable. He would be right, of course, and the Vietnam monument does not profess to be a poem. But Addison's aesthetic has no place for the moving memorial that is not meant to be read, whose power lies in its very unreadability.

iii) in 1984

George Orwell's invention of Newspeak is probably the most influential account of the politicisation of language that our century has produced. Newspeak is a language whose purpose is the reduction of consciousness. The authorities in 1984 have

213

set out to eliminate from language — and so from thought — any possibilities that the authorities wish to suppress, so that 'a heretical thought — that is, a thought diverging from the principles of Ingsoc — should be literally unthinkable.' (Ingsoc — etymologically 'English socialism' — is the political system behind the tyranny of 1984). Newspeak is designed to express all the orthodox meanings of political terms, 'while excluding all other meanings and also the possibility of arriving at them by indirect methods. This was done partly by the invention of new words, and by stripping such words as remained of unorthodox meanings, and so far as possible of all secondary meanings whatever.' The first example given is 'free' which can be used to mean 'this field is free from weeds', but it cannot be used 'in its old sense of "politically free" or "intellectually free", since political and intellectual freedom no longer existed even as concepts, and were therefore of necessity nameless.'

If it is true, this theory is epoch-making; but it isn't true. What does it mean to say that a word 'could not be used' in a certain sense, or that a thought (like 'Big Brother is ungood') could not be sustained 'because the necessary words were not available'? Since the words Orwell mentions did exist earlier, they have become obsolete, and we can therefore begin from what we know about why words become obsolete. This can happen because the objects or ideas designated may themselves have become obsolete (landau, codpiece, prevenient grace: these words are still useful for talking about the past, but not otherwise — unless there are collectors of obsolete carriages, wearers of obsolete clothes, or Calvinists holding to 17th century theology, still extant, or because the word may have been replaced by another (as we say 'tip' for 'vail', or (now) 'gay' for 'queer'). This is not what Orwell had in mind: he meant that it is forbidden to utter the word, or to use it with a certain meaning (as French 'baiser' must be used with care by foreigners). All the terms in 'Big Brother is ungood' *are* in fact available in 1984, but to say it would get you into trouble. The obstacle to utterance is not a matter of language, but simply fear.

The central confusion in Orwell's theory of Newspeak is that it slides at crucial moments between forbidding the use of words by authority, and the much more interesting — but also much more questionable — idea that there could be linguistic means to restrict language. Once again, the concept of register is useful here. If you forbid a word or meaning in one context, you are altering its register: no respectable Englishman, before the mid-twentieth century, would say 'shit' in front of ladies, but this did not of course cause the word to die out; indeed, the strictness with which it was confined to certain registers (colloquial, male, aggressive) probably increased its vitality within those registers simply because it was excluded from more formal and respectable situations. Of course you can punish someone for using the wrong register, but that does not put it out of existence: indeed, unless it existed — and vigorously — in other contexts, there would be no need to forbid it. And of course there are always ways of implying the usages you are not allowed to use, irony being the most obvious.

The reason no one uses irony in *1984* is, quite simply, because they are frightened. Brecht's famous remark after the workers' rising in Berlin in 1953, that the government should dissolve the people and elect another, could have been formulated by Winston Smith, if he were witty enough, but he would not have dared to utter it: even the act of keeping a diary is dangerous. Brecht did not publish his ironic little poem either, through prudence or nervousness, but his fear was as nothing compared with the terror of the inhabitants of 1984. Winston's carefully concealed diary is dynamite, but not for linguistic reasons.

Both Esmond and Winston are being politically incorrect: that is, they are defying the convention of what can and cannot be said, and therefore risking trouble. Esmond's risk is minimal, Winston's is maximal: there are no thought police in 18th century England, and if there were they would not have put the infringement of register very high on their list of crimes, whereas Winston is never safe from observation, and, when observed, from punishment. The price can vary enormously, but where correctness is required, there will be a price to pay for infringement.

iv) today

In 1992 I gave a lecture at the University of Vienna. I sent them, as usual, a list of subjects, and they chose 'The Language of Politics'. This would have the advantage, they explained, of interesting both students of literature and students of language, and in fact I would be part of Prof de Nerval's course on linguistics. Inserting a visiting lecturer into an existing course is common practice in German universities, and given the tyranny of the timetable it makes good sense. This meant that I would have, in effect, two audiences: the regular attenders of the course on structural linguistics and modern English, and those who came along to hear me. It also meant I would be introduced twice: by Professor Bauer, who had invited me, and by Prof de Nerval, whose course it was.

Prof de Nerval's aristocratic French name derived from his being a Saarlander; but he had spent much of his career in America, and he spoke (and dressed) like an American of the 1968 generation. His introduction was brief and formal, leaving the hyperbole to Prof Bauer; but as we shall see in a moment, that did not mean that he intended to play a passive role.

I began with a discussion of George Orwell, who wrote an essay on 'Politics and the English Language', a hotch-potch of good-hearted exhortations that attacks abstraction, euphemism and cliché. Its most interesting moment comes when it refers to cliché-ridden political speaking as a situation in which the speaker 'may be almost unconscious of what he is saying, as one is when one utters the responses in church. And this reduced state of consciousness, if not indispensable, is at any rate favourable to political conformity.' This is the moment which most clearly anticipates Newspeak, which I then went on to describe, and as the students dutifully wrote my account in their notebooks I added my objection, that Orwell does not really show that language itself can reduce awareness, but shifts at crucial points to the more familiar view that saying certain things can get you into trouble. (When the lecturer announces that the view he has just expounded is full of fallacies, some students cross out what they have written, others add the objections, and no doubt some congratulate themselves that they didn't bother to write it down in the first place.) I then suggested that a more valuable theory of language is that which sees it as a system of opportunities. New words arise not only because new things appear and need to be named (aeroplane, computer) but also, and more interestingly, because we are constantly rearranging the complexities of meaning: this rearrangement both reflects and influences the way we arrange our thoughts. From this I moved to Empson, and contrasted Orwell's view with Empson's theory of complex words. A complex word, for Empson, is not a term like 'transcendental phenomenology' but one which we might normally think of as a very ordinary word. It is a word whose meaning includes important areas of our beliefs and values — roughly, a word which has a long entry in the Oxford Dictionary. 'A word may become a sort of solid entity, able to direct opinion, thought of as like a person; also it is often said (whether this is the same idea or not) that a word can become "compacted doctrine", or even that all words are compacted doctrine inherently.' The words Empson mainly discusses are *fool, dog, honest* and *sense.* Interesting uses of these words assert unexplained relations between two or more of their many meanings; and these relations he represents by equations. He does not deny that such uses affect our emotions, often very powerfully; but his theory is a rejection of the idea of emotive language, since the best (even the only) way to explore the emotional aspect is to study meaning. I explained that I preferred Empson's theory to Orwell's because it was a theory about the political dimensions of language based on a more perceptive understanding of how language operates.

I concluded my lecture with a discussion of political correctness. It is not possible to spend time on an American campus nowadays without encountering this movement, which can be described as an attempt to police the language, to forbid 'sexist' terminology and hate speech, and to punish people for insults. In my last years at Vanderbilt I used to receive a paper called *Heterodoxy,* which appeared unasked in my pigeon hole every month or two. It was filled with stories of the latest examples of politically correct intolerance, lengthy and detailed stories which, if true, were certainly disquieting: they told of universities in the intolerant grip of non-smoking pacifist feminist homosexual liberals, determined to stamp out the expression of opposing views. (In American terminology it is no longer a paradox to refer to liberals as intolerant, since 'liberal' now means more or less the opposite of what it used to mean to Gladstone and Mill). I did not regale the Viennese audience with the more lurid tales from this paper, but chose feminist language as my example, claiming that I was both sympathetic to the feminist dislike of patriarchal vocabulary, and more aware than most feminists seemed to me to be of the practical problems involved in trying to correct the language. The point I thought would appeal particularly to a German-speaking audience was the way feminist reformers tended to be monoglot, uninterested in whether the patriarchal speech they castigated was specific to English or common to all languages. An obvious example is the use of 'man' to mean 'human being' so that 'the story of mankind' can be a covert way of insisting that men did it all. There are plenty of reactionary jokes about this attempt to suppress the generalised use of 'man' (such as renaming the Isle of Person), but there are serious points to be made as well, one of which is of course that the situation is different in German, which has two different words for 'man not woman' (Mann) and 'man not animal' (Mensch). This means that German is free of this particular patriarchal locution, just as French is free of the awkward choice between 'his' and 'hers'. But there is no evidence, I claimed, that this has made German and French society any less sexist than Anglo-Saxon society; from which I concluded that though sexist language might be distressing to some people in itself, there is no evidence that it causes or even strengthens patriarchy as a system of power. (I did not then know that there have been attempts to cleanse spoken German of the use of 'man' (meaning 'one', but far more commonly used than the English pronoun), replacing it with 'man und frau' or — ingeniously — 'fra', dropping the final letter as in 'man'. I have never heard anyone say 'fra sagt das nicht', and I don't know how many Germans would understand it.)

Prof de Nerval did not like my lecture. Indeed, that is an understatement. As soon as it was over he leapt to his feet and began a counter-lecture. It was clear that the political gap between us was immense, and he delivered an impassioned radical critique of bourgeois, patriarchal society and its oppressive practices. There was, I suppose, an irony in being rebuked by a professor of linguistics in terms that contained even less in the way of linguistic concepts than my modest amateurism had run to. His main point was that so called political correctness was, in the larger social context, not at all correct, so that the believers in it are not time-servers but dissenters. This is certainly true: American society as a whole has never incorporated the clichés of egalitarianism, multi-culturalism and minority rights into its conception of proper speech, and in the 1990s less so than ever. Every time I opened my copy of *Heterodoxy* I marvelled that a conservative newspaper should use that title: clearly it saw the universities, with their 'liberal' orthodoxy, as centres of opposition to the more sane and acceptable orthodoxy of society as a whole. I had been careful to say this in the lecture, but Prof de Nerval, scenting a political enemy, did not pause to admit that I had already made his point.

He must have spoken for ten or fifteen minutes, and showed no obvious sign of sitting down, inviting me to reply, or inviting the audience to join in; so I seized a momentary pause to stand up and reply to him. I then invited the audience to comment, or to make fresh points, which some did, and the occasion concluded more or less as planned, with a vote of thanks by Professor Bauer.

Two years later I spent a semester as visiting Professor at Vienna. I found that this lecture had stuck in the minds of my colleagues, and several of them offered vicarious apologies, explaining that they had been embarrassed by Nerval's discourtesy, as they saw it. I insisted that I had not minded, and was well able to defend myself; but when I suggested to one colleague that I should seek out Nerval to say hello and invite him to continue the discussion, he shuddered in horror, and urged me not to. In fact, I never exchanged a word with him during the whole of my stay (it is not difficult, in a German or Austrian university, for colleagues to ignore one another): my impulse to seek out those I disagree with and engage in discussion with them was clearly not shared by Nerval. But in an interestingly indirect way our paths did cross.

I had been asked to lecture on literary theory. I explained that I did not like discussions of literature that remain on an abstract level, that I believed generalisations only take on meaning when applied to actual examples, and that when lecturing to students on theory one never knew whether they were familiar with the examples chosen and thus able to listen critically. I was aware that this is an unfashionable view in these days of literary theory, but I stuck to it, and therefore proposed a course of lectures called 'Critical Interpretations of Literature', in which I would choose a small number of primary texts, would insist on the students reading them, and indeed would begin by lecturing about them before going on to expound and compare what different critical schools made of them. My texts were Donne's love poems, Shakespeare's sonnets, *Jane Eyre* and *King Lear.* I began the course with an overview of what I saw as the main theoretical positions from which literary criticism could be written, then I moved to the texts, and in each case gave a lecture on the literary text itself before I moved to discuss the critical approaches, usually for two or three lectures. I tried to represent as many critical schools as I could: inevitably, since it was 1994, feminism loomed large, and I included a number of recent female critics struggling with the politically incorrect attitudes to women in Donne's lyrics. Slightly mischievously, I said that if anyone wanted to come to the 'primary' lectures but miss those on the criticism, that would be all right with me, but I asked them not to do the opposite.

I did not know that Prof de Nerval was also lecturing that semester on Literary Theory, a fact which I learnt from Heinz. Heinz (as I shall call him) also attended the small informal class on creative writing that I had been asked to run in addition to my more academic activities, and I therefore got to know him well. He was an admirer of Prof de Nerval, and a keen reader of literary theory, as well as being the students' representative on the committee that ran the department. Not only did Heinz go to both these lecture courses, he wrote a review of them in the student newspaper, *Arglistik* (the wordplay is untranslateable, but the flavour of the paper can be gauged from its cover message, 'Beat AIDS. Use a condom').

Heinz's article (which incidentally used 'man/frau' instead of 'man') began with praise of my lecturing style and sympathetic manner, but complained that the lectures were in several ways unsatisfactory. He had liked the introductory survey of theoretical positions, but objected to having a whole lecture devoted to the reading of five or six poems by Donne. This example of 'conventional, text-immanent' criticism was an activity which all students were — or should be — familiar with. He had criticisms, too, of my discussions of the critics, because they often seemed based on the idea that the critic was the servant of the poem, and should be judged by what he tells us about its meaning; Prof de Nerval, in contrast, saw literary theory as the expression of a social discourse, and set out to reveal the ideological purpose and epistemological assumptions of such discourse. Heinz recognised that this made his lectures difficult, but congratulated him on following this 'revolutionary procedure'.

I decided to respond to Heinz's article in two ways. First, I wrote a reply, saying among other things that I had devoted a lecture to the Donne poems not in order to illustrate formalist or text-immanent critical method, but in order to make sure that everyone was familiar with the poems themselves, and would therefore be in a position to respond critically to the ensuing lectures on the critics. I gave the reply to Heinz, who said he would be glad to publish it, but that the next issue of *Arglistik* would not appear until the following semester. Second, I asked him if he would like to make some of his criticisms orally during my next lecture, so that we could hear the views of other students, and, with luck, unleash a profitable discussion. He said he would be glad to do this, but added that he was now much less critical of the lectures. He had liked the most recent lecture much better than the others, but it had been too late to modify the article. To my surprise I found myself offended by this remark in a way I had not been by the review itself; the reason, I decided when I thought about it, was that it made him more like an examiner than a critic, and assumed that the aim of my lectures was not to do justice to the subject but to satisfy him.

I discussed it all with my colleague Prof Bauer, who had shown me the review in the first place. He was very anxious that I should write a reply, and told me that if the paper did not publish it he would rebuke them publicly, saying they were not interested in dialogue. He also urged me not to give Heinz a platform without the consent of the other students. So I began the next lecture by saying that no doubt some of them had seen the review of the lecture course in *Arglistik,* and that I had invited Heinz to give a short talk in which he made his criticisms clear, in the hope that this would then lead to a useful discussion. But I don't want to do this, I said, without your consent. How many of you would like it? Nobody's hand went up. I paused, to make sure, and there was an embarrassed giggle, but still no hands went up. Well, I said, it looks as if there'll be no discussion, and I went on with the lecture.

What had I learnt? That Viennese students are naturally deferential, that they want to listen to their professor without being distracted by student comments? Perhaps; but walking back after the lecture I fell into conversation with Christopher, perhaps the liveliest and most intelligent of my students, and we discussed what had happened. 'None of us agrees with Heinz,' he said. 'In fact,' he added, 'that lecture on Donne's poems which he objected to was the one we all liked best.' Donne speaks to his mistress, in one of his elegies, about

> that remorse
> Which my words masculine persuasive force
> Begot in thee.

Politically correct, in the patriarchal society of the 1590s; highly incorrect in academic discourse today, but Christopher did not mind.

The Revolution in English Studies

May you live in interesting times, runs the old curse. Professors of English do, at the moment; and the older ones ask themselves whether they were happier two generations ago, when all was (or seems in retrospect to have been) calm in the academy, and the study of literature did not lead, so quickly and so inevitably, to political and ideological clashes. Of course the clashes have built-in damage limitation: academic politics have the advantage over ordinary politics that what is at stake is only ideas. Only? *Only* ideas? Ideas, in the long run, surely, are what really change the world. If Shelley was right, and the poets are the unacknowledged legislators of the world, if Michel Foucault and his followers are right, and discourse is the way in which power is exercised, and changes in discursive systems bring about many of the more obvious changes that historians notice, then the unofficial assembly of words over which poets and professors preside, with no powers and no bureaucracy to enforce their decrees, might turn out in the end to have wielded the real power.

The debates in that assembly may destroy reputations, cause misery, deprive people of jobs, but they do not kill or maim. The paradigm shift through which literary studies are now passing has the attraction of vigorous intellectual debate, and the damage it can do to your life, though real, is limited, or at any rate distant. If the price of living through such an interesting period is, at the worst, anger and unemployment, it may be worth paying. What has actually happened to the study of literature in the last 25 years? Literature is being destroyed, say some: we have awoken from our dogmatic slumbers, say others. We need, perhaps, to try and see it through the eyes of the young, so let's invent a graduate student, and call her Jane. The first thing Jane meets in graduate school is a dragon called Literary Theory, and the thought of riding it fills her with exhilaration: she is the new generation, and here are the new ideas. So she signs up for all available courses on literary theory, or those taught by those she perceives to be radicals. But what exhilarates some may distress others, so we need another graduate student, whom we'll call John. What brought John to graduate school was his love of literature, and now he has to watch it being destroyed, as he is told that the very concept of literature is suspect because it conceals ('occludes' is the jargon term) what are really ideological questions, that his task as a literary critics is not to love poems but to subvert and interrogate them.

Paul Ricoeur can provide us with a useful phrase here: 'the hermeneutics of suspicion'. In the old days, critics and teachers of English saw themselves as the handmaids of literature, helping their students and readers to appreciate the masterpieces they were proud to serve. Looking back on that image in the 1990s, we cannot fail to notice the gender: these professors were almost all men, but they had no objections to being (metaphorical) maidservants. Was this because they were so imperceptive they didn't notice what they were saying? Or because they were so lofty they didn't care, so confident of their status that they could despise mere metaphor? Jane has no intention of regarding herself as a handmaid, and looking round her she does not see any of her female professors using the term. They may still love literature (though their enemies doubt if they do); but in their professional role, they now feel called on to be suspicious of it.

The new style literary critic looks at the literary text no longer with deference, but with power. No longer to spell out lovingly its intrinsic beauties, but to tell us what the text can't or does not dare to say. Jane and John have little doubt there is a revolution going on, and they argue endlessly about it. Jane christens her opponents the traddies, and John christens her friends the trendies. As they look round they see quarrels everywhere, colleagues accusing each other of plotting and malpractice, appointments decided less on merit than on ideological adherence. Literary criticism has been invaded. In fact it has been invaded twice, from philosophy and from politics.

The Philosophic Invasion

First, structuralism. The snap definition of structuralism is that it treats any area of human behaviour like a language.

From Saussure we have learned that a language is a system of differences, not a set of positive terms: it does not correspond in a simple one-to-one fashion with a world that exists independently of it, as the philosophers of Laputa believed: it is more like a way of shaping our awareness of reality.

*Jane:*Take the two pairs of terms river/stream in English, fleuve/rivière in French. The difference between the first pair depends on size, between the second on whether it flows into the sea or into another river: thus the Missouri is a river in English, but is not a fleuve in French. This simple example shows that it is not enough to be acquainted with the physical world in order to describe it correctly: it is also necessary to be familiar with the system of differentiation you are using. 'River' is a linguistic concept, not part of the physical world.

John: Does this mean that the Missouri has a purely linguistic existence?

Jane: No, it means that Geography is a discourse. It means that we have no access to the physical world except through language.

John: No. You must say that we have no access to *studying* the physical world except through language. We can always kick the stone, like Dr Johnson, or jump in the river — as I'd like some professors to do.

L: This particular example is one of which English and French speakers are (or can easily become) conscious. But languages have deep structures, which their speakers use correctly though they are quite unable to formulate them. Linguistics is not a way of learning foreign languages, it is the attempt to discover and formulate these structures;

Jane: and similarly, the project of literary structuralism is not to help us understand particular poems, but to formulate the deep structures of literary systems, or — as Roland Barthes claimed — not to interpret texts, but to study the conditions under which texts mean.

John: What about all those old fashioned literary critics, who were interested in rhyme schemes, figures of speech or dramatic conventions. Weren't they studying the conditions under which poems mean?

Jane: The difference is that the conventions and devices they looked at were consciously used by the writers. The deep structures of the new poetics, which Barthes called codes, are stated in far more abstract terms, and have greater autonomy: they control the writer as much as he controls them.

John: Codes. I don't think we should call these conventions 'codes'. Once a convention has been understood — once we know that a sonnet has 14 lines with a particular rhyme scheme, or that disguise on the Elizabethan stage is supposed to be impenetrable — it does not lose its validity or its interest; but to speak of codes suggests that once the message has been deciphered it is no longer needed. It looks like a claim that successful criticism renders the literary work somehow superfluous.

Deconstruction

L: Instead of dwelling on that alarming suggestion, let's move on to deconstruction. Structuralism has been around for some time now, and Jane soon takes the next step, into deconstruction, a theory based on the radical instability of language, on the endless deferral of that longed for moment when we shall at last break free of linguistic play and find ourselves in direct contact with reality.

Jane: Deconstruction sets out to cure of us of this longing, which it calls logocentrism, by showing that it is impossible to break out of *différance*: there is no such thing as extra-textual reality. And so in one way, for the deconstructionist, poetry is the most valuable kind of language there is, because it shows awareness of our imprisonment by textuality. Literary texts refuse any definitive interpretation: their rhetorical strategies are ways of showing that the message they ostensibly offer cannot really be stated.

John: So the reason poetry is valuable to you is not because there are particular poems that you value, it is a theoretical reason, that poetry offers us a theory of language that appeals to the deconstructionist.

Jane Correct. The deconstructionist critic is like a poet: he is constantly on the hunt for the aporia, or undecidable moment, in each text.

John: Well some poets may be. Wallace Stevens is, I suppose, or Mallarmé. The poets I like are on the hunt for ways of expressing their feelings.

L: And so if we ask each for his or her definition of poetry, John will perhaps get his from Matthew Arnold:

John: The best that has been thought and said in the world,

L: and Jane from Roman Jakobson:

Jane: The projection of the principle of equivalence from the axis of selection into the axis of combination.

John: Well that's hardly a definition that would cause Keats or Milton to catch his breath in delighted recognition.

Jane: You wouldn't expect me to care much about that, would you? Keats and Milton were fine fellows but they weren't literary theorists.

L: I called this the invasion of literature by philosophy, but in theory it is just the opposite.

Jane: Since literature is the form of writing that admits its own rhetorical basis and the instability of all meaning, deconstructive philosophy needs to take on the status of literature in order to escape its logocentric delusions.

John: I suppose I should be pleased to hear that. But it does not mean, does it, that the philosophers must study Keats or Stendhal, it means they must study Derrida and De Man. It is the *idea* of literature, as offering only aporias and misreadings, that has so much to teach the philosophers — an idea that emerges not from the poets themselves but from the new literary theories.

The Lover's Gift

L: So the dragon is empowered. John has realised this, and he turns up one day with a copy of Congreve's comedy, *The Way of the World,* written in 1700.

John: Jane I've got something to show you; read this.

Jane: (reads) 'Nay, 'tis true: you are no longer handsome when you've lost your lover; your beauty dies upon the instant: for beauty is the lover's gift; 'tis he bestows your charms — your glass is all a cheat. The ugly and the old, whom the looking-glass mortifies, yet after commendation can be flattered by it, and discover beauties in it: for that reflects our praises rather than your face.'

Well, I haven't been reading many Restoration comedies lately, but that's certainly a very intelligent one.

John: Now we'll have Millamant's reply.
(reads) 'O the vanity of these men! If they did not commend us, we were not handsome. Now you must know they could not commend one, if one was not handsome. Beauty the lover's gift! Lord, what is a lover, that it can give? Why, one makes lovers as fast as one pleases, and they live as long as one pleases, and they die as soon as one pleases: and then if one pleases one makes more.'

O, the vanity of these critics. If they did not commend our poems, they were not poetry! Now you must know, they could not commend them, if they were not poetry.

Jane: I see the point. Mirabell is the critic, Millamant is the poet, and of course I think Mirabell is quite right: if there was no sexual attraction, and consequently no lovers, there would be no concept of beauty; if there were no readers who like to be shown how rhetorical strategies defeat themselves, there would be no literature. Poems do not exist until we have a concept of poetry, so criticism has priority.

John: Well, of course I think Millamant is right. Reading is a process of responding to a text, beauty is a process of responding to a face, and the reader did not write the text and the lover did not make the face. If the face and the text did not exist first, then the statement 'Millamant is beautiful' or '*Adonais* is a fine poem' would be meaningless: so the Millamant-poet is obviously right.

L: If both are right, then we need a philosopher to sort things out — but philosophers, so expert at analysing such disputes, never settle them, and perhaps both Millamant and Mirabell would be disappointed if they did.

Now John predicts that Jane will grow tired of being a dragon. Her hot deconstructive breath always seems to have the same effect on the texts she breathes on.

John: Surely you must notice, Jane, that if literature is the form of writing that is aware of its own rhetorical structure and the impossibility of successful communication, then the critic always knows what to look for. When Paul De Man has shown that poem after poem drops us into the void of incommunicability, when Hillis Miller has shown that novel after novel is about the untrustworthiness of the narrator and the misfit between rhetoric and reality, we begin to wonder if there is only one subject for literature, if we can always know what a poem is about, even before we start to read it.

Politics

But at this point Jane begins to turn from philosophy to politics, and she has a new kind of fire in her mouth. Her presiding spirit is no longer Derrida, but Foucault, and her main concern is with the way writing is an expression of power. Now she reads the literary canon conscious of who wrote it, and who was silenced by it, and demands to hear the voices of the poor and the slaves, outcast races and women — especially women.

Jane: Most of our apparently disinterested activities — the search for knowledge, the attempt to give organic unity to a poem — are shot through with claims to power. Take, for instance, all those Victorian novels about industrial England which depict class conflict and strikes, and end on a plea for brotherhood and co-operation. That plea is not disinterested, for the doctrine of harmony of interest between classes was itself a bourgeois doctrine, its function being to avert proletarian revolution.

(This comment seems to owe more to Marx than to Foucault, but it is no longer easy to distinguish the Marxists from the Foucauldians, since the central Marxist concept of class has now been modified, as depending too simplistically on a crude materialist analysis. There is no longer one ruling class and one disempowered proletariat, there is a complex set of interacting discourses, all of them imbued with claims to power.)

John: Now I must ask you whether this claim that writing is not as disinterested as it seems applies to you and me. Are you mainly concerned to show that George Eliot and Thackeray are apologists for the status quo, or that their interpreters — you and me, especially me — are also wicked reactionaries?

Jane: Well I don't go round accusing people of wickedness: that's a moralising terminology that we're better without. But of course the critic is complicit. In some ways it is the critic who concerns us more than the original author, since he is interfering in *our* cultural situation. Shakespeare exists in our society through the Shakespeare industry, so of course we need to examine that.

John: But the more we look at the Shakespeare industry — the more we look at ourselves and our colleagues — the less we look at Shakespeare. We are splendid people, you and I and our colleagues, but we're not as interesting — or as important — as Shakespeare.

Jane: But what do you mean by 'Shakespeare'? You seem to believe that he is some kind of absolute signified, that his plays exist independent of the reader, or the audience.

John: Not independent, but not altogether dependent either. If you think of all the men who've told us about their experience of Shakespeare, then they've all got something in common. That common element is independent of the individual men with their personal responses.

Jane: All the men. It had to come out, didn't it? The common reader you set such store by is a male reader. Reading books by males.

John: I know — dead white males. As you say, that had to come.

Feminist Criticism

There are a lot of reasons why feminism is turning out to be the most important of the new critical schools. First we can look at what's happened to the academic world.

Vanderbilt University in the sixties had an all-male English department, and those in charge were determined to keep it that way; when I arrived there in 1985, there was one tenured woman and four women in probationary or temporary posts, out of a department of about 25; now nearly half the department is female, including two holders of distinguished chairs. Multiply this by the number of universities: there are thousands of women teaching English literature, and of course they are aware that their presence is something new. How can we fail to believe, asks Jane, that it will influence the way we read?

John: But that's not what really matters, is it? The reason feminism is important in literary criticism is that novels and plays are full of female characters.

Jane: But feminism is just as important for studying male characters. Gender is important because so much of our experience is traditionally seen in terms of the masculine-feminine dichotomy. The commonest subject for poetry has been love between the sexes. If feminism teaches us to reassess the way we look at gender it will teach us to reassess the way we look at love, the way we look at all experience.

John: So how does feminism change the way we look at literature?

Jane: Let's start from the simplest and most basic point. The books we ask our students to read have traditionally all been by men, the anthologies are filled with poems by men. Since the women have been silenced for so long, we need to make amends. Revising the canon is the necessary starting point for feminist criticism.

John: But that will soon get monotonous. If every book by a man elicits the comment, Well, that's what you'd expect men to say; if every book by a woman has to be dug up and studied just because it's by a woman, we're once more only looking for one thing. It's like the kind of history which tells us that there's just been one long story, of male supremacy and female oppression.

Jane: And hasn't there?

John: Yes of course, but once you've said that a few times you can't go on saying it for ever. Affirmative action is all very well

in the practical world, but it makes for very monotonous arguments. I don't mind you telling us to read lots of George Eliot
and Emily Dickinson, Virginia Woolf and Madame de la
Fayette, as long as you're not telling us to stop reading Milton
and Dickens and Lawrence.

Jane: Well, Milton, that's going a bit far: 'He for God only, she
for God in him'. But OK, you can indulge yourself in all that
rolling blank verse if you insist. For me it's a kind of frivolity, in
a world where so much is wrong.

John: Putting the world right, and trying to understand literature: they are quite different enterprises, and you deceive
yourself if you think one is a way of doing the other. There are
more interesting questions for literary critics than who should
or shouldn't be on the syllabus, counting the number of men
and the number of women. We ought to be asking whether
women really do write differently from men. There are too
many feminist critics who just assume they do, and who try to
settle the matter by only reading women.

Jane: Well of course there are plenty of feminist critics who've
asked your question, and have come up with sophisticated
answers. We've passed the days of what you call affirmative
action feminist criticism. There's Elaine Showalter, who claims
women have had a literature of their own, and Julia Kristeva,
with her theory of *écriture féminine.* These are not hysterical
females, they're among the subtlest critics now writing.

John: Ecriture féminine, I've read about that. It seems to be a
claim that women are more ready to disintegrate the conventional structures of language, are more ready to dislocate
language, to musicalise it, in order to capture the normally inarticulate bodily experiences through which the world can be
feminised.

Jane: Not bad: I see you've done your homework. And isn't this
a view of language that matters — and that will surely appeal
to what you like to call the literary mind?

John: Of course it is, but it's one we know about already. You
know where I got those crucial terms, *dislocate. musicalise,*
don't you: from Eliot and from Valéry. What I've been describ-

ing is modernism; and modernism isn't a movement only or even mainly by women: Mallarmé and Rimbaud, Brecht and Trakl, Eliot and Stevens — I'm afraid most of the great modernists were men.

Jane: And who's counting heads now?

John: Touché. Let's agree to stop counting, and turn our attention to the concepts of masculinity and feminity. What do they mean? Do all feminists mean the same by them? Do they really correspond to the differences between men and women?

Jane: Yes, but only as long as you don't treat it as an idle academic speculation. You have to remember that these concepts are about power: masculine is empowered, feminine is weak, that has always been the basis. The stamp of patriarchy has been pressed onto all our experience, often in ways we don't notice. Look at love poetry: it idealises women to keep them from having any real independence.

John: I presume you don't want any more love poems telling you that you're a goddess, comparing you to the Virgin Mary, worshipping you from afar. They might come from Jonas Chuzzlewit.

Jane: Oh dear, another clever literary reference.

John: Well, Jonas allows Pecksniff's daughter, when he's courting her, to indulge in the female privilege of holding herself aloof and being temperamental. And why? 'Ecod my lady, you'll catch it for this when you are married... Make the most of it while it lasts. Get your hay in while the sun shines. Take your own way as long as it's in your power, my lady.'

Jane: Well I think I prefer that to all the flattery. If Jonas is a bully, at least he admits it. He's quite a literary critic, in his crude way. He's showing us that the idealisations of love poetry come out of patriarchal society, that the woman is idealised in a situation where she is really powerless, that the conventions of worship emerge from a very different power-structure from the one they proffer.

John: He's not a literary critic, he's a literary theorist. He can't tell a good poem from a bad, and he's not interested in that difference. As I fear, Jane, you aren't either.

Jane: It's all very well to keep saying that some poems arc better than others. What you keep dodging is the fact that your Jonas Chuzzlewit principle applies to them all, good and bad alike.

John: Well I'm touched that you're willing to take on the repulsive Jonas as an ally: it's often the villains who provide us with the insights. But perhaps you'd like someone more presentable — like Jane Eyre. She's the right sex at least.

Jane is used to John's habit of providing her with allies from literature itself, and has learnt to tolerate, even to enjoy it. So she waits for him to explain.

John: Jane Eyre didn't want Rochester to woo her in the vocabulary of the Minnegrotte, the cave of love of the medieval poets. 'I never can bear being dressed like a doll by Mr Rochester, or sitting like a second Danae with the golden shower falling daily round me.' Her rejection of the literary conventions of love is a way of asserting her independence, of treating love as a way of genuinely escaping from the embedded power relations of patriarchy.

Jane: But you can't escape them. Not so easily.

John: Well I suppose you think you've escaped them, don't you?

Jane: That's cheap, John. You know what I mean: you can't escape them when there's no feminist consciousness.

John: Jane, sometimes I think you don't realise how strong are the allies you have among all the writers who weren't feminists. Of course there have always been ways of escaping: one of them is love.

Jane: Love. It's one of your favourite words, but you're never really clear what you mean by it.

John: Well, I'll give you a definition. Love is a relationship in which there is no element of power.

Jane: That's sentimental. You like to think we can just shed power relations because we're happy. They're not so easy to get rid of.

John: I've never thought it's easy. I'm not sure there's ever been a perfect love relationship, though some poetry at least gives us a blueprint. But if there was one, that's what I think it would be like. That's why Jane could stand up to Rochester by refusing to be absorbed into the literary tradition he was trying to drag her into. Charlotte Brontë was quite a literary critic, in her way: she had looked at the tradition with her eyes open.

Jane: The trouble with you, John, is that you think you can make up your own feminist criticism — and you make it up to suit you. You ought to start from the feminist criticism that there actually is. You're always telling me about Congreve and Dickens to show that I haven't read enough literature, so I'll tell you about the feminists to show you haven't read enough criticism. For instance, Nina Auerbach's book on *Communities of Women.* According to Auerbach, if you compare the way in which all-male and all-female communities have been represented in fiction, you find that the bands of brothers are complete and satisfying, 'symbolised by uniforms, rituals and fiercely shared loyalties', whereas sisterhoods tend to be seen as mutilated. Brotherhoods are often engaged in a quest, whereas the women tend to be rooted in one place. Yet at the same time, perhaps despite the opinions of the author, the depiction of the community of women — especially if the author is a woman — tends to show us positive elements: it is 'a rebuke to the conventional ideal of a solitary woman living for and through men, attaining citizenship in the community of adulthood through male approval alone.'

Take as example Elizabeth Gaskell's *Cranford.* This rural idyll used to be the most popular of her novels, much loved for its delightful picture of an English country town, protected from industrialism and progress, and for its heroine, the harmless, sweet-tempered old maid, who receives the tribute of the book's last, sentimental sentence: 'We all love Miss Matty, and I somehow think we are all of us better when she is near us.' Auerbach sets out to 'redeem' *Cranford* 'from familiar critical assumptions about women without men.' Surely this is preferable to the generations of male condescension which described the book's episodes as 'strung together with easy grace, like a wreath of flowers and ivy-leaves.' Auerbach has read the novel with far more intelligence and insight than any of the patronising male professors who professed to love it so: which of them would ever have thought of putting together the description of Miss Matty trying to protect her carpet from sunlight by putting down newspapers ('and lo! in a quarter of an hour the sun had moved, and was blazing away on a fresh spot; and down again we went on our knees to alter the position of the newspapers') with Miss Matty's remark that she 'never could believe that the earth was moving constantly...it made her feel so tired and dizzy whenever she thought about it', to conclude that 'a world in motion is a world Cranford denies', and then comparing that to the mad astronomer in Dr Johnson's *Rasselas* to conclude 'Cranford would have been defined by Deborah's beloved Dr Johnson as insane.'

John is impressed, and takes the book home to read. The next day he is back. A little reluctantly, he agrees that Auerbach (he has the tact not to refer to her as Nina Auerbach, let alone Miss Auerbach) reads with a probing intelligence that is absent from the male traddies.

Jane: But that's not enough. What matters is not just whether Auerbach is a good critic by your standards, but the fact that she is able to achieve her insights because of the feminist intelligence that is now available to us.

John: Well, yes. Or rather yes and no. (He smiles, to ward off Jane's remark that he loves saying 'Yes and no'.) There are qualifications to add. In the first place, the patronising or sentimental critics now consigned to the shelf of history were not all men; there is no reason to think that Victorian women read *Cranford* any differently from their husbands. Even the great George Eliot, praising the book, used the now suspect word 'charm'.

Jane: But of course those were women in a patriarchal society.

John: As of course most women have been. But I want to say something else, something that may shock you. (Jane smiles, to show that she is not easily shocked). I'm not sure that all this probing intelligence is an unmixed blessing; intelligence likes to score points over judgement, so that although we now have more perceptive critics we also have more who are luridly absurd.

Jane: And are you claiming you found absurdities in Auerbach's book?

John: Well, only one: that was the comparison between Miss Matty and Jael. That was her bit of bra burning: to show that she didn't find the book charming, she had to have one really militant touch. But actually, in the end, I thought she wasn't suspicious enough; she grants to the community of women more durability than Gaskell herself did. The novel begins with the famous sentence: 'In the first place, Cranford is in possession of the Amazons; all the holders of houses above a certain rent are women.' Of course this is an ironic remark: the women of Cranford are not Amazons, and they're not really in charge of their lives. Every now and then a man appears, a marriage takes place, and we're made to realise that no society can keep going without men and marriage. At crucial moments, Auerbach forgets the irony: she speaks about the *triumph* of Cranford, or about its *durability* as a community. At such moments, she is more Victorian than I am, and less shrewd than Elizabeth Gaskell.

Jane: It doesn't matter how good the feminist critic is, you have to find something to object to. You couldn't bear just to say how good she is.

John: Well that's obviously true, but where did I get it? How many feminist critics are content to say of their male predecessors, See how good he is, and leave it at that? I suppose I'm reacting to that. That's what happens when there are two sides, fighting each other.

Jane: The question is, has there really been a paradigm shift in criticism? Of course I believe there has: we notice things that people didn't use to notice. It doesn't matter how good a reader you were, before things were opened up there were connections you just didn't see — or wouldn't see.

John: The question for me is, are they things which the novelists didn't see? Let's have a final example, and let me turn again to the literature directly.

When Tom Tulliver catches his sister Maggie in her secret meetings with Philip Wakem in the Red Deeps, he behaves in a strongly masculine manner. Philip is the son of lawyer Wakem, whom their father hates, and regards as responsible for his ruin, and Tom insists that his sister break off all relations with him; he accuses the sensitive, deformed Philip of underhand conduct, and compels Maggie to stand by and listen while he refers to Philip's 'crooked notion of honour' and his 'puny miserable body': 'I'll thrash you — I'll hold you up to public scorn. Who wouldn't laugh at the idea of *your* turning lover to a fine girl.' The situation is complicated: Maggie is not in love with Philip but values his friendship; she feels some guilt because she has concealed the meetings (in order not to hurt her father), and she is moved to genuine admiration when Tom tells her — as part of his reproach — that he has now saved enough money to pay off the family debt. So she agrees not to see Philip again without Tom's knowledge, but tells him, 'But yet, sometimes, when I have done wrong, it has been because I have feelings that you would be the better for, if you had them.' This draws his scorn: 'Pray, how have you shown your love, that you talk of…by disobeying and deceiving us. I have a different way of showing my affection.'

'Because you are a man, Tom, and have power, and can do something in the world.'

Jane: Hooray — you've got there! It took you a long time, but you have found a crucial remark in one of your beloved Victorians. The novel has put its head above water, and offered a sudden clear-sighted awareness of the nature of patriarchy. It shows us that patriarchy is not the order of nature, that in a different (and possible) society, women too could do something in the world. Maggie could have received the classical education that Tom was so unsuited to, and that she would have appreciated. If she'd had a profession she could have saved money to pay her father's debts. That's what *The Mill on the Floss* is about, in the end. For the traddies, it's about personal relations, the love and the clash between brother and sister — something nice and timeless. They don't want it tainted by what they see as abstractions. But these abstractions of social analysis are the world that the characters live in. We can't pretend they aren't there.

John: Do you expect her to say these things — in the novel?

Jane: Well, it came out in 1859, and in 1859 there were people who said them — men and women.

John: The question for me is whether you want the novel to be different, whether you want Maggie to go on and talk like John Stuart Mill, whether you think that what we're seeing here is fresh evidence of the silencing of female consciousness.

Jane: But it wasn't silenced. Maggie's remark is there, in the book.

John: Yes, and it's a wonderful moment, that's why I brought it up. Now we have three possible critical positions. We have the traddie, as you call him, who wishes the remark wasn't there, it's a distraction from the emotional situation. He's waiting for the great orgasmic climax, when the brother and sister are united in death, and the social issues can be forgotten. Then we have the crude feminist who insists that Maggie must go on and say that she should have been allowed to become a doctor, or a professor, or whatever, and patriarchal society prevents her from doing so. I want you to say that's silly.

Jane: And in between? Of course you want an in between, you always do.

John: In between we have the position that it's a wonderful moment of insight, but the novel would be ruined if politics was then thrust into it, and Maggie went on to set forth a programme that a girl like her, at the beginning of the 19th century, could never have thought up. If you'd suggested that to George Eliot she'd have been appalled, it would have ruined her novel.

Jane: I guess I'm willing to accept that what we've got is the right way to do it, though I'm not as horrified as you are by what you melodramatically call the sacrifice of art to politics. What I want you to say is that without feminism you'd never have picked out that remark, you'd never have realised it's a crucial moment in the novel.

John: Labels. Who cares about labels.

This is as near as they will come to agreement, but perhaps it is nearer than either of them admits; when they look scrupulously enough at an actual literary text, their theoretical differences can meet in the middle. But there is one last point. What is the connection between the two invasions of criticism which we have looked at, that by philosophy and that by politics? Are they natural allies?

Jane thinks they are: one form of radicalism leads to another.

John: That's all very well if we're talking about radical temperaments. Trendy in one thing, trendy in everything. But I'm asking about the logic of the positions. I don't see that deconstruction, really, has anything to do with feminism.

Jane: Deconstruction gives us a kind of negative power; it enables us to reveal the blatant contradictions in patriarchal discourse.

John: If the contradictions which deconstruction tells us about are inevitable constituents of all discourse, they are no disgrace to patriarchy. What feminists are after is ordinary oppressive contradictions, not those which patriarchy shares with any other system, and which are manifested only in rhetoric. Politics is for real. If I were a dictator determined to stay in power, and my spies told me that the universities were full of radicals denying that there is any extra-textual reality, I'd be delighted. Keep them busy with that, I'd say. Just make sure they keep away from real politics.